BUTCH QUEENS UP IN PUMPS

TRIANGULATIONS
Lesbian/Gay/Queer ▲ Theater/Drama/Performance

Series Editors
Jill Dolan, Princeton University
David Román, University of Southern California

TITLES IN THE SERIES:

UP IN PUMPS

BUTCH QUEENS

Gender, Performance, and Ballroom Culture in Detroit

Marlon M. Bailey

THE UNIVERSITY OF MICHIGAN PRESS

Ann Arbor

Published in the United States of America by
The University of Michigan Press
Manufactured in the United States of America
♾ Printed on acid-free paper

2016   2015 2014   2013   4   3   2   1

A CIP catalog record for this book is available from the British Library.

Library of Congress Cataloging-in-Publication Data

Bailey, Marlon M., 1969–
    Butch queens up in pumps : gender, performance, and ballroom
culture in Detroit / Marlon M. Bailey.
        pages cm.—(Triangulations: lesbian/gay/queer theater/drama/
    performance)
    Includes bibliographical references and index.
    ISBN 978-0-472-07196-8 (cloth : alk. paper)—ISBN 978-0-472-
05196-0 (pbk. : alk. paper)—ISBN 978-0-472-02937-2 (e-book)
    1. Gay and lesbian dance parties—Michigan—Detroit.   2. Female
impersonators—Michigan—Detroit.   3. Gay culture—Michigan—
Detroit.   4. African American gays—Michigan—Detroit.   5. Sexual
minorities—Michigan—Detroit.   I. Title.
GV1749.5.B35   2013
793.3086'64—dc23

                                                        2013015604

For Xavier,
    Ballroom "kids" everywhere, and
    in memory of Noir Prestige; may your life
    continue to inspire others as you inspire me

Preface
Courageously Queer

I first learned the meaning of queer family as a teenager in the 1980s at Cass Technical High School in Detroit. My friends and I—five men and three women, all *queer* in the full sense of the term—called ourselves "The Family." Most of us attended Cass Tech, and we always hung out together—as a family—whether it was at a high school event or going to a gay club. In a sense, we were typical kids participating in the usual heteronormative high school activities, such as hayrides, homecoming, and prom. And likely because most of us were performing arts majors at Cass Tech, we inherited the residual *faggot, sissy, dyke,* and *freak* markings placed on people in the arts. The name-calling was only one of the ways in which our lives existed in tension with those of our classmates and how they were coming to understand their racial and sexual selves. In spite of derogatory names and the relatively hostile environment we experienced at school, we continued to do everything together, and with a rebellious flamboyance and flair, as if to say, "Eat it!" In this queer family, we supported and provided for each other in ways in which our biological kin, for a variety of reasons, could or would not.

When I was a sixteen-year-old Black gay teenager, still trying to figure out and grasp my Black gender and sexual selfhood, my "bestie," a burgeoning lesbian, took me to my first Black gay bar/club. We had acquired fake IDs so that we could go to Black LGBT nights at Todd's, a popular nightclub on East Seven Mile Road and Van Dyke that we affectionately called The "Tabernacle" to signify its role as a space of Black gay sanctuary. Soon going to Todd's became a weekly ritual that my group of friends—none of us yet eighteen—attended as a family.

But there was danger there. I was still a naive teenager, and men old enough to be my daddy were trying to swoop me up. The more experienced members of The Family tried to protect me, especially my gay sister, who would snatch me away as soon as she saw one of those "vipers," as she called them, look at me. "He's with me," she would always say. Yet we did not perceive the space as dangerous but as a refuge where we could be our queer selves in ways that we could not in a city hostile to our presence. In the Detroit environment, going to a gay bar or simply being around other Black LGBT people is a way of coming out, regardless of whether you announce it to your family or anyone else for that matter. We grew up marginalized or on the fringes of our families, churches, peer groups, and social institutions of origin. Reflecting on my own life and those of other Black LGBT people I know and love, it is clear that exclusion from and marginalization within Black belonging has had an indelible impact on us.

We engaged in a lot of risky sexual behavior back in those high school days, simply because we did not know any better. I used to hang out at the infamous Palmer Park in the gay ghetto on Detroit's northwest side, where late at night, sometimes with friends and sometimes alone, I would cruise guys on the strip. Cruising was the way many of us found sex partners, tricks, and even romantic partners. This was very dangerous because the guys walking the streets were often hustlers and drug dealers, and Palmer Park was known as a place where gay people often were bashed, robbed, or arrested.

When HIV/AIDS came on the scene in the early eighties, it seemed a scary but altogether distant problem. One of my first jobs was as a sexuality educator for Planned Parenthood, cautioning others about risky behavior, but in my mind the warnings seemed not to apply to me. HIV/AIDS was just not on my radar at the time. In Detroit, where the gay population was racially segregated, we assumed that the only people who "got AIDS" were the White gay guys that hung out at Menjos in the heart of Palmer Park, or so we thought.[1] The entire city of Detroit seemed to be in denial about HIV/AIDS and perhaps ignored the disease to a greater extent and for a longer time than other cities did.

In the late 1980s many of my friends became infected with HIV and some eventually developed full-blown AIDS at a young age. There were no life-prolonging forms of medication at the time—at least none to which my friends had access. For the most part, when my friends tested positive for HIV, it was indeed a death sentence. Many of the people I knew who were infected have since died of complications resulting from AIDS.

One of my first direct encounters with the epidemic, a situation that put my notion of queer family to the test, was when a member of The Family, my gay friend/brother Kendall, tested positive in 1988, during my first year of college and his first year in the U.S. military.[2] He was just nineteen years old, Black, gay, and HIV-positive, "doing time" in the mil- itary before the era of "Don't ask, don't tell." Who could he talk to back then about his seroconversion?[3] He had no access to any kind of counseling services to deal with the trauma of such a diagnosis. There were no HIV/AIDS prevention or treatment organizations that he could turn to for help at that time. He certainly could not tell his biological family. His family was poor (hence his motivation to join the military, so he could obtain a postsecondary education) and they were neither understanding nor supportive of his sexual identity. He had no conventional means through which to seek help coping with the dire consequences of an HIV-positive diagnosis, particularly at a time when his prospects for survival were far bleaker than they would be today.

At least he could talk to *me*, but, then again, who was I? I was only nineteen and grappling with a wide range of issues such as trying to figure out how long I was going to be doing the "gay thing." My family was finding out about me, and, as my mother's suspicions were growing stronger as the days went on, she was tightening her grip, trying to "de-gay" me. For me, and I suspect for Kendall as well, the moment of clarity about the vital role of our courageously queer kinship occurred during a phone conversation when in tears he said, "Marlon, I am going to die," and, I, also in tears, provided the only response I could: "But we are all going to die; we just have to do the best we can while we are alive." At that moment, I had to console my Black gay brother, for whom I felt responsible, because I had brought him into the Black gay world as it were. I am happy to say that Kendall has been living with HIV for almost twenty-five years now and is healthy with a successful career. I like to think that our relationship has played a key role in his life. We have maintained our relationship over the years, and from what I have observed, he has always surrounded himself with people who value, love, and care for him. However, it was only while writing this book that the magnitude of what my friend must have gone through became clearer than ever to me. Indeed, he was and is courageously queer. This concept of family—the kind of bond that two Black gay teenagers who are not blood relatives formed at that moment of crisis—is the true subject of this book.

All Black LGBT people, including many in the Ballroom community, continue to struggle against the disproportionate impact of the HIV/

AIDS epidemic on our community. Many of those diagnosed with HIV are living with it and continue to look to other LGBT people for social support and strategies for survival in the face of perilous consequences. For concomitant to this struggle against HIV/AIDS is an effort to love ourselves and each other in the midst of a society that is largely hostile to Black LGBT people. This book is about how Ballroom culture, a Black and Latino/a LGBT community, uses performance to forge and celebrate alternative gender and sexual identities, kinship, and community and continues to create livable lives for its Black LGBT members in Detroit and throughout North America. This is the same kinship and community I experienced when I was coming of age in Detroit, when I was most in need of social support: my queer family was there for me. And now, as a grown man and a college professor in another state, the most important people in my life remain my Black queer kin—including those who are LGBT and those who are not. They saved my life. This book is for all of those Black queer people who lived courageously and have passed on and those who continue to live with courage despite the difficulties and challenges that we face.

Acknowledgments

This has been a very long journey, and I have been blessed with enormous love, care, and support throughout. I am deeply grateful first and foremost to everyone in the Ballroom community in Detroit and various cities throughout the country for sharing their stories for this project. Without my fellow Ballroom members and my Black LGBT comrades, including those who have passed on, this book would not have been possible. I would like especially to thank the Detroit, Los Angeles, and San Francisco Bay Area chapters of The Legendary House of Prestige (as well as all its national members) for welcoming me into their respective Ballroom families without hesitation and generously sharing their experiences, perspectives, and skills while I conducted research for this book. I offer special thanks to Duchess Prestige, the former housemother of the Detroit Chapter, and Father Alvernian, cofounder and overall housefather of The Legendary House of Prestige. I also want to thank the Board of Directors of The House of Blahnik for recently inviting me to join their organization, and the National House and Ball Community Change Coalition for giving me an opportunity to remain an active member of the Ballroom community as a researcher and advocate.

Many community-based organizations (CBOs) in Detroit gave me timely assistance in recruiting Ballroom members to participate in the study, as well as information about balls, HIV prevention, and other community-level developments that could not easily be obtained otherwise. For example, Jonathon Davis (Father Infiniti) was extremely generous in providing invaluable knowledge and support. He gave me his time, opened up his office so that I could conduct interviews with Ballroom members, and showered me with his vast knowledge of the Ballroom scene in Detroit. I also appreciate my experience working at Men of Color Motivational Group, Inc. Although I traveled a rocky road with the organization, they made me aware of HIV intravention as a form of prevention, and for that I am grateful. I am thankful to Laura Hughes, the Executive Director of the Ruth Ellis Center, for a very informative interview and tour of a facility that renders crucial services to Ballroom community members and Black LGBT young people in Detroit. I thank the AIDS Project of the East Bay for giving me my first job in HIV prevention as a street-level outreach worker. Overall, my heartfelt gratitude goes to Black LGBT communities everywhere but particularly in Detroit, the community in which I grew up.

The research was made possible, in part, by very generous funding resources and time off from teaching, which was granted so I could conduct further data collection and analysis and writing for this book. I cannot thank Indiana University, Bloomington enough, particularly the College of Arts and Sciences, for providing the lion's share of research funding and support for release time for this project. The research for this book was also supported by a Chancellor's Postdoctoral Fellowship in Gender and Women's Studies at the University of California, Berkeley; a Dissertation Fellowship in Black Studies from the University of California, Santa Barbara; an Arcus Endowment Award; and a Woodrow Wilson Foundation Humanities at Work Grant.

I am enormously grateful to the many mentors and colleagues who have supported me tirelessly and unconditionally throughout this project. First, I want to give a very special thanks to my dearest friend, "my brista," my mentor, and my dissertation adviser, E. Patrick Johnson. Patrick has been my intellectual and academic rock, and I am so very fortunate to have him in my life in every way imaginable. Words cannot express how grateful I am for him. I thank his wonderful partner, Stephen Lewis, for welcoming me into their beautiful home with open arms whenever I needed to get away from the stresses of my life in Indiana. I thank all of my other mentors, advisers, and friends (and people who inspire me), such as Percy C. Hintzen and Paola Bacchetta—thank you for supporting me when I needed it most—Dwight McBride, Gayatri Gopinoth, Judith Halberstam, José Muñoz, Stephen Epstein, Emily Arnold, Martin Manalansan IV, Roderick Ferguson, Marlon Ross, Susan Stryker, Cathy Cohen, Sandra Richards, Michelle Wright, Rinaldo Walcott, Shaka McGlotten, Celeste Watkins-Hayes, Nitasha Tamar Sharma, Barrie Thorne, Linda Carty, D. Soyini Madison, Gayle Rubin, Charis Thompson, and the late Dwight D. Conquergood and Barbara Christian.

My professors in the departments in which I received my training deserve recognition here. I thank the faculty and staff in African American Studies, Gender and Women's Studies, and Theatre, Dance, and Performance Studies at the University of California, Berkeley. And I am grateful for my stellar dissertation committee: E. Patrick Johnson, Charles Henry, Paola Bacchetta, and Percy Hintzen, as well as an incredible PhD cohort: Xavier Livermon, Ivy Mills, and Libby Lewis.

I benefited from the invaluable comments of some of my closest friends and colleagues in the Black Sexual Cultures Writing Group: Mireille Miller-Young, Matt Richardson, and Xavier Livermon. Thanks to each of them for reading every chapter closely and helping me shape this book. I am honored to be among the brilliant, progressive, and supportive scholars in the Black Sexual Economies Working Group (BSE) at Washington University in St. Louis. I am so very thankful that Adrienne Davis and Mireille Miller-Young, the coconveners, invited me to join the group. The BSE has enriched my scholarship on race, gender, and sexuality studies. In addition, I thank my colleagues in the Black Gay Research Group (BGRG) for teaching me HIV/AIDS prevention studies. I am particularly thankful to Leo Wilton and LaRon Nelson. I would not be the HIV prevention scholar I am now without them.

My friends and colleagues at Indiana University have inspired and supported me through this process every step of the way. I am most appreciative of my mentors, LaMonda Horton Stallings and Scott Herring. I am also indebted to Mary Gray, Shane Vogel, Colin Johnson, Claudia Breger, Sara Friedman, Brenda Weber, Lessie Jo Frazier, Maria Bucur-Deckard, Karma Lochrie, Jen Mayer, Fedwa Malti-Douglas, Marvin Sterling, Amrita Meyers, Purnima Bose, Khalil Gibran Muhammad, and the late Alex Doty—you are sorely missed. I want to send a shout out to the Gender Studies staff: Nina Taylor, Kristin Brand, and Barbara Black-Kurdziolek. I thank the many others I do not have the space to name here. I also thank the departments of African American and African Diaspora Studies and American Studies for their support since I arrived at Indiana University, especially Micol Siegel, Stephen Selka, Matt Guterl, and Michael Martin.

I have learned a great deal and benefited immensely from working with graduate students at Indiana University. I thank all of the graduate students from my Gender Studies seminars, such as Cultural Politics and Twentieth Century Sexuality, Researching Gender Issues, and Cultural Politics of HIV/AIDS. I especially want to thank my research assistant and grader, Walter Tucker IV, and the other graduate students with whom I have worked closely since joining the faculty, such as Katie Dieter, Dana D. Hines, Samantha Schalk, LaNita Campbell, Nickolas Clarkson, Laura Harrison, Joselyn Leimbach, Betsy Jose, Victoria Crump, Cierra Olivia Thomas Williams, and my favorite mentee, Kiwan R. Lawson. They are why I love working with graduate students. I am especially appreciative of the undergraduate students who took several courses with me and always helped create a very engaging and exciting classroom. Students like Erika Sutton, Julia Napolitano, Sloka Krishnan, Clarence Hammoor, Sarah Hughes, Lucas Zigler, Barton Girdwood, and many others who have made teaching Gender Studies at IU a joy.

I could not have come this far without a very supportive and loving community of LGBTQ people and progressive allies, some of whom include Rashad Shabazz, Patrick Anderson, Roshanak Kheshti, Sara C. Kaplan, Kristie Dorr, Marques Redd, Chris Lewis, Matais Pouncil, Marvin White, Tim'm T. West, David Malebranche, Jeffrey McCune, Thabiti John Willis, Paul Dunoquez, Stewart Shaw, Cedric Brown, Frank Leon Roberts, Michelle Tellez, Jafari Allen, Jeffry Thigpen, Randall Washington, Sylvester Bennett, M Donivon Blue, Johari Jabir, Ramón Rivera-Servera, Edgar Rivera Colón, Zakiyyah Jackson, Lance McCready, Zuwarah Muenda Jahi, Antonio Espree (my dearest cousin), and a host of others; I deeply love and appreciate these folks from the bottom of my heart.

I am very thankful to LeAnn Fields, Senior Executive Editor at the University of Michigan Press, for her support and commitment to this project from day one. She won me over at our very first meeting. I also thank Editorial Associate Alexa Ducsay and the staff at the University of Michigan Press. I am honored and thankful that my book is included in the prestigious Triangulations Series, coedited by Jill Dolan and David Román. I am grateful to both Jill and David for their support of my project. I thank Barbara from New England Transcripts and my wonderful copyeditor, William Barnett of WordCraft Editing & Writing Services. I thank Chris "Snaps Monroe" Cushman, Thabiti John Willis, Frank Leon Roberts, and Mireille Miller-Young for allowing me to include in this book many beautiful photographs they took at ball events in Detroit, Indianapolis, New York City, and Toronto.

I also thank my mother, Evelyn C. Barnett, for raising a Black gay scholar/professor/artist/activist, whether she planned to or not. Most of all, I thank my very best friend in the whole world and life partner Xavier O'Neal Livermon. He has been my primary source of emotional and moral support since we met nearly fourteen years ago. He also reads everything that I write. He is a brilliant and beautiful person. I would not be the person, the scholar, the artist, or the activist that I am today without him in my life.

I want to commemorate Noir Prestige—his spirit lives on—and all of those who pioneered the Ballroom community and have since passed away, those we call Immortal Icons such as Pepper LaBeija, Dorian Corey, Eriq Christian Bazaar, Willie Ninja, and many others. All of these people made *Butch Queens Up in Pumps* possible.

Contents

ONE

Introduction

Performing Gender, Creating Kinship, Forging Community

It is my contention that the doing that matters most and the performance that seems most crucial are nothing short of the actual making of worlds.
—JOSÉ ESTEBAN MUÑOZ, *DISIDENTIFICATION: QUEERS OF COLOR AND THE PERFORMANCE OF POLITICS*

The House of Supreme International Ball

I attended my first ball on a snowy evening in January 2001 while home for the holidays. Since leaving for graduate school in California a year and a half earlier, my visits to Detroit had been infrequent. On a previous trip to visit friends and family, I had met several members of The House of Ford, who informed me of an upcoming ball that I should attend if I was interested in learning more about an emerging Ballroom scene in the city. The House of Supreme International Ball was being held at Club 2000 on East Woodbridge in the Warehouse District near downtown Detroit. Located just east of the General Motors World Headquarters building, the tallest building on Detroit's skyline, the Warehouse District is a mixture of downtown renewal and urban blight. In this district, new loft apartments, law offices, condominiums, and restaurants stand side by side with abandoned buildings. Resting on the waterfront of the Detroit River, the body of water that separates the city from Canada, the close proximity of new and dilapidated buildings explains why many residents describe Detroit's cityscape as "spotty." It is against such an urban backdrop that I would attend that first ball.

This Sunday is a typical cold January night in Michigan. At about 10:30 p.m., I am driving down Jefferson Avenue heading east. As I make a right turn toward the river to Woodbridge, I recall going to Club Taboo on the same street in the late 1980s to see Sylvester, the flamboyant Black disco diva, in concert. When I look at the building now, I remember that Club 2000 used to be the Warehouse Club, a straight club that could be rented out for a variety of events, including those attended by Lesbian, Gay, Bisexual and Transgender (LGBT) patrons. As I pull up in front of the building, I see very few cars on the narrow street where I want to park. I must be early. The street is desolate and the place feels tucked away, hidden from the rest of what is going on in the city, even for a Sunday night.

Once I enter the building, I am frisked meticulously by security at the club entrance. I pay $25.00 at the table just beyond the entrance and proceed into a large room. House music beats are pumping. An internationally popular music form, particularly in Black gay urban spaces, house music is the signature sound of Ballroom culture.[1] I see two rows of tables, each decorated and bearing signs indicating the names of houses: "Reserved for The House of Prada," "Reserved for The House of Ford," the signs read. Houses, which are like families, pay money to reserve their tables so that their members can sit together. As I walk toward the center of the room, I see the "runway," a long platform adorned with red ribbons, situated between the two rows of tables and chairs, extending the length of the entire room. This runway is where the participants perform in each category in front of the judges during the competition portion of the ball. My early arrival allows me to see the setup, snap some pictures, and find a good viewing spot, which is important since it is my first time attending a ball. Yet I quickly learn a lesson that will hold true for every other ball I attend: balls never start on time, at least not by the time indicated on the ball flyer. A ball begins only when its commentators arrive, and no commentator takes the microphone on this night until approximately two hours after my arrival. I feel fortunate that The House of Ford has invited me to sit at its table because, by the time the ball starts, the hall is full of people. I see Black LGBT people everywhere. "D.J., give me a muthafuckin' beat; let's get this shit started. And where's my cocktail?" admonishes the commentator. Finally, the ball begins.

Once the ball starts, all I can hear is house music blasting over the large speakers elevated in various places throughout the room. After the commentators announce upcoming balls around the country, they begin the "Legends, Statements, and Stars" portion of the ball. "I wanna see that legend femme; I wanna see her voguing femme, that pussy, pussy, dainty femme," the commentator yells in sync with the throbbing house music beats. It does not take me long to realize that balls are very structured and, despite always starting late, they exhibit an amazing continuity.

Moments later I notice that there are only a few lights on and they seem to be blue and red or something close to that. Otherwise, it is rather dark, reminding me of being at a gay bar late on a Saturday night. These lights create a perfect ambiance for the Grand House March, which is an opportunity for the sponsoring house to show itself to the audience through a concerted display of house unity, as the local chapter is often joined by members from other chapters. Contrary to its name, The House of Supreme International is not international, but each of the seventeen house members (I will learn later that this is an unusually small number) walks on the platform with gait accentuated, drawing focus to his or her extravagant clothing. Some members of the house enter the space wearing little more than tight-fitting underwear with see-through backsides. Some are shirtless, exposing their perfectly chiseled torsos. Members of the crowd scream "You give me trade boy!" commenting on a Butch Queen—a gay man. I see another Butch Queen wearing red pumps—what we call a "Butch Queen up in pumps"—prancing down the runway in high-fashion celebrity model style. Other members sashay fervently across the walkway. Many wear long, flowing silk capes and gowns. "You wear that suit, Miss Thing," someone says from the audience. Most of their gaits exude glamour and grandeur as their garments swish and swirl behind them.

In the midst of all the excitement, I sense a few people looking at me as I jot down notes in my little notebook. Later, during the competition portion of the ball, a couple of inquisitive guys approach me. One of them asks, "Why are you taking notes?" Then the guy sitting next to me chimes in, "Yeah, you've been writing in that little book since you got here. Whatcha writin' about? Write *my* story," he says jokingly.

Among all the memorable aspects of that night, that gentleman's seemingly playful comment stayed in my mind throughout my subsequent work on Ballroom culture. As I mobilize various theories to analyze this cultural phenomenon, that request—"Write *my* story"—reminds me that this project is ultimately about everyday LGBT people. The Black LGBT people on whom I focus are poor or working class and must struggle against the odds to find and make meaning in their lives. These Black LGBT people occupy one of the most marginalized social locations within blackness in Detroit. Therefore, chiefly, this book is about how these Black LGBT people, who are marginalized in so many ways, perform gender, create kinship, and forge community despite their marginalization. I ask what can be learned from everyday Black LGBT lives in Ballroom culture, particularly those who are largely ignored in dominant academic and sociopolitical discourse.

What Is Ballroom Culture?

Sometimes called "house/ball culture," Ballroom culture was first captured in mainstream media in Jennie Livingston's popular documentary film *Paris Is Burning* (1990). Livingston's documentary was the first work to bring mainstream exposure to Ballroom practices in the late 1980s in New York City, and it continues to be the film most often screened and referenced, even by Ballroom members. Given the limits of documentary film, *Paris Is Burning* provides only a glimpse into the world of this cultural practice. The films *The Aggressives* (2005) by Daniel Peddle and Wolfgang Busch's *How Do I Look* (2006) capture Ballroom culture in its more contemporary form. Ballroom culture has also received popular exposure through music videos and live performances by entertainers such as Madonna in her notorious video *Vogue* (1990), which features members of the Ballroom community "voguing." Vogue, a dance form created by the Ballroom community, has been appropriated by entertainers like Madonna without properly crediting the community that created it. More recently Ballroom community members and the culture have been represented in the popular media by the dance group Vogue Evolution and in an episode of *Noah's Ark,* a Black gay television series that aired on the LOGO Network. This commercialization of Ballroom culture has overshadowed the daily practices and functions of the community, which this book seeks to redress.

Three inextricable dimensions constitute the social world of Ballroom culture: the gender system, the kinship structure (houses), and the ball events (where ritualized performances are enacted). What members refer to as the "gender system" is a collection of gender and sexual subjectivities that extend beyond the binary/ternary categories in dominant society such as male/female, man/woman, gay/lesbian/bisexual, and straight. Ballroom members conceive of sex, gender, and sexuality as separate but inextricably linked categories. Ballroom gender and sexual identities serve as the basis of all familial roles and the competitive presentation and performance categories at ball events.

Houses and balls are inseparable core social dimensions of Ballroom culture. Houses are family-like structures that are configured socially rather than biologically. Most houses are named after *haute couture* designers, but some are named after mottos and symbols that express qualities and aims with which the leaders want a house to be associated. Houses are also alternative families that are led by "mothers" and "fathers." House parents provide guidance for their "children" of various ages, race/ethnic identities (usually Black and Latino/a), genders, and sexualities, who come from cities and regions throughout North America. In general, a "house" does not signify an actual building; rather, it represents the ways in which its members, who mostly live in various locations, view themselves and interact with each other as a family unit.

The most conspicuous function of houses is organizing and competing in ball events. The gender system and kin labor create a close-knit community, and that community expresses its essence at these events. Thus, house parents recruit, socialize, and prepare their protégés to compete successfully in categories based on the deployment of performative gender and sexual identities, vogue and theatrical performances, and the effective presentation of fashion and physical attributes. Participants compete vigorously on behalf of their respective houses, and at times as individuals, in which case they are "free agents" and "007s."

Although contemporary Ballroom culture has existed for at least five decades, this community of Black and Latino/a LGBT people remains largely underground. Since its beginnings in Harlem, Ballroom culture has expanded rapidly to almost every major city in the United States and Canada. There are major Ballroom scenes in Chicago, Atlanta, Baltimore, Washington DC, Charlotte, Los Angeles, and Philadelphia. Cities like Cleveland, St. Louis, Newark, Columbus, Miami, Buffalo, Pittsburgh, and Richmond have smaller Ballroom communities but thrive all the same. There are regional Ballroom scenes that include collaborative relationships between scenes in two or more cities, such as The Kentuckiana scene, involving Louisville and Indianapolis; The West Coast scene in California, consisting of Los Angeles and the San Francisco Bay Area; and The Carolina scene, which includes Charlotte, Fayetteville, and Raleigh/Durham joined with cities in South Carolina. Recently a Ballroom community has emerged in Toronto, Ontario. Ballroom participants in the United States have helped to cultivate house/ball practices in the United Kingdom, Japan, Russia, and Sweden. Clearly, Ballroom has gone global, and there are many more cities in which Ballroom is growing and its members participate in balls throughout the world.

During this culture's early years in New York City, older Black and Latino/a LGBT people made up the majority of its membership. Yet, in just the past decade or so, members of Ballroom scenes across the country have become markedly younger. Indeed, especially for LGBT people of color in their late teens and early twenties, this community offers an enduring social sanctuary for those who have been rejected by and marginalized within their families of origin, religious institutions, and society at large.

From 2001 to 2007, the period in which I conducted most of my ethnography, the Ballroom community experienced rapid change and growth. Technology has played an integral role in the expansion of Ballroom culture, allowing its members to stay connected throughout the globe. For instance, the national Ballroom scene uses websites, such as walk4mewednesdays and thehouseofballs, as well as Yahoo groups, electronic mailing lists, and blogs that are set up and maintained by houses and individual members in order to connect with the community at large and to communicate with their chapters throughout the country.[2] More recently members of the scene have begun to network through Facebook and to post performances on YouTube. Members use all of these social media to announce balls, discuss the highlights of previous balls, organize events, and gossip about the scene. Ballroom culture also has a presence in magazines, a few of which focus on Ballroom in their entirety and others of which devote several pages to it, such as *Swerv, CLIK,* and *Ballroom Rockstar.*

Several organizations hold balls annually within the context of HIV/AIDS prevention efforts that target the Ballroom community. For example, organizations such as The Gay Men's Health Crisis (CHMC) in New York City, The National AIDS and Education Services for Minorities (NAESM) in Atlanta, and The Minority AIDS Project in Los Angeles sponsor annual "prevention balls." Finally, The National Confederation of Black Prides is an umbrella organization that works with citywide Black Pride festivities to bring together Black and Latino/a LGBT members of the community to participate in national balls.

Shared race/ethnic identity and class status in the United States shape the demography of Ballroom communities in all cities in which there is a scene. In New York, Newark, San Antonio, and Miami, the community consists of Black and Latino/a LGBT participants, whereas in most other locations membership is almost exclusively Black LGBT people. The cultural critic and former member of The House of Ninja in the New York City scene, Tim'm T. West aptly explains how the intersections of race/ethnicity, class, and sexuality affect the makeup of the community, particularly in a city like New York:

> You have Black people in New York City who are very much embedded geographically in Black communities. New York is a very segregated city, so if you are Black and from New York, chances are you grew up in a Black neighborhood or maybe even a Black/Latino neighborhood. Therefore, you are not just dealing with coming into your gayness, but it's like finding a space where both your blackness and gayness can evolve in tandem. So, for the culture that you grew up in, there is a sort of recognized cultural fluency that you share with other Black gays. [Ballroom] houses sort of help to facilitate and maintain that.

Notably, most of the Latino/a participants in New York City and Newark are Puerto Ricans, many of whom identify as Blaktino (Black Latino/a).[3] Thus, West suggests further that, in addition to the shared race/ethnicity of Ballroom members, "the house scene," as he calls it, consists of "kids" who are urban and lower class. "We are talking about kids who are much more latch-key, who have a lot more independence as teenagers to leave and roam about."

West's point is important because it speaks to the cultural norms that Ballroom members adopt, norms that represent a shared race/ethnic and class position. The Black or Latino/a LGBT people who are in the Ballroom scene come from families, communities, and neighborhoods in which they have had to navigate the often difficult terrain of the streets, which means facing homophobic and transphobic violence and abuse, homelessness and hunger, insufficient education, under- and unemployment, and general sociocultural dispossession. For most, the Ballroom scene becomes a necessary refuge and a space in which to share and acquire skills that help Black and Latino/a LGBT individuals survive the urban world. Much of what constitutes the cultural labor of Ballroom reflects the realities of the worlds in which its members live in the everyday.

Detroit, where I grew up and came of age as a gay man—not New York City, Newark, Miami, or San Antonio—provides the sociocultural geography in which I situate Ballroom culture and, by extension, the larger Black LGBT community.[4] The Ballroom scene in Detroit consists of mostly poor and working-class Black LGBT people who live within larger Black communities in the city. Some of my interlocutors were unemployed,[5] and some lived off of government assistance. Others were underemployed in low-wage retail or other service industry jobs. One of my interlocutors worked for one of the "big three" car companies in the city. And some of them worked for nonprofit HIV/AIDS prevention agencies. A few were college students, and two interlocutors were professional artists: one a classical violinist and the other a drag performer and makeup artist.

The ages of most members range from as young as sixteen to as old as forty-five. Note, however, that in Ballroom culture chronological age is not emphasized as a personal identifier as it is in larger society.[6] Although Ballroom participants are mostly urban, Black, LGBT, and working class, the overall involvement in the Ballroom scene in Detroit is becoming increasingly diverse in terms of race and cultural heritage, age, gender, sexuality, and geography. This community not only consists of competitors or "ball-walkers," it also includes those who just attend balls or follow Ballroom scenes via YouTube and other forms of social media. Therefore, as a community, Ballroom culture creates a multidimensional world in which Black and Latino/a LGBT people, as well as various people throughout the globe, can reconstitute, affirm, and celebrate their LGBT identities and lives.

Why Detroit?

Among the many North American cities with a Ballroom scene, Detroit was an especially rich and compelling site to choose for my research on Ballroom culture. Detroit has the most distinctive racial and class demographics of any large US city, with a large Black working-class population that has lived there for decades. According to historian Thomas Sugrue, in the 1940s, during the influx particularly of southern Black people who moved to the North for greater opportunities and freedom during the second Great Migration, Detroit was a thriving industrial boomtown with one of the fastest-growing populations and economies in the nation.[7] During that decade, Detroit's overall population grew enough to make it among the largest cities in the United States. Notably, between World War II and the advent of the Civil Rights Movement, the African American population in Detroit was the third highest in the country.[8]

However, according to US census data, beginning in the 1950s, Detroit began to experience a rapid decline in population, losing over a million residents by 2010. Furthermore, for over six decades, ongoing deindustrialization has caused the city to hemorrhage manufacturing jobs at alarming rates.[9] Deindustrialization, ghettoization, and racialized poverty in Detroit and other cities like it, according to Sugrue, were largely a result of bad political and economic decisions, protracted corporate union-busting efforts, and entrenched race and class segregation and strife, which have subjected Black Detroiters, in particular, to extreme forms of racism and discrimination.[10] He argues that, even though in recent years Detroit has endured a series of postindustrial crises that have sent the economy spiraling downward and caused continued population loss, the current fate of the city is a result of a long-standing inequitable distribution of power and resources.[11]

Although Detroit remains a very large city, its population has been in steady decline. From a peak of about 1.8 million people in the 1950s, the population dropped to 951,270 residents in 2000, and dropped further to 713,777 residents in 2010.[12] Nevertheless, in 2000, one year before I began my research, Detroit was still the largest city with a Black majority in the United States, with 83 percent of the population identifying themselves as Black or African American.[13] Notwithstanding the large Black population sustained in the city over several decades, the general racial/ethnic landscape of Detroit remains troubling. For instance, the 2010 US Census ranked Detroit as the fourth-most-segregated city in the country.[14] Such segregation functions on several levels, but primarily in terms of race/ethnicity. Blacks, whites, Arabs, Latino/as, and other groups all tend to live and socialize in separate domains. This segregation is often accompanied by extreme racial hostility, antagonism, and strife that make difficult any sociopolitical mobilization and coalition building across race/ethnic difference.

In terms of socioeconomic status, combined with a growing disparity between the wealthy and the impoverished, Detroit has one of the poorest populations in the country. In 2000 the city had a 7.8 percent unemployment rate. Over the course of my research unemployment increased consistently and was at 17 percent when I concluded data collection proper in 2007. According to the 2000 US Census, between 26.8 and 33.4 percent of individuals in Detroit reported living in poverty.[15] Detroit's poverty places a heavy burden not only on families as a whole but on young people in particular. The *Detroit Free Press* reported that 47.8 percent of the city's children lived below the poverty line in 2004.[16] Laura Hughes, Executive Director of the Ruth Ellis Center, a service agency that serves LGBT youth in Detroit, estimates that about 10 percent of the fourteen thousand youths in the Child Welfare System in the State of Michigan are LGBT. According to the center's website, nearly eight hundred homeless LGBT youths are on the streets of Detroit every day.[17] And many of the LGBT youths who the Ruth Ellis Center serves are Black, perhaps reflecting the city's extreme segregation, which exacerbates its poverty. Many are also members of the Ballroom scene.

With its large working-class Black population, Detroit has been viewed as a counterhegemonic social geography in which prominent Black cultural and labor movements have helped shape the socio-political landscape in the United States. However, due in part to its history and reputation, for a long time the city has been the target of protracted and aggressive attempts to dismantle its social, political, and economic infrastructure by hostile governments at the state and federal levels. Yet, in the midst of these struggles against various forms of social and economic domination, rich and resilient forms of Black cultural expression have served as a powerful source of resistance and resilience within an urban sphere that is increasingly powerless and deprived.[18]

In addition to its distinctive racial and class character, Detroit has a history of tolerance for gender and sexual nonconformity that is little known or, if so, rarely acknowledged. In general, contemporary Ballroom culture emerges out of a long history of nonconforming gender and sexual practices and nonnormative kinship formations that have been inherited and adopted by those referred to as Black LGBT individuals today. It is well documented that, since the early twentieth century in Harlem, Black people who did not conform to the gender and sexual mores of the time forged discrete spaces of gender and sexual fluidity, participated in transgressive forms of gender and sexual expression, forged alternative kinship relations, and developed new performance styles for pleasure and survival.[19] Ballroom communities have drawn from these early and ongoing Black LGBT cultural practices, such as male and female impersonation and costume balls.[20]

Here, I am most interested in the fluid gender and sexual relations among Black people that emerged in spaces such as speakeasies, rent parties, and "buffet flats" (so named because every sexual behavior was, as it were, "on the table"). Historian George Chauncey has described how, usually during the late hours at speakeasies in Harlem, gay, lesbian, and sometimes straight men would engage in sexually charged behavior, at times in full view of other patrons.[21] Many historians of LGBT life have cited East Coast or northern cities like Harlem, Washington DC, and even Chicago as cities where gender and sexual nonconformity was engaged in and tolerated both privately and publicly.

What is far less well known and documented are what practices of gender and sexual nonconformity among Black people in Detroit looked like and the spaces in which they occurred during the early to mid–twentieth century. Indeed, Detroit has a rich history of nonconforming gender and sexual communities and spaces that allowed for more fluid gender and sexual practices, a history largely unknown to my interlocutors, who view Detroit as a socially conservative and homophobic city. And, although a comprehensive historical analysis of homophobia in Detroit is not within the scope of this project, it is important to provide some historical context, however limited, for the experiences with homophobia that my interlocutors regularly encounter. Furthermore, this book highlights the continuity that exists between spaces created and practices enacted to combat homophobia back then *and* now in contemporary Detroit.

"Underground" Black LGBT communities, broadly defined, have existed in Detroit since before the second Great Migration in the 1940s.[22] Early on, Black LGBT people forged spaces in which they could be and do whatever they wanted. Chris Albertson's 1971 interview with Ruby Walker, famous blues singer Bessie Smith's niece (through marriage), elaborates this point. While she speaks of Detroit as having been very "open" during the 1920s, she also describes discreet buffet flats where Black gender and sexually transgressive people socialized:

RUBY: Yeah, Detroit . . . that is where the faggots used to dress like women there and it wasn't against the law you know. That was an open . . . a real open house for everybody there in that town. That's where they had that party that time and I went to it. Bessie and I and all of us got drunk there at that house, a woman's house who is some friend of Bessie's. The woman has a house there, a buffet flat.
CHRIS: What is a buffet flat?

RUBY: A buffet flat is nothing but faggots and bull-daggers and, uh, an open house. Everything goes on in that house.

CHRIS: But it was strictly a gay place?

RUBY: Very gay.

CHRIS: And it was strictly for faggots?

RUBY: Everything that was in "the life," everybody that was in "the life."

CHRIS: So why did they call it a "buffet flat"?

RUBY: 'Cause buffet means everything.[23]

There is an important distinction to note here about the role of buffet flats in a larger Black LGBT social practice. As can be imagined, buffet flats offered the privacy that drag balls could not provide because balls have always been open to the public.[24] During this time in Detroit, although drag balls, rent parties, house parties, and other gatherings provided spaces for Black LGBT socializing, buffet flats were more exclusive and allowed patrons to be themselves, to do "everything," to explore new gender and sexual identities and experiences, to socialize and enjoy one another sexually, and to celebrate their nonconforming gender and sexual lives inconspicuously.[25]

One of the most known and celebrated underground spaces in Detroit that Black LGBT people frequented was the home of Ruth Ellis and Ceceline "Babe" Franklin. Yvonne Welbon's documentary film *Living with Pride: Ruth Ellis @ 100* (1999) chronicles the life of the late Ruth Ellis, a Black and "out" lesbian who lived to be 101 years old. From 1946 to 1971, Ruth and Babe, her partner of thirty-four years, had a house in Detroit that was widely known as the "gay spot." This house was not only a place in which to socialize and perform; it was also a space where the labor of familial and community building was enacted. Before Ruth died in 2000, she gave an agency in the Detroit area permission to use her name and carry on her legacy of helping people in need. Hence, since 1999 the Ruth Ellis Center has provided a short- and long-term residential safe space and support services for runaway, homeless, and at risk LGBT youth.[26]

Historians Thaddeus Russell and Tim Retzloff, in their respective historical research on Detroit, highlight the notorious James Francis Jones, known as Prophet Jones, a flamboyant minister of one of the largest Pentecostal congregations in the city in the 1940s.[27] According to Russell, Prophet Jones was arguably one of most popular religious figures among the Black working class in Detroit. By all accounts, Jones maintained this celebrity-style popularity among his hundreds of followers in Detroit, as well as garnering positive coverage in the Black press despite his well-known homosexuality. I asked my mother about Prophet Jones, and she said, "Oh everybody knew who Prophet Jones was, and he used to come on the radio." Before I could ask my mother about his homosexuality, she said, "And he was gay; people knew about that."

Interestingly, Jones remained hugely popular until the Civil Rights Movement took hold in Detroit and national Black leaders like Adam Clayton Powell and Martin Luther King Jr. began to speak directly to the issue of homosexuality, or what they called "sex perversion," arguing that it threatened Black peoples' pursuit of integration into the national polity as respectable people deserving of full citizenship.[28] Detroit was an important proving ground for the Civil Rights Movement, particularly to leaders who prescriptively linked civic responsibility with sexual restraint, especially among the Black working class. The Black working class was considered the most seriously in need of social rehabilitation and management on behalf of the race. Thus, during the Civil Rights Movement's high point, historians mark the occurrence of a palpable shift in the Black press—from celebratory coverage of figures such as Prophet Jones and others who could be considered gender and sexually "queer" to condemnation.[29] I am not suggesting that Detroit happily accepted gender and sexual nonconformity before the Civil Rights Movement; rather, I want to bring into focus sociopolitical factors that played a role in refracting public displays and practices of Black gender and sexual diversity in the past.

The final and perhaps most important reason for focusing on the Ballroom scene in Detroit is the Black LGBT community's resilience and endurance despite the difficult conditions under which its members live. The Detroit in which I grew up and conducted this research presented challenges for Black LGBT people that are both similar to and more severe than those of Detroit's earlier days. Black LGBT people in Detroit exist within a marginalized and fragmented sociogeographic space, one that is split by the politics of race, as well as the politics of gender and sexuality. As a Black cultural formation, Ballroom culture materialized within the convergent histories of Black racial pride and socioeconomic deprivation in Detroit. Nevertheless, the Ballroom community in particular and the Black LGBT community in general still thrive in the city despite daunting obstacles.

One such obstacle is the fact that gay communities in Detroit are as segregated by race and class as heterosexual communities are. Black LGBT people stand apart from their White counterparts socially, politically and, in many cases, economically. Black LGBT social spaces are almost exclusively Black, and White gay spaces are exclusively White. White gay social spaces exist mostly in middle-class suburbs such as Royal Oak and Ferndale. Black LGBT people generally do not socialize in such areas. These are areas in which my interlocutors are made to feel unwelcome. Gay and straight spaces of all kinds are clearly demarcated, so straight people of any race/ethnicity rarely visit gay establishments. LGBT people who go to straight bars are well aware of their surroundings and usually carry themselves accordingly. And, because Black LGBT people have very few spaces of their own, their events happen on particular nights at otherwise straight establishments or in "hole-in-the-wall" spaces.

Balls are thrown on late Sunday nights in various spaces throughout the city, wherever the houses can find a venue that is not too expensive to rent. For instance, while conducting this research, I attended several balls at the Tom Phillip Post Lodge on Gratiot Avenue, an after-hours Black gay spot on the east side of Detroit, one of the most dangerous parts of town. Due to widespread homophobic violence, which ensures the social transience of the larger Black LGBT community in Detroit, Ballroom is always on the move, holding balls at a variety of venues throughout the city in an effort to identify inexpensive spaces that are safe from violence and surveillance.

The Black LGBT community in Detroit must also overcome being silenced and demeaned by political and community leaders. Because of the nonnormative gender and sexual identities and practices of its members, Ballroom culture, as an everyday practice of resistance and survival for Black LGBT people, stands in tension with one of the most powerful forces in the city—people I call the Black political elite. Ostensibly, the political sphere in Detroit has been—at least for the last thirty years—dominated by Blacks. This political elite consists mostly of career politicians and members of the clergy, all of whom represent a socioeconomically privileged class in Detroit. These politicians and public officials are often politically liberal in the Civil Rights tradition of racial inclusion and equality but very conservative on social issues such as gender, sexuality, marriage, and family.

A separate book could be written about the difficult relations between the Black LGBT community and the Black political elite in Detroit, but

I have space only to recall one incident involving former Detroit mayor Kwame Kilpatrick. Although Kilpatrick's stint as mayor ended in scandal, the Kilpatrick family had been one of the most prominent political families in Michigan and Detroit for three decades.[30] During the Kilpatrick administration, debates about LGBT rights, same-sex marriage, and HIV/AIDS prevention resulted in politicized confrontations, one of which occurred between members of the Black LGBT clergy in Detroit and Mayor Kilpatrick himself because of disparaging statements he had made about gay people on a conservative radio show during his mayoral campaign: "'I don't want Jelani and Jalil out there, you know, even seeing that type of lifestyle,' he said." Mayor Kilpatrick went on to suggest that there are things he does not want his two young, impressionable children to see, such as "a man kissing a man" or "a woman kissing a woman," because he wants to "raise strong, proud men that love women." He was elected despite the uproar from the Black LGBT community over these comments. Black community leaders have also used Black LGBT people as political foils to deny resources or limit the implementation of more effective HIV/AIDS prevention efforts. All these incidents, combined with widespread homophobic violence, make Detroit, in the eyes of many Black LGBT people, a city that is hostile at all levels of government to Black gender and sexual minorities.[31]

Apart from the Black LGBT community's outcry against Kilpatrick's comments, I have seen few public responses to the homophobia to which gender and sexual minorities are consistently subjected in Detroit. Still, such incidents and the HIV/AIDS epidemic have created unlikely platforms on which Black LGBT people, many of whom are Ballroom members, can enter the political sphere as staunch advocates for LGBT rights and programs that raise awareness of the HIV/AIDS epidemic and its devastating impact on the community.

Overall, Detroit's unique race and class demography; its historical, though little known or acknowledged, tolerance for gender and sexual nonconformity; and the resilience of its Black LGBT community in the face of recent hostility and marginalization make for a rich, distinct, and complex social-geographic context in which to situate this ethnography of Ballroom culture. In many ways, this book demonstrates how the Ballroom community in Detroit constitutes a means by which Black LGBT people have and continue to contend with the social challenges they face regularly.

Redefining Labor: Performance as Cultural Labor

Although I deliberately privilege the quotidian theorizing of my Ballroom interlocutors (or what queer of color scholars refer to as "theories from the flesh"),[32] this interdisciplinary project draws extensively on queer theories of performance, gender, and sexuality, and of family and kinship, as well as on cultural studies analyses of HIV/AIDS. Yet, to redress the paucity of scholarship on Black LGBT cultural formations, this project also intervenes critically in the aforementioned literatures. For instance, Black feminist and queer scholars have aptly theorized how Black gender and sexual minorities are scapegoated for the so-called moral turpitude and social perils associated with and assumed to be characteristic of Black communities, particularly relating to gender and sexuality. But there is a dearth of scholarship that examines how some Black LGBT people create culture, other forms of belonging, and alternative ways of being and forging community, using performance to withstand the social, political, and economic marginalization and exclusion with which they are confronted. Consequently, *Butch Queens Up in Pumps* is an examination of Ballroom culture that brings it into rare scholarly focus by providing a critical lens through which to understand its formation and its endurance.

This book argues that members of the resilient Black LGBT community rely on cultural labor not only to survive but also to enhance the quality of their lives. Taking into account the history of labor in Detroit, I examine how and why Ballroom culture forces a redefinition of the entire notion of labor. Given the high rates of under/unemployment and poverty in Detroit, many members of the Ballroom community have been excluded from or marginalized within the labor force in the city. In part this expansion of the concept of labor reflects how creating culture, family, language, gender, and community requires constant and strenuous work—labor. Overall, performance provides a means through which Black LGBT people undertake this necessary "work" to sustain themselves as a minoritarian community.

For instance, the cultural theorist and historian Robin D. G. Kelley's notion of *cultural labor* is useful in highlighting the critical role that performance plays while examining the practices that members undertake. In *Yo' Mama's Disfunktional! Fighting the Culture Wars in Urban America,* Kelley argues that the cultural expressions deployed by urban Black youth in the face of social and economic deprivation are forms of cultural labor.[33] Kelley also suggests that, for African American youths, constructing gender identities and engaging in pleasure, play, and cultural expression constitute the labor that is necessary to survive the social, political, and economic crisis of the urban ghetto.[34] Throughout this book, I use the terms *gender labor, performance labor, kin labor,* and *discursive labor* to argue that for Ballroom culture these are forms of cultural work on which this community formation depends and are akin to what Kelley theorizes in his book.

I draw from queer theories to examine each facet of this cultural formation. My use of the term *queer* as a theory and a concept of analysis is consistent with theorist Siobhan B. Somerville's definition of *queer* as a way to denaturalize and destabilize categories, such as lesbian/bi/gay and straight/heterosexual, and male/female and man/woman, as well as notions of family and community.[35] *Queer* reveals these categories as social and historical constructions that have been used to "police the line between the 'normal' and 'abnormal.'"[36] Ballroom members queer hegemonic gender and sexual identities and familial and community formations. In this book, I demonstrate that the Ballroom community's performative revision and expansion of gender and sexual subjectivities, its construction of alternative kinship structures, its creative response to the HIV/AIDS crisis, and its overall creation of a minoritarian sphere are all, as I theorize them, forms of work, of *queer cultural labor.*[37]

Broadly, my use of *performance* draws from a definition widely used in the field of performance studies. According to performance studies scholar Susan Manning, to perform generally means to carry out, undertake, complete, and accomplish. To enact, take on, or revise a gender identity in the everyday and at balls is referred to as gender performance.[38] Performance, in more theatrical terms, is to act out a role in a play, execute a dance step, or play a musical instrument. For example, ritualized practices and voguing at balls that I describe throughout reflects my theorization of performance at ball events.

Since performance constitutes this queer cultural labor, *Butch Queens Up in Pumps* examines three forms of performance labor that members of the Ballroom community undertake: (a) performativity/performance for individual and communal self-fashioning,[39] (b) performance as the construction of a minoritarian community, and (c) performance as a critical and creative response to the HIV/AIDS epidemic. This study explores how Black LGBT people perform gender and sexual identities not only to survive the dangers of the urban streets but also to engage in play, pleasure, and competition. Performance makes it possible to revise, negotiate, and reconstitute gender and sexual categories and norms, enabling Ballroom members to reconfigure gender and sexual roles and relations while constructing a more open minoritarian social sphere. Therefore, instead of capitulating to gender and sexual norms, completely reinscribing them, or rejecting them outright, Ballroom members have constructed and thereby enact what performance theorist José Esteban Muñoz calls a *disidentifactory performance*. Muñoz argues that minoritarian communities adopt a strategy of disidentification to negotiate and contend with—working on and against—the ubiquity of dominant gender and sexual norms, the very machinery that undergirds State power.[40]

The performative identities that help Ballroom members construct the gender system of Ballroom culture extend beyond the ball events into practices of self-identification and self-fashioning in their everyday lives. These are subjectivities insofar as Ballroom members identify and fashion themselves by and through the intersecting notions of gender and sexuality that arise within Ballroom culture and are imposed on them outside the culture.[41] Ultimately, Ballroom culture provides channels for gender and sexual self-fashioning through performances that are not always available to them in the larger world they must navigate at least part of the time.

Performance is also the primary theoretical lens through which I analyze how Ballroom members create a cultural formation that consists of queer forms of kinship and community. This approach extends a recent trend in performance studies to explore how, through performance— both theatrical and quotidian—human beings fundamentally make culture, affect power, and reinvent their ways of being in the world, especially for those with limited or no access to State power and privilege.[42] Indeed, for this study, Muñoz's notion of *world-making* best captures another essential role that performance labor plays in Ballroom culture.

> World-making delineates the ways in which performances—both theatrical and everyday rituals—have the ability to establish alternative views of the world. These alternative vistas are more than simply views or perspectives; they are oppositional ideologies that function as critiques of oppressive regimes of "truth" that subjugate minoritarian people. Oppositional counterpublics are en-

abled by visions, "worldviews," that reshape as they deconstruct
reality.[43]

When members of Ballroom culture undertake performance labor,
kin labor, and ultimately a labor of care, service, critique, and competition, they are effectively taking on the work of family and community
that the larger Black society fails to do. Conditions of marginalization
within and exclusion from Black communities and society necessitate
an alternative terrain for members of the Ballroom community. In discursive terms at least, performance is a critical means through which
gender and sexual minorities survive in an oppressive world; it is also
tantamount to creating a new one. In Ballroom, as in the larger society,
performance is a site of conflict, contradiction, negotiation, and transformation. Members of the Ballroom community negotiate, and at times
struggle, between capitulating to ubiquitous gender and sexual norms
and employing the labor involved in the pursuit of transformation and
freedom.

Furthermore, Black LGBT kinship has been markedly absent from
scholarship on Black families and queer kinship. Black LGBT members
of the Ballroom community often grow up and live within Black families that subscribe to heteronormative logics that emphasize blood bonds
and fixed gender and sexual roles. Conversely, Black LGBT people have
always revised kinship by engaging family as a social practice or a form
of "kin" labor. For example, as I elaborate in Chapter 4, houses are often
literal homes for Black LGBT people who have been kicked out of their
biological families' homes because of their nonnormative gender and
sexual identities. Thus, joined with performance, the notion of kin-labor
has formed the basis of how Black LGBT people in Detroit and throughout the country have created alternative kinship structures and gender
and sexual relations within them. By extension, I argue that, for Ballroom members, performance is at once a means of altering their ways of
being in the world and of creating an *alternative world* altogether.

Finally, in his book *Performance in America: Contemporary U.S. Culture and the Performing Arts,* performance theorist David Román con-
vincingly argues that performance, particularly theatrical performance,
plays a critical role in shaping ways of thinking in American culture,
specifically about social crises such as HIV/AIDS.[44] For Román performance also enables the development of perspectives on HIV/AIDS that

are counter to dominant views, while revealing new forms of agency for those marginalized groups that are disproportionately impacted and disadvantaged by the epidemic. Although Román mostly discusses theatrical performance and the performing arts, his point underscores my theorization of how Ballroom culture undertakes performance labor as a means through which to intervene in the HIV/AIDS crisis within houses and at ball events.

The crucial role that performance plays in HIV/AIDS prevention became very clear to me while I was conducting this research. As I discovered the devastating impact of HIV/AIDS on the Ballroom community, I also observed and actively participated in performance designed to combat the rapid rise of infection rates within the community. Performance labor is a creative and crucial response to a crisis insofar as it challenges the dominant discourses that construct the epidemic. As performance ethnographer Margaret Thompson Drewal notes, through performance, people reflect on their current condition, define or reinvent themselves and their social world, and either reinforce, resist, or subvert the prevailing social order.[45] Thus, performance makes alternative representations of the epidemic possible, charting a new course for community action against it. Hence, taken together, balls (performance labor) and houses (kin labor) constitute the community's creative response to the HIV/AIDS crisis, a response that heretofore has not been taken seriously in prevention research. HIV/AIDS prevention scholarship in public health has failed to take into account or to examine the range of Black LGBT community-defining practices that are, at times, deployed in addressing a community crisis such as HIV/AIDS. By revising and reconstituting gender and sexual identities and reconfiguring kinship while developing communal responses to HIV/AIDS, Black LGBT people construct this minoritarian sphere/alternative world of Ballroom culture.

Performance Ethnography

I was born and raised on the northwest side of Detroit and came of age in/among Black LGBT communities during the 1980s and 1990s until I moved to California in 1999. In *Butch Queens Up in Pumps*, I draw on these experiences to co-construct the lens through which this community is revealed. Since the Black LGBT scene in Detroit was then and is now an underground community, my relationships with people there provided me with access to the major players in the Ballroom scene, most of whom are interlocutors in this study. As both an insider and an outsider at various moments over the course of my study, I share similarities with those in the Ballroom community, but my life differs in important ways from the lives of many of its members. Therefore, I sometimes mobilize my reflections on, my experiences with, and my participation in the community and join them with the detailed memories and experiences shared by my interlocutors in the Ballroom scene in particular and the larger Black LGBT community in general to examine these rich, rapidly evolving cultural practices. This multidimensional examination reflects the ongoing, vexed relationship between Black LGBT people—who are central to but marginalized within this predominantly Black working class space—and Detroit.

I conducted fieldwork on this community for more than six years, during five of which I was an active member of The Legendary House of Prestige in three chapters: Detroit, Los Angeles, and the San Francisco Bay Area. I also conducted subsequent, periodic fieldwork between 2007 and 2012. I interviewed thirty-five members of the Ballroom community, some of them multiple times.[46] In terms of race/ethnicity, most of my interlocutors were Black/African American. Only one of my interlocutors identified as White. Most of my interviews with Ballroom members were with Butch Queens (gay men). This is not surprising because Butch Queens dominated the Ballroom scene in Detroit during the time of my research. Out of the thirty-five Ballroom members I interviewed, only five were Femme Queens (transwomen), two were Butches (transmen), and one was a cisgender lesbian woman, all of them were between the ages of twenty and forty-five at the time of the interview. All of my interlocutors were either working class or poor and from the Detroit Ballroom scene or from other scenes throughout the country. I attended and competed in over thirty ball events in Detroit, Atlanta, New York City, Philadelphia, Miami, Louisville, Charlotte, Indianapolis, Oakland, and Los Angeles, and I participated in house meetings and activities. I worked as a staff consultant for a now defunct HIV/AIDS prevention organization, Men of Color Motivational Group (MOC), which ran a prevention program that targeted the Ballroom community in Detroit and was funded by the Centers for Disease Control (CDC).

Because performance is the primary way in which the Ballroom community organizes and sustains itself, this project necessarily presents a *performance ethnographic* study of this culture. This methodology allowed me to assume the role of what the late performance ethnographer Dwight D. Conquergood called a *coperformative witness*. This approach requires one to perform and lend one's own body and labor to the process involved in the cultural formation under study, particularly when it involves a struggle for social justice. Performance thereby becomes the vehicle for moving across seemingly disparate social locations and registers of knowledge. In this context, rather than being simply a participant/ observer, I was coperformer, member, and community advocate, as well as theorist and critic.[47]

In this capacity, I joined the Detroit chapter of The Legendary House of Prestige, while working on HIV/AIDS prevention in the Ballroom community at MOC. I also found it necessary to participate in competitive performances at balls. At balls everyone assembled participates in what I refer to as the "performance system" of Ballroom culture. Because balls are communal events, one contributes to the performance labor as a commentator, an audience member, a judge, or a performer. There are, however, moments at balls when all elements of the performance system come together, and all those attending become coperformative witnesses to epiphanic moments of performance.

Coperformative witnessing not only structures my participation in the competitive performances at the ball events, it also informs the scope of my engagement with other aspects of the cultural labor of the Ballroom community. Although my fellow house members were aware that I was conducting research, when I competed at ball events the participants from the larger community had no way of knowing that I was a researcher. Therefore, my body was on the line and my performances were subjected to scrutiny, just as were those of all the other participants. This approach assumes an experientially focused, participatory epistemology that not only accesses hidden knowledges that are constitutive of the clandestine practices in the community but also is guided by ethical underpinnings and political commitments to the community. Hence, I sought to know "the how and who" in the everyday lives of Black LGBT members of Ballroom culture.[48] Furthermore, as a researcher whose life experiences are similar to those of most of the members of the community, I maintain an advocacy relationship with Ballroom culture, as well as Black LGBT people generally. While the principles of coperformative witnessing require the researcher to engage directly in the performances deployed in the culture, there is an ethical dimension to this approach that pushes the researcher to work beyond the site and ball events. Performance at balls largely dismantles the wall of division between spectator and spectacle, for me dissolving the line between the researcher and the researched. It also blurs the line between the performative and other aspects of everyday life. Performance undergirds members' commitments to and participation in their houses. Performance also helps some members generate income while playing a central role in HIV/AIDS awareness and prevention activities undertaken by others.

Butch Queens Up in Pumps is not a history of Ballroom culture; instead, it presents a genealogy of the contemporary scene's communal practices, situating them in historical Black LGBT culture. Each chapter offers an ethnographic examination of one dimension of Ballroom culture, contextualizing it within and linking it to earlier practices. If we are truly to understand Ballroom culture and its core dimensions, we must take seriously the histories from which they emerge. Hence, *Butch Queens Up in Pumps* is as much an examination of Black LGBT cultural formations in the United States and North America as it is an ethnographic account of Ballroom culture in Detroit.

It is necessary to provide a few caveats. I use the term *queer* to refer to the practices of identity, kinship, and community making in which the members of Ballroom culture are engaged. I do not claim, however, that members of this community use the term as a way to identify themselves. Instead, I refer to my interlocutors as LGBT throughout to convey the primary identities in terms of which members are understood and refer to themselves in the dominant world. And, as I elaborate throughout but most extensively in chapter 2, within the Ballroom scene, members of the community identify as being in one of the six categories in the gender system. Ultimately, I deploy queer theory to examine what members of the Ballroom community *do* as opposed to who they *are*.

Second, many of my interlocutors would not reveal their chronological age to me, and I did not require them to. I refer to interlocutors primarily by their Ballroom names, unless they asked me to use their given first name. In general Ballroom members choose their first name and use the house to which they belong as their last name. Finally, I want to make clear that *Butch Queens Up in Pumps* is only one story of many that can and should be told about Ballroom culture. The scene is huge and complex, expanding throughout the globe; thus, what is revealed in these pages captures only a small dimension of this overall phenomenon in primarily one social geography—that of Detroit.

Chapter 2, "'Ain't Nothing Like a Butch Queen': The Gender System in Ballroom Culture," delineates and examines the Ballroom gender system. Members of the Ballroom community function under expanded notions of sex, gender, and sexuality. Unlike the dominant US society, Ballroom communities view and adopt categories of identity as malleable and mutable. The "gender system" in Ballroom culture consists of six gender (and sexual) categories, and, while these categories do not break entirely free of hegemonic notions of sex, gender, and sexuality, the Ballroom gender system accepts more categories of identity and articulations of sex, gender, and sexuality than are claimed in the world outside this minoritarian sphere.

Although members call it the *gender* system, each category implies sexuality, at least implicitly, by demarcating the system in terms of meanings that are embedded in each of the categories. Therefore, in my analysis, I suggest that the gender system in Ballroom culture is always about sexuality and reflects the pervasive conflation of sex, gender, and sexuality in overall society. However, this system also reveals gender and sexual fluidity and multiple configurations of romantic, sexual, and nonsexual affinities and interactions among the members.

To elaborate on the expansive yet seemingly contradictory nature of the gender system (it is limited, yet fluid), I focus on the category of the Butch Queen. On the one hand, the Butch Queen is a good example of how, to a certain degree, these categories operate on fixity, as members impose and enforce strict criteria for inclusion in any category. On the other hand, because Black gender and sexual categories reflect the very complicated and often dangerous realities and conditions under which Black LGBT people live, the performance of sex, gender, and sexual categories in Ballroom can be considered an important form of individual and communal self-fashioning. This chapter also theorizes the Ballroom-derived concept of *realness*. In this sense, performance becomes a way for Ballroom members to refract the violence to which Black gender and sexual minorities are subjected in Detroit.

Chapter 3, "From Home to House: Ballroom Houses, Platonic Parents, and Overlapping Kinship," delineates the community-fashioned kinship system using the concept of kin labor or what I refer to as "housework." Ballroom members challenge conventional notions of marriage, family, and kinship by revising the gender relations and redefining gendered labor within the kin unit. Furthermore, I bring into focus the inextricable

linkage between Ballroom kinship and performance and the discreet
subjectivities that they engender.

In Ballroom, parental roles and relationships are based primarily on
the gender system. House parents, or what I refer to as "platonic parents,"
are mothers (men, women, or transgender women) and fathers (men or
transgender men) who, regardless of age, provide parental guidance to
members of the Ballroom community, especially by preparing them to
compete at the balls. This labor helps to constitute a particular form of
family and kinship in the community. Moreover, Ballroom culture exists
within larger Black and Latino/a LGBT communities that engage in what
I call overlapping kin-making practices.

These practices exist outside of what we have come to understand
as marriage, particularly the heteronormative domain from which Black
LGBT members have been or choose to be excluded. For working-class,
Black, gender, and sexual minorities, the precursor to seeking marriage
privileges is claiming a stable gender and sexual identity to gain access
to the benefits that this institution supposedly offers. However, such an
imperative is untenable for the members of the Ballroom community involved in my study. In fact Ballroom members remake the relationships
on which family is based through a flexible and overlapping kinship
structure, whereby LGBT members nurture and look after one another
according to a logic of kinship that exceeds gender and sexual norms, age
hierarchies, and biological ties.

Chapter 4, "'It's Gonna Get *Severe* up in *Here*': Ball Events, Ritualized
Performance, and Black Queer Space," provides a detailed ethnography
of ball events, particularly their ritualized performance system. It elucidates how Ballroom members use performance to create a Black queer
space, where such a space is a sociocultural undertaking rather than a
concrete spatiality (as in gay bars, clubs, and halls). I show that, although
balls happen in halls or clubs, Ballroom members perform social and
performance labor wherever they are to create a more abstract Black
queer space.

To illustrate the importance of balls, I create a composite ball based
on several balls in which I participated in Detroit as a member of The
Legendary House of Prestige. I examine all forms of performance labor
and focus on several important competitive categories. Using performance studies scholarship on ritual practices, I analyze the ritualized
performances undertaken at these events that address the needs of this

community. Members of the Ballroom community draw on performance practices from throughout the African Diaspora to create an occasion and space in which to find social support, affirmation, competition, and critique. Ball events rely on a performance relationship between the commentator, the audience, the runway performers, and the DJ. I delineate and refer to this relationship as the performance system.

Chapter 5, "'They Want Us Sick': Ballroom Culture and the Politics of HIV/AIDS," critically examines the HIV/AIDS epidemic and analyzes how the Ballroom community confronts the crisis and the havoc it has wreaked. The question that guides this chapter is: What does the Ballroom community do on its own to withstand the epidemic that goes unremarked in most HIV/AIDS prevention work, activism, and research?

First, I elaborate on the impact HIV/AIDS has had on the Ballroom community in Detroit. I analyze the extent to which the stigmatization associated with HIV and Black LGBT sexuality structures approaches to prevention. I recount my own experience working at MOC, the aforementioned HIV/AIDS prevention agency that targeted the Ballroom community. I suggest that stigmatization of HIV and Black LGBT sexuality is so far-reaching that the work of this organization was hampered by misogyny, internalized homophobia, femmephobia, and transphobia among its own staff members.

Second, I argue that in general HIV/AIDS prevention programs that target Black communities have relied on research and intervention models that are based on the role of individual sexual behavior and are devoid of cultural contextualization. As a result, the organic practices and strategies of prevention that emerge from within so-called at-risk communities have been woefully neglected by public health officials and prevention workers. For example, three strategies for HIV/AIDS prevention already exist within the Ballroom community and culture. Drawing on my earlier analyses of the gender system, ritualized performance at the balls, and kinship practices, this portion of the chapter elucidates the ways in which, according to one of my interlocutors, Ballroom is already "structured for prevention work." First, the community creates alternative social knowledge about HIV/AIDS to fight the stigmatization associated with Black gay sex and the epidemic. Second, through performance, members fashion prevention messages that are based on Ballroom values and norms. Finally, houses undertake kin labor or social support to help their members survive the epidemic.

The "Epilogue: The Future of Ballroom Culture" discusses the Ballroom scene today [approximately five years after I formally completed most of my fieldwork.]Throughout this book, I discuss Ballroom culture as a minoritarian sphere, one that is inclusive, egalitarian, and fluid in some ways but exclusionary and hierarchical in others. In addition, I discuss the various microscenes that have developed to redress, theoretically at least, the exclusions and hierarchies practiced and maintained in what members now call the "main scene." For example, designed mainly for HIV prevention purposes, the Kiki scene was conceived as a fun and less serious and competitive site for the younger LGBT people who aspire to compete in the main scene. The Women, Butches, and Transgender scene was founded to address the exclusion and marginalization of cisgender feminine and masculine women and transgender men and women in the main scene. In my discussion of the ways in which the scene has expanded throughout North America and other geographies around the globe, I also point out how these micropractices of Ballroom culture have been taken up in various global sites. Yet, as many of my interlocutors observed, while designed to address the limitations of the Ballroom community, these microscenes end up replicating the same hierarchies and regimes of exclusion—and, in some cases, gendered power relations—they were created to challenge and undo. Thus, I suggest that Ballroom is indeed a cultural formation that reproduces itself and expands while not completely eliminating the problems with which its membership struggles. In other words, inherent in cultural formations like Ballroom are conflicts caused by simultaneous possibilities and limits.

This ethnography tells a story that has never been told—Ballroom culture in Detroit—one that reveals, explicitly, the great extent to which this minoritarian sphere adds quality and value to the lives of its members. Black LGBT members participate in Ballroom communities to create livable lives for themselves. As I elucidate throughout, the cultural labor that members undertake helps an increasingly young Black LGBT membership find meaning in their lives under seemingly insurmountable conditions. Thus, for some, Ballroom literally *saves* lives. In Detroit, the familial, socioeconomic, cultural, and communal exclusion of Black LGBT people is increasingly harmful and destructive to young urban Black LGBT people, who suffer high rates of homelessness, unemployment, substance abuse, HIV infection, violence, and suicide. What is at stake for the Black LGBT people in Detroit is nothing less than finding meaning through individual and communal forms of social support and an opportunity to be cared for and nurtured when one's family and communities of origin fail to do so. It is also impossible to overstate the importance of having a space in which to hone one's creative skills through competitive performance. Ultimately, Ballroom culture provides a space in which, unlike in the dominant society, its members can be affirmed and valued as Black LGBT people, despite their poor or working class status.

TWO

"Ain't Nothing Like a Butch Queen"
The Gender System in Ballroom Culture

I see myself as a Butch Queen. A Butch Queen for me is a radical
act of resistance to normative black subjectivity, and mainstream
gay homogeneity.
— CHARLES F. STEPHENS, "PERFORMING BLACK AND GAY"[1]

Ain't Nothing Like a Butch Queen (Baby)

It is a chilly November afternoon, the Saturday of Thanksgiving weekend
of 2003, as I arrive at the Best Western Robert Trent Hotel in downtown
Newark, New Jersey, at about 2:15 p.m. for a national meeting of The
Legendary House of Prestige. The meeting is scheduled for 3:00 p.m.,
with a ball hosted by the house to be held late Sunday night at The Warehouse in the Bronx. The cofounder and overall housefather, Alvernian,
a Butch Queen, had called the meeting but was still in Philadelphia, or
so I am told by Grandmother Prestige, who is also a Butch Queen. Upon
my arrival, I soon realize that I will be waiting in the hotel for a long
time, something to which I have grown accustomed. In Ballroom culture, nothing begins or ends on time.

When I arrive in the hotel lobby, Grandmother Prestige meets me
at the front desk and escorts me to the room in which the meeting is
to be held. There I join Trinity Prestige, the new housemother, and a
few other members from the Detroit chapter who are already there. To
my surprise, a very young White Femme Queen named Princess, from
Flint, Michigan, who is being recruited by Trinity, is in the hotel room.
Liquid, a very popular Butch Queen from The House of Escada in the
Detroit scene, is also in the room, hanging out and having a good time
with us while we wait for the rest of the Prestige kids and Father Alvernian to arrive. As we are all laughing, joking, and "cocktailing," Trinity

and Liquid begin espousing the so-called virtues of being Butch Queens, gay men. They explain how Butch Queens get the best sex, being "versatile in bed." According to Trinity, this is true because "We fuck and get fucked." Of course, this is not always the case, but in the Ballroom scene the Butch Queen is the quintessential sexually versatile subject. Eventually, Trinity and Liquid break spontaneously into song: "Ain't nothin' like a Butch Queen baby; ain't nothin' like a Butch Queen," using the melody and some of the words from the 1967 Marvin Gaye and Tammi Terrell recording, *Ain't Nothing Like the Real Thing*. Trinity and Liquid's spontaneous tune speaks, on the one hand, to the dominance and privilege that Butch Queens enjoy in the Ballroom community while revealing, on the other hand, the pleasure in and transgressive possibilities of the Butch Queen category for a reformulation of the masculine/feminine binary.

This chapter delineates and examines what Ballroom members refer to as the "gender system." I argue here that the gender system and its attendant categories and performance criteria are constructed by Ballroom members' engagement in individual and communal labor. Because it is both produced by and embedded in the performance system and the social relations that develop in Ballroom culture, my discussion of the gender system also highlights the performance categories that this system articulates within the community. Through gender and sexual performativity, Ballroom members create a wider range of gender and sexual subjectivities than is recognized and legitimized in the heteronormative world. These categories include and extend beyond the heteronormative male/female and heterosexual/homosexual binaries. Ballroom members also expose the limits of gay, lesbian, and transgender identities.[2] Performance is a form of cultural labor that Ballroom members undertake to create a minoritarian social sphere. This chapter explores the ways in which quotidian performance underpins the gender and sexual identity formation that is at the heart of this community.

While highlighting the gender system's core function in the Ballroom community, I examine it in four ways. First, I discuss how the six-part system provides the collection of categories from which all members choose one with which to identify. The gender system is queer insofar as it allows for, and in many cases celebrates, sex, gender, and sexual fluidity and diversity. Members of the Ballroom community enact and experience sex, gender, and sexual identification as a performative process rather than as an immutable biological fact. I also discuss how the gender system structures the competitive performative categories at balls. As I do throughout this book, I analyze the gender system from a queer perspective even though members of the community do not refer to themselves as queer. In this chapter, I argue that sex, gender, and sexuality are *what* one *does* rather than inherently *who* one *is*. Similarly, I emphasize that *queer* is not only what one does but is also a framework within which to analyze the practices that drive Ballroom culture.

Second, although members call it the *gender system,* each category implies sexuality, implicitly if not explicitly, by demarcating it in terms of meanings that are embedded in each of the categories. Therefore, in my analysis, I suggest that the gender system in Ballroom culture is always about sexuality and reflects the pervasive conflation of sex, gender, and sexuality in the broader society. This system also, however, reveals the gender and sexual fluidity that plays out in the various configurations of romantic, sexual, and nonsexual affinities and interactions that occur among the members.

To elaborate on the expansive yet conflicting nature of the gender system, I focus primarily on the category of the Butch Queen. On the one hand, the Butch Queen is a good example of how, to a certain degree, these categories do indeed operate on fixity. This is to say that, while categories in the gender system allow for identities and expressions and erotic practices that extend beyond the traditional male/female and gay/bisexual/straight divisions, the members impose and enforce strict criteria determining who can claim or be included in a specific category. For instance, the Butch Queen is a gay man, but his gender performance can fall anywhere on the feminine-to-masculine continuum as long as he is a gay man. Yet transgender men who identify as gay may or may not move into the Butch Queen category. Instead, most transgender men, regardless of their sexuality, claim the gender category Butch (female-to-male, transgendered men at various stages of gender or sexual transformation). Simply put, just as dominant sex/gender/sexual categories in society seem fixed and stable but are not always that way in fact, likewise, the Ballroom gender system can appear to be fixed and stable while some aspects are actually fluid and unstable.

Third, I delineate the concept of and criteria associated with "realness," offering a theory of gender performance and performativity that both emerges from and is applicable to the Ballroom community. Because Black gender and sexual categories reflect the very complicated and often dangerous realities and conditions under which Black LGBT people live, I argue that the performance of sex, gender, and sexual categories in Ballroom should be considered a technology of the self—both individual and communal. Although this technology of the self is undertaken, in part, by individuals, the coproduction, critique, and reformulation of gender and sexual identities happens in the course of a collective process, what I refer to as communal performance labor. In this sense, performance becomes a method—a form of work—through which Ballroom members attempt to refract the violence to which Black gender and sexual minorities are subjected in Detroit. LGBT Ballroom members do not enjoy the race and class privilege that some of their White LGBT peers do, limiting their access to sex reassignment (sex change) technologies, for instance. Therefore, working and negotiating the body through gender performance becomes a viable and desirable alternative to a more conventional (and public) sex, gender, and sexual identification. These transgressive performances of the body are rehearsals and momentary acts of freedom within the liminal space and practice of the ball scene.

Finally, I consider language and consumption practices as additional aspects of the individual and communal performance labor in which Ballroom members are engaged. I examine Ballroom vernacular as another form of individual and collective self-fashioning. Community members create new terms and fashion alternative meanings for standard terms. In many cases, community members recuperate derogatory terms by endowing them with alternative meanings within the Ballroom community context. I suggest that the practice of ascribing alternative meanings to such terms is a form of performance labor, even as the alternative meaning often breaks insufficiently from its pervasive usage in the dominant society.

Similarly, since expressing performative identities through fashion is an integral part of this culture—based on fashion categories and the presentation of bodily and physical attributes at the balls—I address consumption practices in the final pages of this chapter. The relatively low socioeconomic status of most members of the community induce some—not all—to acquire these garments by shoplifting (mopping) and credit card/check fraud (crafting). Although it might seem easy to blame such participation in illegal activity or conspicuous consumption

by Ballroom members on their obsession with material goods and the
lifestyles of the rich and famous, I insist on a more complicated and
nuanced analysis of their pursuit and acquisition of material goods. In
the Ballroom context, consumption can also be understood as an act
of resistance to or survival within the exclusionary practices on which
consumption in our market-driven capitalist system is based. Therefore,
the Ballroom community's consumption behavior cannot be adequately
understood simply as purely criminal on the one hand or wholly resis-
tant on the other.

The Gender System

The performance labor undertaken by Black LGBT people in Ballroom
culture has created the means through which members revise and create
alternative gender and sexual subjectivities. I argue that, for members
of Ballroom culture in particular, gender and sexual performativity are
significant aspects of the cultural work of constructing community. Even
though the performance labor involved in the production of gender
and sexual subjectivities is enacted at the ball events, it is important to
keep in mind that the balls, although they are "many things," are always
linked to community members' quotidian experiences in the larger society.[3] The gender system consists of six gender (and sexual) categories:
Butch Queens (gay men), Butches (female-to-male [FTM] transgender),
Femme Queens (male-to-female [MTF] transgender), Butch Queens Up
in Drag, Men, and Women. While these categories do not break entirely
from hegemonic notions of sex, gender, and sexuality, the Ballroom gender system includes more identity categories and articulations than are
available to members and legible to people outside of Ballroom.

My central aim in this section is to consider what can be learned from
Ballroom culture about sex, gender, and sexuality as these categories of
identity are lived daily both in and outside of the Ballroom scene. Thus,
while I acknowledge the limits of this system of categories, chiefly its
privileging of cisgender men and masculinity, I emphasize how the gender system makes it possible for members to reformulate sex, gender,
and sexual knowledge and practice not only for LGBT people but for all
others as well. I cannot overemphasize that these transitive and discrete
gender and sexual subjectivities are the result of a considerable amount
of work, a form of discursive labor that often goes unnoticed and is taken

for granted by those outside the community. Since all identities are produced in large part through rituals of the self and communal forms of representation, quotidian performance plays a vital part in Ballroom members' reconstitution of their gender and sexual identities.[4] I suggest that performance labor consists not only of the presentation of gender through comportment or behavior but also of one's efforts to reconfigure and fashion the body as a part of constructing and claiming a gender and sexual identity. This performance labor produces a counterdiscourse of identification and serves as the machinery driving social relations in Ballroom culture and the forms of group knowledge that underpin them.

There are three overarching dimensions to the gender system in Ballroom culture: sex, gender, and sexuality. Members of the Ballroom community expand all three. Unlike in the dominant, heteronormative US society, Ballroom communities view and adopt categories of identity as malleable and mutable. In this community, when it comes to sex, gender, and sexuality, most things are open, negotiable, and alterable. These aspects of the gender system are salient revisions of traditional gender and sexual norms. Ballroom members conceive of three categories of sex:

1. Female (a person born with female sex characteristics)
2. Male (a person born with male sex characteristics)
3. Intersex (a person born with both male and female or indeterminate genitalia).[5]

Even though these appear to be delimited categories, Ballroom members do not equate the anatomic sex or genital configurations with which one is born with a rigid, lifelong gender identity. For example, there is a difference between being genetically assigned to the female sex at birth and living as a woman. *Female* or *female bodied* refers to sex and *woman* refers to gender.[6] According to the feminist bioscientist Ann Fausto-Sterling, sex categories receive gender; therefore, in the dominant society, one's sex assignment at birth is believed to coincide with a predetermined and fixed gender. Ballroom members, however, view categories of sex as open and unfinished, just as they do gender.[7] Akin to their notions of gender and sexuality, the sex of a body is the result of an ongoing process or activity as opposed being a biological fact. The sex categories that are linked to the gender system in Ballroom culture differ from the male/female binary in dominant society. This system is constructed through modes of knowing that most accurately reflect the lived realities and conditions that Ballroom members experience because they believe fundamentally that sex categories are malleable and the body can be altered through various means. As I will show, bodily modification is accomplished in Ballroom life mostly through hormonal therapy, padding, hair modifications, and so on. Reconstructive surgery is cost prohibitive for most members of the Ballroom community. And those who, for whatever reason, find themselves uncomfortable or dissatisfied with the sex to which they were assigned at birth can and do refashion themselves through a variety of means to live their lives in sexed categories they choose as alternatives to what had been imposed on them.

As they do with sex categories, Ballroom members also modify gender categories, even though, like sex, gender is not created entirely from whole cloth. This reflects the extent to which all our lives are influenced by notions of gender that are believed to be biologically determined. [Gender categories, however, are socially and culturally produced and imposed on bodies and people rather than being biologically inherent to them.]Ballroom members choose within a system of predetermined gender categories, even though some of these categories are formed and fashioned by the community itself. In Ballroom, categories exclude and delimit, as they do in the larger society. Nevertheless, I am less concerned with the limits of these gender categories than I am with what Ballroom members *do* to gender. To be clear, the genders and sexualities found in Ballroom culture are subjectivities insofar as members identify and fashion themselves by and through the convergent notions of sex, gender, and sexuality within the Ballroom community *and* as those meanings are imposed on them by society. Thus, Ballroom members do not reject dominant gender norms entirely, nor do they desire to do so; rather, by revealing and exploiting the unstable and fluid nature of socially produced and performed gender categories, members forge more creative and expansive ways of living their gender and sexual lives. Ultimately, as Enoch Page and Matt U. Richardson suggest, queer gender subjectivities reflect the multitude of experiences of creatively nonconforming gender identities, sexualities, and bodily configurations, both anatomic and performative.[8]

As noted at the outset of this section, the gender system in Ballroom culture consists of six categories, which I list here again with brief descriptions:[9]

1. *Butch Queens Up in Drag* (gay men who perform in drag but do not take hormones and do not live as women).
2. *Femme Queens* (transgender women or MTF at various stages of gender transition involving hormonal or surgical processes, such as breast implants).
3. *Butches* (transgender men or FTM at various stages of gender transition involving hormonal therapy, breast wrapping or removal, and so on or masculine lesbians or females appearing as men irrespective of their sexuality).
4. *Women* (biological females who live as women and are lesbian, straight identified, or queer).
5. *Men/Trade* (biological males who live as men, are very masculine, and are straight identified or nongay identified).
6. *Butch Queens* (biological males who live and identify as gay or bisexual men and are or can be masculine, hypermasculine (as in thug masculinity), or very feminine.

The term *gender system* is something of a misnomer. Again, it is not about gender only; it is also always about sexuality, which is expressed in either implicit or explicit terms. Therefore, I draw distinctions between gender and sexual categories of identity. In the broader society, gender and sexuality are conflated.[10] For example, in the United States, among gender and sexual minorities, those who identify as LGBT are lumped together as a community, even though *lesbian, gay,* and *bisexual* denote sexual identities and *transgender* is a gender category.[11] Some sexuality categories are combined with gender categories. For example, a Butch Queen is a gay man, but a Femme Queen is a transgender woman. The former is both a gender and sexual identity, while the latter is solely a gender identity.

Furthermore, it has often been assumed by outsiders that all Ballroom members, regardless of gender, claim a gay identity. This is far from the case, as members claim a variety of sexual identities. Moreover, these identity claims do not always reflect the romantic/sexual relationships in which they are involved. For example, Femme Queens are involved in romantic and sexual relationships mostly with men, many of whom are straight identified and *not* in the Ballroom scene. Yet other Femme Queens are involved in gay, lesbian, and bisexual romantic and sexual relationships and identify as such. If a Femme Queen dates or has sex with men, she typically identifies as heterosexual. When I asked Levin, a Femme Queen and free agent, about her sexual identity, she said, "I would say, living as a woman, [I'm] heterosexual. But it's hard to say . . . because you know what other people gone say, you know, 'cus it's really considered you still gay or whatever, but I don't talk to no women, so . . ." Interestingly, Levin's boyfriend does not identify as heterosexual. Despite acknowledging how society might see her as a gay man if someone "knows her business," Levin insists that as a Femme Queen she is heterosexual because she is romantically and sexually interested in male-bodied men, even if her boyfriend does not identify as heterosexual.

Most Femme Queens date masculine or "thuggish" gay men. Brianna Cristal's boyfriend identifies as a bisexual man, and he is not involved in the Ballroom scene, but he wants to walk Thug Realness. Nonetheless, both Brianna and Levin said their boyfriends are very masculine and "look like boys," but neither identifies exclusively as either gay or straight. Although it is far less common, there are also Femme Queens who are romantically/sexually involved with Women, Butches, and other Femme Queens. I encountered few such scenarios while I was conducting my fieldwork, but increasingly in recent years members are engaged in a variety of romantic and sexual relationships with both members and nonmembers. Gender and sexual couples vary in combinations because the gender system creates the conditions for it. Gender performance in Ballroom culture is intertwined with self-identification and implies a wide range of sexual practices and identities. Nevertheless, the fluidity of both gender and sexuality makes identification in Ballroom complicated and multidimensional.

Butch Queens Up in Drag

While drag performances (involving both MTF and FTM) have always been a hallmark of Ballroom culture, new categories have emerged within the scene, and gender and sexual subjectivities have been codified to accommodate the vast diversity of gender and sexuality in the community. As a result, Ballroom members have created separate categories to distinguish drag or Butch Queens Up in Drag—gay men who *perform* as women—from Femme Queens—male-bodied individuals who *live* as women. There is no stand-alone subjectivity for drag kings, and there is no category referred to as butches up in drag in the Ballroom community.

Although he is not a Ballroom member, the best known public example of a Butch Queen Up in Drag is RuPaul, who lives as Andre Charles.
One of the most popular Butch Queens Up in Drag of the Ballroom scene
in Detroit is Diva of The House of Chaos, a house that was formed ex-
pressly for Butch Queens Up in Drag. Diva lives as a gay man. Members
like Diva compete in categories for realness, vogue performance, and
fashion and body presentation. Unlike Femme Queens, Butch Queens
Up in Drag do not take hormones, and they do not get breast implants
or other surgical body modifications. Instead, they use padding, wigs,
and clothing to create their drag appearance. It is worth noting that Diva
makes all of the clothing and costumes he wears when he competes at
balls and performs at drag shows.

Many of my interlocutors maintain that mainstream representations
of the Ballroom scene conflate drag queens with Femme Queens, miscat-
egorizing the entire community as a drag queen community. This point
is evidenced by frequent references to balls as "drag balls." Drag performance and those who identify as drag performers and competitors comprise only one dimension of a much larger panoply of subjectivities and
practices in the scene. The gender system makes this apparent.

Femme Queens

Femme Queens are transgender women at various stages of MTF gender transition. Almost all Femme Queens are preoperative and rely on
other forms of body modification in the transition process. As mentioned, Femme Queen is solely a gender identity in the Ballroom scene.
Femme Queens compete in many performance categories at balls, such
as Femme Queen Body and Femme Queen Face. In terms of realness,
they compete in Femme Queen Realness categories. And, although
mainstream representations of Ballroom culture and LGBT communities tend to conflate drag queens with Femme Queens, as I suggested
above, the Ballroom scene definitively distinguishes Femme Queens and
Butch Queens Up in Drag, the latter being a drag queen category. Among
their fellow Ballroom members, Femme Queens refer to themselves accordingly, but in the outside world Femme Queens tend not to refer to
themselves as transgender or transwomen. Instead, since they live as
women, they tend to identify as such. I take note of what Ballroom Legend Ayanna Christian, a Femme Queen, proudly proclaimed, recently, at

a Ballroom conference in Washington, DC: "I am a Black woman." Such a proclamation is understandable insofar as many Femme Queens report having always felt as though they were women, and it reflects the work required of them to undertake such a transition.

Although Levin said that she wants eventually to have a sex change, she explained that once one decides to transition to being and living as a woman one must take it seriously from then on. For Femme Queens in the Ballroom scene, most of whom are poor and working class, hormonal therapy is the first and most important step in gender transitioning and self-fashioning. Brianna Cristal agreed with this notion and explained her experience: "[But] I mean you have to find out about hormones because I didn't find out about hormones until I was like in drag a couple of months and then that's when I heard about the shots and bought me some. Once you start hormones you start seeing the results in like a month or two, if you keep on them like you are supposed to." Another aspect of gender transitioning involves breast implants. Levin said her breast implants cost her about five thousand dollars. Alternatively, some Femme Queens undertake the very dangerous option of silicone injections, which unfortunately are often provided by people who have no idea how to administer them. Finally, Levin and Brianna Cristal emphasized the importance of hair and the options of hair weaves or simply allowing the hair to grow long enough to be styled in a manner that enhances a would-be Femme Queen's femininity. Some Femme Queens already have what the community refers to as a "female figure," or feminine qualities. As Brianna Cristal explained, "I was always thin, so I always felt like a woman even when I was a boy, so no matter how I dressed or whatever, I still felt like feminine." Therefore, for some Femme Queens, always feeling like a woman, along with the attributes they already possess, adds to whatever body modification efforts they undertake.

Despite the impression that the subjectivities in the gender system are fixed and stable, and that there are clearly defined characteristics that determine who is a Femme Queen and who is not, some Ballroom members treat their identity claims within the scene and in their lives very fluidly. For instance, Lovely, a Femme Queen member of The House of Mohair during this study, opts for neither hormones nor breast implants. Instead, Lovely pads her chest, hips, and buttocks. She identifies and competes as a Femme Queen in the scene, but she does not consider herself a transgender woman and does not identify as a Butch Queen Up in Drag. Rather, she considers herself androgynous. Lovely is, then, one example of the fluidity in the gender system, making evident some of the ambiguity that exists between gender identity claims in the Ballroom scene and the lives that members lead in the world outside of it. Perhaps most important, just as transgender lives, knowledges, and practices have done more broadly, Femme Queens—as transgender women—call into question the commonsense notion of "woman" as a social category in the larger society. Moreover, as transgender studies scholar Susan Stryker insists, "Transgender phenomena challenge the unifying potential of the category 'woman' and call for new analyses, new strategies and practices, for combating discrimination and injustice based on gender inequality,"[12] and, I would add, for understanding sex and gender as social and cultural categories.

Butches

Like the Femme Queen, the Butch is explicitly a gender category, while multiple sexualities are implied. Butches are transgender men at various stages of FTM gender transition. At balls, Butches compete in various performance categories, but mostly in Butch Realness. Butches identify as gay or lesbian, straight, bisexual, or sexually fluid. Butches in the Ballroom scene have become more prominent recently, in part due to the release of the documentary film, *The Aggressives,* which features Black, Latina, and Asian American Butches, lesbians, and female-bodied women who are masculine or identify as "aggressive." Some of the Butches in the film are involved in the Ballroom community. Interestingly, in Black LGBT communities, drag king performance does not enjoy the same prominence as does drag queen performance. Again, in the Ballroom scene there is no butches up in drag category. Instead, the Butch is a kind of catchall gender category for biological females that consists of FTM transgender men, masculine lesbians, aggressives, tomboys, studs, drag kings, and so on. There is, however, at least a tacit acknowledgment of a difference between an FTM who *lives* as a man and one who only *performs* and competes as one.

Over the course of my study of and participation in the Detroit Ballroom scene, only a few members of the community identified and competed as Butches. Most Butches take hormones to produce body hair, particularly facial hair, a lower voice, and other physical changes, such as clitoral growth. Many Butches wrap or bind their breasts, or have them removed altogether, but this is usually the extent of the surgery they are willing to undergo. As is the case with most Femme Queens, surgery is cost prohibitive for Butches, so hormones are the cheapest and most accessible means of undergoing a gender transition. All of these changes produce what is believed to be masculine bodily characteristics. They also prepare the Butch body to compete in Butch Realness categories, as it is common for a Butch to remove his shirt and reveal a muscular chest and chiseled torso. As I discuss in chapter 4, Godfather Reno, a member of the Philadelphia chapter of The Legendary House of Prestige, was famous for winning Butch Realness categories at balls.

In the gender system, the Butch category encompasses a whole range of individuals, including female-bodied women who are "masculine appearing." Since there is no category specifically for lesbian women (irrespective of being masculine or feminine) as there is for the Butch Queen—a gay man—in the gender system, Butch becomes one of only two categories that include female-bodied women, the other being Women. Furthermore, Butch is the only category in the gender system in which both female-bodied women and female-bodied men are included in the same category. I reiterate that the Femme Queen category consists of male-bodied women only; the Butch Queen Up in Drag category is only for gay men who perform as women; the Butch Queen and Men categories consist only of male-bodied men. These elisions in the gender system indicate that power and privilege are accorded to gay men and masculinity within the community. I suspect that, as the participation of anatomic females and women in the scene continues to grow, the Ballroom community will be challenged to expand its gender system to reflect its membership more accurately. Nonetheless, for Butches, Femme Queens, and even Butch Queens Up in Drag, the fluid nature of Ballroom categories allows members who cannot afford a sex reassignment or do not want one the latitude of exercising their chosen gender and sexual identities and leading their lives based on their own life preferences and experiences.

Women

The Woman category is a gender identity and represents, in many respects, a contrast to the other categories, for it is the only category exclusively for female-bodied (cisgender) women who live as and, at the very least, appear as women. While the Woman category can include women who are straight, lesbian, or bisexual identified, and whose self-performances fall along the continuum from masculinity to femininity, there is no separate category for women who live as women and are lesbians. I reiterate that his distinguishes their place in Ballroom culture from that of gay men, who have the Butch Queen category available to them. Moreover, unlike the Man identity in Ballroom culture, on which I elaborate below, the sexual identity or practice of a Woman is not apparent. She is neither always straight identified, nor is she always a lesbian. Her sexuality is understood to fall within a wide range of possibilities. Increasingly, Women are joining the Ballroom community but on a limited basis in the Detroit scene. As the presence of Women increases in the scene, the number of competitive categories for Women at balls increases as well. During the course of my study, The national secretary of The Legendary House of Prestige, based in Philadelphia, was a Woman who identified as straight, and the housemother of the Detroit chapter of The House of Prodigy was a woman whose sexuality was fluid.

Men

In the gender system of Ballroom culture, Men participate in the community, either directly or indirectly, and are usually romantically involved or have sex with Butch Queens or Femme Queens. Men do not typically identify as gay, often identifying as straight or bisexual instead. Men are usually very masculine and, if they participate in balls, they compete in realness categories. Some Men participate in house activities but do not walk balls. The Man category is both a gender category and a sexual one because of the joined ideas of sexual practice embedded in and ascribed to the identity. Men are similar to what is known as *Trade* in Black LGBT culture at large. To be known as *Trade* is to be known as a straight-identified man who is paid either to have sex with a man as a *trick* or who dibbles and dabbles in homosexuality but does not consider himself to be gay or bisexual.[13] Men also have romantic and sexual relationships with Femme Queens, which is consistent with their identifying as straight because Femme Queens live as women. Conversely, a few Men who are involved in relationships with Femme Queens do identify as bisexual even if they do not see themselves as gay; hence, they are not Butch Queens. Brianna Cristal's boyfriend, for example, identifies as bisexual, according to her. Another example is Lovely's boyfriend, a Man who, according to Lovely, had never "messed around" before. Lovely considers her boyfriend to be a Man "because he doesn't do what bisexual men do. I don't date men that suck penis or bend over. If they want to play with the penis that totally defeats the purpose for me." Lovely's statements demonstrate the Ballroom view that Man as an identity is constituted by both gender and sexuality or, more precisely, sexual practice and position. A Man is one who does not "suck penis"; rather, he gets his penis sucked. He is not a bottom; he is a top.[14]

Being a Man/Trade bears some resemblance to being an MSM (a man who has sex with men), a term used in public health discourses to describe men who do not identify as gay but nonetheless engage in sex with men or male-bodied women. The category Man relies on a kind of representational masculinity that marks a man as heterosexual or at least a masculinity that does not signal strong or consistent same-sex desires or practices. In addition to what I have suggested here, the Man identity in the gender system creates a space in the Ballroom community for men who are sexually curious or fluid, are engaged in sex work, or fall in love with or are attracted to a Butch Queen, Femme Queen, or Woman. This allows them to belong to the Ballroom community in some way without having to identify as one of the more commonly claimed identities.

Butch Queens

The Butch Queen identity or the gay man is a normative category in Ballroom, just as Black gay men dominate the larger Black LGBT community. Butch Queens comprise the vast majority of the membership in the Ballroom scene throughout North America. Most of the roles in the kinship system are undertaken by Butch Queens; we will see in chapter 3 that most of the housemothers and housefathers in the community are Butch Queens. For example, Alvernian, the cofounder and national housefather of The Legendary House of Prestige, is a Butch Queen, and Duchess and Trinity Prestige, both of whom served as housemothers of the Detroit chapter, are Butch Queens. Tino and Noir Prestige are both masculine Butch Queens who walked realness categories, Thug Realness and Schoolboy Realness, respectively. All of the national and most of the local commentators of whom I know are Butch Queens, such as Jack Givenchy, Selvin Kahn, and Kodak Kadinsky. Furthermore, most of the more prominent members in the Detroit scene are Butch Queens, such as Mother Goddess and Diva D Bvlgari. Many of the houses in this study are or were Butch Queen houses, such as The House of Ford, The Cash Money Boys (CMB), The House of Prodigy, and The Legendary House of Prestige. Finally, I am a Butch Queen, and so are the majority of the interlocutors represented in this book.

Although it is claimed almost exclusively by cisgender men and forms along a continuum from masculinity to femininity, the Butch Queen category includes very masculine and very feminine individuals as long as they identify and live as gay men. Butch Queens are therefore not confined by dominant notions of masculinity and deploy a variety of conflicting performances. In some ways, then, Butch Queens push the limits of masculinity, thereby challenging assumptions about Black men in general that are shaped by essentialist notions of race, class, gender, and sexuality.[15]

While it is no coincidence that Butch Queens are men who are gay—reflecting the privileging of men in Ballroom culture—this category that wraps gender and sexual identity into one also reflects a collapse of the masculine/feminine binary of gender presentation and performance. Mainstream notions and representations of Ballroom culture associate gender transgression with Femme Queens, Butches, and Butch Queens Up in Drag. These categories of identity are understood to be the quintessential examples of how Ballroom culture challenges, revises, and reconfigures gender norms. Because Butch Queen is primarily a sexual category, it tends to be overassociated with sexuality and underestimated as a site for the practice of gender transgression. As I demonstrated at the opening of this chapter, even Ballroom members emphasize the so-called sexual versatility of the Butch Queen without considering how he represents more expansive and fluid forms of masculinities and femininities within the one category. Notwithstanding the substantial prominence in the Ballroom scene that Butch Queens enjoy, insufficient attention has been paid to them as a transgressive category of gender.

To claim the Butch Queen identity is to commit what writer and critic Charles F. Stephens calls "a radical act of resistance to normative black subjectivity and mainstream gay homogeneity."[16] Kali, a Butch Queen from The House of Ford, described his Ballroom gender and sexual identity as representing one who can be very feminine or very masculine or both simultaneously. He explained further, "Butch Queens can be bangy, meaning they are gay black men that act straight. And on the other hand, gay men that are boyish act feminine, too." Kali Ford emphasized, in so many words, that a Butch Queen's gender is flexible, fluid, and contingent. Explained another way, when the Butch Queen "boy" has to walk the runway at a ball, he performs femininity and enacts the runway strut that "serves the kids." Yet that same Butch Queen needs to and can act like a boy or a "thug" when he is walking Butch Queen Body. In this category, the body and the gender expression go hand in hand to produce a performance that will be recognized and affirmed by the community.

There are times, however, when the movement from one side of the masculine-to-feminine continuum to the other cannot be viewed as progressive. For instance, I was struck when Diva D announced to me that he was changing from being the housemother of The House of Bvlgari to ✨ being the housefather for, as he put it, masculinity reasons. And, interestingly, other members confirmed that the decision was a house decision, not a decision made unilaterally by Diva D. In cases such as this one, a house sometimes wants a father figure who is also pursuing a masculine gender whether or not the actual person presents himself as a masculine Butch Queen. Nevertheless, only the Butch Queen is allowed to change from mother to father or vice versa and maintain the same identity in the gender system.

Gender system identities derive most of their coherence from the multitude of performance categories at the balls, reflecting how the performative identity of Ballroom members is inextricably linked to the categories they walk/perform at the balls. Ultimately, in the Ballroom scene, the conventional terms and conflations used for gender and sexual identification (such as male/female and man/woman or gay, lesbian, transgender, and straight) are unreliable monikers because they do not accurately reflect the complexities of gender and sexuality in the community.

Gender as Communal Performance Labor

The gender system and its attendant categories and meanings are a form of individual and communal self-fashioning. Specifically, however, gender self-fashioning is constituted by a form of communal performance labor whereby the community creates, recognizes, and confers legitimacy on particular performances of gender and sexual identity. To be clear, this communal performance labor is undertaken not only within the context of balls but also in the daily lives of Ballroom members, thereby inform-

Fig. 1. A Femme Queen contestant walking in a Femme Queen Body category in the "Love Is the Message" Ball in Los Angeles in 2005. (Photograph by Marlon M. Bailey.)

ing both aspects of their lives. Fashioning the self requires considerable exertion, which LGBT members of the Ballroom scene take pleasure in doing and view as a necessary life strategy. This section discusses both the pleasures and the high stakes involved in gender performance labor, as well as some of the internal hierarchies and struggles involved in gender that play out within the community.

Since, as Susan Stryker reminds us, gender is *what* we *do* not *who* we *are,* I reiterate that Ballroom members undertake cultural labor in a variety of forms.[17] All of these forms are underpinned by performance, which is the basis on which this community constitutes an alternative space in which members are affirmed, celebrated, supported, and constructively critiqued. To argue that the gender system in Ballroom is based on communal performance labor, I borrow from what the feminist and queer studies scholar Jane Ward theorizes as gender labor. In her essay "Gender Labor: Transmen, Femmes, and Collective Work of Transgression," Ward insightfully describes gender labor as

Fig. 2. A Butch contestant walking in a Butch Face category at the "Love is the Message Ball" in Los Angeles in 2005. (Photograph by Marlon M. Bailey.)

the affective and bodily efforts invested in giving gender to others, or actively suspending self-focus in the service of helping others achieve the varied forms of gender recognition they long for. Gender labor is the work of bolstering someone's gender authenticity, but it is also the work of co-producing someone's gender irony, transgression, or exceptionality.[18]

While what I describe about Ballroom culture departs slightly from what Ward offers here, the gist of her argument illuminates the function of communal performance labor that I discuss. Members create, sustain, and affirm forms of presentation and performance in the community.

Ballroom itself is a result of the collective efforts of its members to create a minoritarian sphere for those who are excluded from or marginalized within the majoritarian society. This minoritarian sphere enables individuals, houses, and sectors of the community to undertake a process of identity making and remaking, against pervasive notions of identity that are fixed and permanent. For many of my interlocutors, Ballroom culture is what Diva D Bvlgari called a "fictitious existence." When I asked him whether "low self-worth" was a motivating factor for Black LGBT people to join the Ballroom scene, he responded by saying:

> Yes, it gives them a brand new identity; it gives them a brand new slate. If your family don't care about you because you are gay and what not or if you can't get a job, the Ballroom scene helps you start anew. It creates a brand new identity that you can feel comfortable with. No matter what you had to do to get it . . . steal, kill, or what have you.

Therefore, as the members of the community work to create this sphere, this "fictitious existence" that is at the same time very real—and necessarily so—they individually and collectively revel in the opportunity to explore the creative potential that this sphere enables. Prince J, a Butch Queen from The House of Prodigy, in echoing this point, told me, "I feel like if you can't be creative then you can't be innovative and you can't grow. You can't bring new things to yourself . . . or to your house or to anywhere, really. You have to be creative." Prince J highlights the need for an individual member to always consider what he or she brings to the house and thus to the larger community. "Bringing it," as Ballroom members say, to the larger community is the means through which one engages in a dialectic of gender performance. In other words, one brings his or her ideas and creativity to the ball to be judged and critiqued, and this process no doubt plays a crucial role in self-fashioning.

Having to live under difficult conditions in the urban space, that is to say, in impoverished, rough, and violent neighborhoods, many members come to the Ballroom scene to hone what Tim'm T. West calls "a broader range of gender performance." This begins the learning process. Upon entering the scene, one has to learn the performance norms, not only in terms of the competitive categories but also in terms of how one presents and lives one's subjectivity. Although the process is not unique to Ballroom members, teaching and learning gender is crucial in the scene. Housemothers teach their children who are Femme Queens when and how to take hormones, how to don fashionable garments, and how to present themselves and walk and perform at balls in order to avoid getting chopped—being eliminated from the category as opposed to getting a score of ten from each judge—and survive the first cut in the category.

Levin taught her "gay" daughter Brianna the steps involved in the process of transitioning from a Butch Queen Up in Drag to a Femme Queen. Levin guided her through hormone therapy, a hairweave, and gender self-fashioning so she could be as competitive as possible at balls and simultaneously blend into the larger society when necessary. It is worth mentioning that Levin's "gay mother" Tori did the same for her. Although this communal performance labor happens at various levels and in various domains within the Ballroom scene—including in individual houses and larger Black LGBT communities—what I describe as told to me by my interlocutors is that which communal performance labor entails. Teaching and learning gender is an ongoing process, as gender and sexual identities are always constructed, revised, and enacted on demand within a given context.

It is worth noting how members of the community use performance to work within the system to transgress and expand even the categories that are most often delimited and policed. Moreover, as I have suggested, many Ballroom members' gender and sexual identities within the system are different from what they live in the outside world. Paradoxically, in *The Aggressives,* Tiffany identifies as a faggot—a Butch Queen—who has heterosexual sex with transgender women or those who are "female appearing." She is not attracted to male-bodied men, male-appearing females, or masculine women. Tiffany is represented as a Butch in the film, yet the activities in which she participates in the Ballroom scene are more associated with Butch Queens. She is shown commentating at balls and doing street outreach for HIV/AIDS prevention in the scene. These activities are typical of those undertaken by and associated with Butch Queens in the Ballroom scene.

A slight variation on this example would be Onyx, a Butch, who suggested that his gender and sexual identities are based on his current romantic relationship: "I usually just say I'm queer, but I identify depending on who I'm with. It's emotionally safer and easier to identify as a Black gay man." Nevertheless, Onyx's partner, when I spoke with him, was a female-bodied woman who was, according to Onyx, "attracted to boys." She, too, identified as queer. In the Ballroom scene, Onyx is a Butch, but it is worth noting that he said that emotionally, in the outside world, it is easier to identify as a gay man. Yet he is not considered a Butch Queen in the Ballroom scene, and it is safe to assume that he can freely identify as a Butch. Like other interlocutors who discussed similar experiences, the gender system and the Ballroom community in general allow one to engage in and enjoy the process of self-fashioning and gender and sexual identity formation through communal performance labor. This speaks to potential and possibilities. Yet sometimes such potential and possibilities go unrealized while at other times they are refracted by the social prism of the scene. Even as the Ballroom scene offers a space and an occasion for gender and sexual transgression, various forms of gender and sexual bias continue to persist within the community.

During the time of my study, gender diversity in the Detroit Ballroom scene was limited, and I observed a significant amount of drama or bias and struggles over gender. In other words, there were, and still are, forms of exclusion that primarily Butch Queens enact in order to maintain their prominence. Femmephobia and transphobia continue to exist in the scene. Yet, reminiscent of all struggles, those who occupy positions of power and privilege in a particular sphere do not always succeed in maintaining it. In Ballroom, Femme Queens, Women, and Butches continue to challenge exclusionary practices and push against the boundaries and hierarchies that subordinate them. In some ways, this is accomplished by their mere presence and increased participation.

The first house I considered joining was the Detroit chapter of The House of Prodigy. Noir Prestige, who was a Prodigy at the time, was my main contact and made efforts to get me into the house. This house was led by the notorious Cage Prodigy, the housefather, a masculine Butch Queen who, by the way, had been married with children in the outside world and did not identify as gay until he joined the Ballroom scene. The housemother was a Woman who was queer or fluid sexually. I ended up not joining The House of Prodigy. Instead, I was invited and agreed to join The Legendary House of Prestige. I chose the latter mainly because of its HIV/AIDS prevention focus. During an interview with Noir Prestige a couple of years later, however, he explained that, upon joining the house, the members had agreed that it would be a house of masculine Butch Queens only; that meant no Butch Queens Up in Drag and no Femme Queens. Noir further suggested that Butch Queens Up in Drag and Femme Queens are viewed as "messy" and always creating drama. I found this to be a common stereotype applied to Butch Queens Up in Drag and Femme Queens that is based on the femme- and transphobia that existed, in the Detroit scene, at least during the time of this study.

Because of such exclusion, which afflicts Butch Queens Up in Drag in particular, some of them, along with a Butch Queen as housefather, established The House of Chaos, which my interlocutors referred to as a drag queen house. One of its most prominent members from the Detroit scene was Diva. I observed evidence that Butch Queens Up in Drag feel mistreated in the Detroit scene when, at The House of Ninja ball in 2003, The House of Chaos walked out—but not before the housefather, who was incensed by what he believed to be mistreatment of and bias against drag queens by other houses, announced that he was taking his house out of the scene. I must say, it made for a very dramatic spectacle as the Butch Queens Up in Drag walked out of the hall one by one at approximately 2:00 a.m. From Prince J Prodigy's perspective, this femmephobia in the Ballroom scene is peculiar to Detroit. According to Prince J, "Ballroom in Detroit hasn't embraced the queen. Like, on the East Coast, most of the housemothers of the houses out there are queens." What Prince J describes is a kind of femmephobia that is directed not only toward Femme Queens but also, and mainly, toward Butch Queens Up in Drag or those "queens" who are neither Femme Queens nor Butch Queens. Rather than fitting neatly into a familiar category, they exist in an undefined space formed by the interstices between Femme Queens, Butch Queens, and Butch Queens Up in Drag.

I have also observed tension between Butch Queens Up in Drag and Femme Queens. Butch Queens Up in Drag are afforded less respect from Femme Queens because they are viewed as less authentic. Butch Queens Up in Drag dress and perform as women but live as gay men; therefore, to some, they enjoy undeserved male privilege. However, Butch Queens Up in Drag *are* gay men, and, for the most part, they do not perform the kind of masculinity that has social currency outside of Ballroom culture. In other words, as gay men who perform as women and are usually more feminine in their comportment, they do not fit into the rigid strictures of masculinity that are pervasive in the larger society. It is clear that gender is viewed as malleable in Ballroom culture, but particular members and even sectors of the community invest in policing the boundaries around categories in the system. At the same time, other members insist on being limited neither by the boundaries nor by the efforts deployed to erect and maintain them.

Gender performance also provides insight into the ways in which working-class or poor Black LGBT people in Detroit perform gender and sexual identities to contend with and navigate through the high risk of being victims of homophobic, femmephobic, and transphobic violence. Examining these practices requires attending to subjectivities and experiences that are simultaneously impacted by race and class oppression. On July 16, 2003, Duchess, a Butch Queen and housemother of The Legendary House of Prestige at the time, called me crying hysterically because he had been chased by a man after leaving his apartment to walk to work at MOC, the Men of Color Motivational Group, Inc.,[19] which was located on the far north side of Detroit.[20] Duchess said he had followed his normal route (he didn't have a car) and that there was limited public transportation in his neighborhood. He encountered a man who asked for a light (to ignite his cigarette). After firing off a series of questions, the man asked Duchess for money in exchange for sex. When Duchess refused, the man chased him until Duchess ran into a restaurant and asked the employees to call the police. The aggressor disappeared, but Duchess was concerned that the man had possibly seen where he lived.

It is not only Butch Queens who must negotiate violence in urban environments (some of which is influenced by homophobia), but so must other nonconforming gender and sexual subjects. Onyx, from the St. Louis Ballroom scene, describes a transphobic altercation he experienced in Austin, Texas.

> I got into an altercation with a group of Black men. It was in front of my girlfriend, which made it worse. I usually don't get read [as transgender] in public and if I do they don't usually say anything. We were sitting out on the curb. I'm talking to my girlfriend and the men pull up. We were sitting outside of the hotel and they yelled out the car, saying, "Are you a boy or a girl?" Then I went inside and they were walking and passing the door of the hotel and bamming on the door, yelling, "Are you a boy or a girl?" and laughing. I called the police and filled out a report, but they didn't do anything of course. I wanted it to be a part of public record.

As for Detroit, when I first started going to clubs in the 1980s and throughout the 1990s, most of the bars and clubs that Black LGBT people frequented were located in "rough" parts of town. During my younger years of attending these Black gay bars, my friends and I would, at times, rush to our cars to avoid being seen coming out of the club by people driving by, particularly if there were people coming out or standing in front of the club whose gender performance and presentation we believed marked the club, and therefore us, as LGBT. On some occasions, cars would pass by the club and someone would yell "fucking faggots" as they sped past. At other times, people would hurl not only expletives but also physical objects from their cars. The constant threat of gender and sexual violence that Black LGBT people endure in both public and private spheres should not be ignored. For instance, as Diva D Bvlgari explains, the street is especially dangerous for Femme Queens.

> Detroit is very homophobic, even in the way the boys dress is homophobic. If it's fashionable it is seen as gay. If you wear tight pants you might be seen as gay. It makes people not want to walk the street and be themselves. Femme Queens, real as hell, won't go out during the day.

Although Diva D is talking mostly about his experiences as a Butch Queen, he poignantly describes the rigid criteria of masculinity and gender normativity to which Black LGBT people are forced to adhere in order to avoid being *seen* in ways that subject them to persecution and violence.

For men, Diva D's comments, as well as those expressed by other Ballroom members, allude to the notion that masculinity comprises a set of signifiers that connote heteronormative manhood within a given cultural framework.[21] However, these definitions of masculinity change, and so do their attendant signifiers. Wearing "tight pants" has not always been a marker of femininity or gayness. Such definitions are fluid and change as particular cultures define and redefine them. Nevertheless, for the Black LGBT people I interviewed, homophobia is embedded deeply in shifting notions of Black masculinity and performances thereof. These performances of Black masculinity are expressed more explicitly in certain social geographies. Hence, Black LGBT people in Detroit believe that they are required to perform double labor—the work of material survival and the work of self-presentation through the performance of gender and sexual disguise—in order to negotiate and survive the rigid heteronormativity that they confront in their everyday lives.[22] Most of all, Diva D signals the integral role that performance and body presentation play in the daily lives of Black LGBT people, irrespective of subjectivity.

It is also helpful to consider the perspectives of Brianna and Levin, who are both Femme Queens. When I asked Brianna whether she views Detroit as homophobic, she said, "For a minute because like when I was younger I used to always just hear people talking about gay people. So I like never really like came out like that, but they could always, you know, just notice about me. Now it's a lot of gay people in Detroit . . . you see a lot of gays just like walking around freely." Apparently for Brianna, seeing "a lot of gay people" in Detroit represents a certain amount of progress, a decrease in homophobia; mere presence, openly, means less hostility toward gay people. This is complicated by race and class because, generally, for poor and working-class Black LGBT people in Detroit, the hostility and threat of violence are still very real in the city. When I asked Brianna and Levin whether they had experienced a certain kind of freedom since choosing to live as women that they did not experience as men, Brianna chimed in, "Not necessarily. It's like you live the life, so it's hard." Overall, both Brianna and Levin point to the difficulties associated with being Femme Queens—living as transgender women—they face among their biological families and communities within the urban space of Detroit.

In much of her book *Undoing Gender,* Judith Butler emphasizes the quotidian danger associated with gender nonconformity and unintelligibility, and thus she calls for scholars to examine and learn from the practices that LGBT people deploy to avoid or survive phobic violence.[23] Ballroom community members use performance to unmark themselves as nonconforming gender and sexual subjects.[24] Unmarking oneself through performance, or "passing," is a necessary strategy by which to avoid discrimination and violence in the urban space. As I discuss later, Ballroom members literally perform and present their bodies to influence how they are "seen" in a society in which the Black body, specifically, is read as a text. And if such a person's body or performance is read as "queer" or nonconforming in terms of gender and sexuality, he or she will be treated as such, making him or her vulnerable to a tragic end in a homophobic and transphobic environment.

When Diva D suggests that Femme Queens who are "real as hell" fear going out during the day in Detroit, he brings into focus the perilous consequences that Butch Queens, Femme Queens, and Butches believe they might face if or when they are *seen* as queer gendered. Notwithstanding the use of gender performance for survival, Tim'm T. West brings up an important point about "passing" in the urban sphere: "Passing for a lot of girls [Femme Queens] is just about if I look just like a woman and [if] no one is able to clock me, then I have won. But then you haven't won as a transgender person. You are just seen as a woman. You haven't done anything to a system that has disenfranchised people who are transgender." West offers a valid point, but, as I argued in chapter 1, Ballroom members are neither interested in nor able to dismantle the systemic forms of race, gender, and sexual hegemony that disenfranchise them. Rather, survival and the pursuit of a better quality of life are the aims of members. And performance is the means through which these aims are pursued in the everyday.

Apropos of my point, Diva D's use of the term *real* is significant here because it reflects the integral function of the concept of realness within the Ballroom community, a concept that also helps to explain the efforts of its members to avoid discrimination, violence, and exclusion. In the final analysis, Ballroom members have to live in two worlds (at least). One of these worlds imposes strict prescriptions of gender and sexual meaning and behavior. The other one allows members to choose and fashion their gender and sexual subjectivities through performance. Much of the recent popular and scholarly—albeit limited—preoccupation with the Ballroom community underemphasizes the oppressive nature of the conditions under which its members live and their use of performance as a way to survive such conditions.

Gender/Racial Realness

How do LGBT members of the Ballroom scene use performance to unmark themselves as nonnormative? What Ballroom members refer to as "realness" has remained the fundamental criterion for performance in the culture throughout the more than five decades that it has been in existence. As a Ballroom-created standard, this criterion requires adherence to certain performances, self-presentations, and embodiments that are believed to capture the authenticity of particular gender and sexual identities. These criteria for performative gender and sexual identities are established and function within a schema of race and class. Racialized, classed, gendered, and sexualized performances, self-presentations, and embodiments give realness its discursive power in both the Ballroom scene and the larger society.

In the community, realness serves two primary functions. First, it is a guide that members use to construct, rehearse, and hone their performances and the presentations of their bodies to compete, be judged, and snatch trophies at balls for enacting the most "real" gender performance for a given realness category. Second, realness is based on the individual and communal recognition of what I will suggest is the way in which members enact their realness performances to create the illusion of gender and sexual normativity and to blend into the larger heteronormative society to avoid homophobic discrimination, exclusion, violence, and death.

Before I illustrate the two inextricably linked functions of realness in the Ballroom scene, I should explain that the theory of realness emerges from the Ballroom community itself. Realness as a theory of quotidian performance offers a way to understand, primarily, how, in society beyond the Ballroom scene, all gender and sexual identities are performed. Ballroom members use performance to play a greater role in how they are interpellated—seen—as particular gender and sexual subjects. This means that one's sexuality, for example, is perceived based on the appearance of one's body, gender performance, and the clothes one wears. This interpellation is based on racialized and classed notions of gender embodiment and performance in the urban arena. In a society in which, as the feminist scholar Robyn Wiegman aptly states, "vision is the privileged sense of modernity," meaning is conferred onto bodies through a visual epistemology of race and gender. Bodies are located in and viewed through a frame or visual epistemology that determines what is considered "real" through naturalizing discourses that render the body as a true text.[25] Accordingly, such a text requires certain behaviors, certain performances, and certain representations that are supposed to guarantee the authenticity of a given subject.

Ballroom members deploy this strategy because they know that their black bodies are read in the dominant world within what the cultural studies scholar Maurice O. Wallace refers to as a form of sociovisibility. For Wallace, sociovisibility is the corporeally arresting consequence of a kind of picture-taking racial gaze that fixes or frames black subjects within a rigid and limited grid of representational possibilities.[26] At times Ballroom members use sociovisibility to their advantage, as Onyx elaborated.

> My blackness helps me pass. I rely on people's stereotypes about black masculinity to pass. My father is 6'5 and 100 percent Mandingo, and from Monrovia, Liberia. My mother is 6'1, and my grandmother 6'5. My largeness makes it very easy to pass. I think there is an intimidation factor, so I feel like I have to be super nice. There is a fear of blackness and black masculinity, and I have never felt more visible than I do now.

Black LGBT people are not only subjected to a white supremacist gaze within majoritarian society, but they are also seen simultaneously through a heteropatriarchal gaze within Black communities. In both cases the sociovisibility through which Black LGBT people are seen functions at the behest of a gender and sexual normativity that is racialized and seeks to police and discipline Black gender bodies, identities, and practices both inside and outside of Black communities.

Completely aware of their sociovisibility, Ballroom members use performance as a survival strategy. Because the black body is read through and within a visual epistemology in which race, gender, and sexual hierarchies are corporeal, Ballroom members refashion themselves by manipulating their embodiments and performances in ways that render them visible and remarkable within the Ballroom scene, particularly at ball events, while being invisible and unmarked in the world outside of it.

What constitutes the performance strategy that Ballroom members deploy to contend with the sociovisibility through which they are seen in the outside world? Performance theorist E. Patrick Johnson proposes the concept of racial performativity as a way to theorize the performance strategies that Black LGBT people create and deploy. Drawing from dance scholar Susan Manning's conceptualization, Johnson suggests that "racial performativity informs the process by which we invest bodies with social meaning."[27] For the Black LGBT members of the Ballroom community, the discursive meanings of race and gender serve as the means through which racialized gender and sexual identities are rehearsed at ball events and performed in the public sphere. Ballroom members take up, coconstruct, and rehearse the normative but shifting scripts of Black femininity and masculinity to have them judged by the "experts," as it were, in the Ballroom community. For example, as I will elaborate, "thug" masculinity is a particularly racialized and gendered performance that has to be read/seen as "hard," dangerous, aggressive, and "street," and one that signifies not only straightness but also fitness for the role of sexual penetrator. What human geographer Rashad Shabazz refers to as "prisonized masculine performance," thug masculinity is "characterized by baggie pants, exposed boxer shorts, large T-shirts, bandanas, and tattoos.[28] This Black masculine aesthetic emerged from prison culture as a result of the mass incarceration of Black men and has infused hip-hop culture and thus quotidian articulations of Black heteromasculinity.[29] Therefore, in Ballroom culture, "thug realness" is taken up, rehearsed, and mastered within the Ballroom community and deployed on the urban streets in cities throughout North America, like Detroit. This one example of race and gender performativity illuminates how performance enables Black LGBT people to have agency in their own identity formation, self-image, and self-fashioning.[30] This strategy is necessary not only for enhancing Ballroom members' quality of life but also, and mostly important, for ensuring their safety.

Realness as a Criterion (The Realness Kids)

Unlike in the outside world, where the desire to blend into heteronormative society is assumed for most people, Ballroom members assemble their gender performances to be remarkable and exceptional at ball events so as to distinguish themselves from their competitors and to snatch trophies and garner approval and recognition from their peers. Realness categories serve as a means through which to achieve this goal. Realness categories constitute the performative nexus between competitive categories at balls and the gender and sexual subjectivities of Ballroom participants. Combined with the experiences of the members, realness furnishes the meaning behind the subjectivities and, at the same time, underpins the criteria by which categories are judged.

Some categories are arranged in groups based on the criterion of realness. Members of the Ballroom community call them *realness categories* and call the members who walk them *realness kids*. Realness most commonly includes Butch Queen Realness (sometimes thug realness), Executive Realness, Schoolboy Realness, Femme Queen Realness, Butch Realness, and Butch Queens Up in Drag Realness. For all of these categories, to be "real" is to minimize or eliminate any sign of deviation from gender and sexual norms that are dominant in heteronormative society. For Butch Queen, Femme Queen, Butch, and Butch Queens Up in Drag realness categories, the person must not only perform heteronormative gender and sexuality, but he or she must also embody the so-called markings of masculinity or femininity by altering the body through, for example, hormone therapy and body modifications, such as breast implants and padding for hips and buttocks. The central goal here is to be undifferentiated from the rest of Black working-class people in the urban space—particularly in Detroit for most of my interlocutors.

Realness criteria for various categories are often spelled out in flyers and are reiterated and enforced at balls by commentators and judges.

Here I enumerate typical descriptions that appear in ball flyers. Ball participants use flyers for upcoming balls as guides as they prepare their performances and presentations for the given categories in which they plan to compete. For Butch Queen Realness categories, typically, variations on the same criteria appear on all flyers. Butch Queen Realness competitors need to "bring it" like "The Athletic Man (Basketball, Football, Boxing etc.)" or "Ovah trade," performing a rough straight thug from the streets. Considering the category Butch Queen Realness as a Team, The International House of Supreme's ball flyer describes Butch Queen Realness or Thug Realness as a way to "bring it so that people cannot figure out 'who's zooming who'" or, in other words, who is fucking whom. This presumes, of course, that thug masculinity is enacted by a sexual top. Again, in Ballroom, gender performance always implies sexual identity as well as sexual position (in this case top) and practice (penetrator).

The aim for the Executive Realness category is to perform heteromasculinity for "Wall Street," to be seen as a gender-normative businessman. Flyers describe this category thusly: "The Board of Directors is having a meeting and it's your day to give the presentation." Executive Realness also allows one to perform masculinity as an academic or professor. I walked this category, for instance, and snatched a trophy at the Love is the Message ball in LA in 2005. The Detroit chapter of The Legendary House of Prestige gave me the Ballroom name "Professah Prestige" because of the unique performance I created for this category as a university professor. Similarly, as in Executive Realness, the primarily Butch Queen competitor walks the runway as though he is going to work on Wall Street. In the Schoolboy Realness category, one has to perform "grade school aged" normative masculinity. As the commentator Junior LaBeija says in reference to the schoolboy category in *Paris Is Burning*, he should be "going to school, not here," as in not going to a ball. On flyers the description for the Schoolboy Realness category reads, "Whether you're prep, nerd or thug, you must bring the judges something to show that you're in school." Or "Come with books, bags, backpacks, school ID, laptops, and a lunch pail." For these categories, realness is achieved if the competitor unmarks himself as sexually queer through his gender performance. The emphasis is primarily on sexuality and using racialized and classed performances of gender to perform straightness.

However, for Femme Queens, Butch Queens Up in Drag, and Butches, the focus of realness is primarily on gender identity and unmarking oneself as gender nonconforming or as transgender. For example, the same guidelines appear for the Butch Realness category; however, the differ-ence is that Butches are not Butch Queens. For the "Eric 'Zontae' Dior" ball in Detroit, the expectation for Butches on the flyer read, "Butch Realness [must be] unstoppable and unclockable. You look like a thug from the hood." On other flyers, the criteria for the category reads, "Your mother can't tell; your father can't tell." This means the Butch must be "unclockable" as a transgender man.

Criteria for the Femme Queen Realness and Butch Queens Up in Drag categories require that participants be "unspookable" as transgen-der women. Regardless of the important distinction between Femme Queens—people who live as women—and Butch Queens Up in Drag—gay men who perform and compete as women—both of these realness categories require participants to appear as female-bodied or cisgender women. Moreover, to perform effectively as female-bodied women these competitors must be able to be seen as "real women" in the outside world.

Some flyers present criteria for the Femme Queen Realness category with a question: "Can you walk through the roughest neighborhood in your city and not be spooked for being a man?" Other flyers explicitly state the realness criteria. For instance, a flyer for The Legendary House of Prestige's "Domination Ball" in Detroit in 2003 captures Butch Queen Up in Drag Realness: "You can't be clocked. You can't be stopped. Make the girls know [you] as either the only baby momma or as the only wifey." I have read other flyers that instruct Butch Queen Up in Drag Realness competitors to "get through with No Work," meaning without hormones or implants. Butch Queens up in Drag do not take hormones or get im-plants unless they are undergoing a gender transition.

At ball events, commentators help to discursively produce the gender and sexual formations that are so integral to the overall community. For instance, at The House of Ford ball in Detroit in 2001, when commenta-tor Jack Givenchy asked the judges "Is she real?" or "Is he real?" he was asking them to determine who (or which body) presents and performs the coded aesthetic imperative that defines style and deportment to re-create and re-present the discursive ideas of masculinity and femininity in a given category.[31] In terms of masculine realness, during Butch Queen Realness competitions, the commentator will chant, "We can't tell who's fucking who." For each of these categories, the particular expectations of realness and what one needs to do to execute it are known and ac-cepted throughout the Ballroom community. The ultimate aim is for the competitors to perform realness better than their opponents do. Thus,

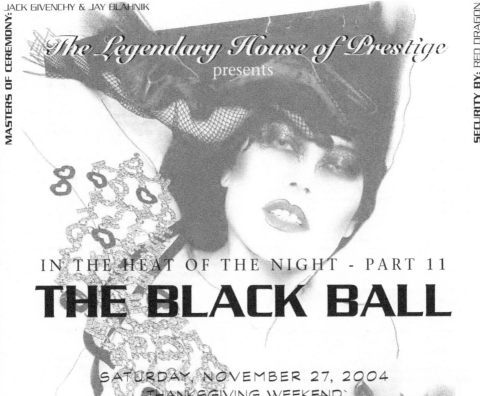

The Legendary House of Prestige
presents

IN THE HEAT OF THE NIGHT - PART 11

THE BLACK BALL

SATURDAY, NOVEMBER 27, 2004
THANKSGIVING WEEKEND

CELEBRATION HALL
2709 Cecil B. Moore Ave, Philadelphia, PA

$20 DRESSED IN ALL BLACK / $30 EVERYONE ELSE
9PM UNTIL 4AM

Tables $75
-Seats 10 people with Champagne & Gifts-

MUSIC BY: DJ CARLTON

Fig. 3. The flyer for "In the Heat of the Night II: The Black Ball,"
an Overall Ball hosted by The Legendary House of Prestige in
Philadelphia in 2004

BUTCH QUEENS

New Face - An Ovah Entrance and a Sickening Exit, this will get you prepared for the big boys

Realness - The Athletic Man (Basketball, Football, Boxing, etc.) vs. The 9 to 5 Working Man vs. The Pretty Boys vs. The Catholic School Boys in the name of Quasim, Kyree, Rayvon, Mello, Damarco, I.Q., Larry, Denim, Greg, Angel, Domingo. K.C., Abdul, and Bow Prestige

Mr. Prestige 2004 (Face, Body, & Realness) In a 2 piece suit, peeling into designer underwear

Sex Siren (I'm a Slave Forever) Sell sex in S&M attire, black leather, whips, and chains, etc. and maybe I'll set you free $$

Virgin Runway - You've watched Econ, Chiffon, Chyna, Junior, & the kids turn it out at the other balls and you've wanted to walk. With whatever you have on, hit the floor and show us what you've been working on, but you better turn it

Face w/performance - Serve that face w/style and grace. Remember we're looking for both face and performance

Sexy Body - (Models vs. Muscular) Coming from a Foreign Country, Africa, Brazil, Japan, Egypt, Etc...in the name of T.C. and Marquis Prestige

American Runway (Wild, Wild West) Let's go Texas style again. This time make it an Ovah Fall/Winter Western look $$

New Way - In a stunning cat suit who can twist and bend and start a trend, use their feet to catch a beat while causing confusion with a sickening illusion?

The Old Way (Principal of Precision) Lots of attitude, classic style, eye catching moves. Example: Malez and the legend Father Alvernian Prestige)

Vogue Femme Phantom - Concealed from head to toe, serve those sickening moves, and slay the girls one after the other until only one masked menace remains victorious. The catch is you will automatically be disqualified if your mask is removed (under any circumstances) before the last battle, your face should be 100% covered. In the name of Lucus, Darnell and Antwon $$

Face w/an Attitude - Done in all black! You declare war! The battle you have been waiting for. The category no doubt is face! Storm whom ever is on the runway. Creating a process of elimination not to be forgotten in the name of Kevin Prestige (Light vs. Brown vs. Dark vs. Big vs. Legends) 5 trophies, one cash!

Battle of the Streetwear (Hi Fashion European vs. Urban) 2004/2005 pieces only!

Labels (American Fashion Exhibit) American designers are often criticized for following their European counter-parts, but tonight's the night to end this madness. Come done head to toe in 5 or more American designer pieces 2004/2005 to upset the Europeans $$

Team Performance (Wonder Twins Annihilate) Whether it's old, new or femme, two individuals dressed alike, coming to cause HAVOC, not bothered by any other team walking, because this night your gonna let them have it!!

Realness w/a twist - Part 1: Come dressed thugged out in all black, Part 2 : Come dressed cunt out in a black mini skirt in the name of Ellis, Black. 2 way, and Nabisco Prestige $100

SPECIAL CATEGORIES

Best Dressed Spectator - Elegant with a touch of self expression, tastefully dressed

Philly's Finest (Male Figure) in Hi Fashion Fall/Winter Sportswear, you are the most alluring and eye catching male Philly has to offer. No one can ever come close to you. You have always served the purpose, and tonight you will let us know it. Done in III Fashion Sportswear. Who will it be?

Mr. Out-of-Towner - In head to toe overness. Across the waters you came and tonight is just not going to be the same. Your done from head to toe, but no one knows what effect you'll bring so send your competition home in a flash and you will gladly receive the trophy and the cash

Philly's Finest (Female Figure) in Hi Fashion evening wear. The season is here. You bring the look, from your creative mind or out of a story book. Fall is the season summers behind us, now show us why you are Philly's finest $$

Ms. Out-of-Towner - You're visiting Philly, and you are the Diva! In Hi Fashion evening wear the season is here you bring the look, from your creative mind or out of a story book. Your competition home in a flash and you will gladly receive the trophy and cash

Models Magazine Face (The Unpublished Black Photos) We need (4) photos in black and white 8x10 or larger 1 eveningwear, 1 Hi Fashion sportswear, 1 streetwear, and 1 sleepwear. Hit the runway selling the new makeup line on your face. You're auditioning to be a model for their next magazine layout $$

House Chants - Nick Nack Paddy Wack, give a dog a bone, which house is gonna chant Ms. Selvin's song?

International Punck Rock, Futuristic or Bazaar Masquerade Choas

Team Battle - The Three Magnificent Wonders of the World invite you all to learn the taste, as they rock, sock and shake the ballroom floor serving models effect, performance and face; but which team has what it takes, to cause a great deal of commotion in the place and snatch the grand prize? Because there is no first place. (3 People from 3 different house)

Hands Performance - dressed in all black ready to attack! Concealed, never to be revealed until one is defeated $$

Figs. 4, 5, and 6. These pages of the flyer illustrate typical descriptions of the competitive categories that are linked to subjectivities in the Ballroom community gender system.

BUTCHES

Realness - The Athletic Man (Basketball, Football, Boxing, etc. w/ Accessories) vs. The 9 to 5 Working Man w/ Accessories in the Name of the Legendary Reno & Jerri, and the New School Dee, Nino & Shyquan Prestige

Hi Fashion European Labels - Tonight is your night, it's time for the kids to learn that Butches do know the taste. Come turn it in one rock socking ensemble from head to toe, and make us gag $$

Performance - You've seen the B.Q.'s slay, now bring it in all black w/a pair of white gloves

Face w/an Attitude - Done in all black... You declare war, the battle you have been waiting for. The category no doubt is face! Storm whom ever is on the runway. Creating a process of elimination not to be forgotten in the name of Nino Prestige

WOMEN

The Scandalous Madame X - Beautiful but sinister. We're looking for the ultimate face, body and attitude in that scandalous little black dress $$

Sexy Body - Coming from a Foreign Country (Brazil, Africa, Egypt, India, Japan, etc...)

Performance - In all black..Ready ready to attack! In the Name of Jamila Prestige

Face of the Year - Make your presence known, by making a dramatic grand entrance into the ballroom, totally done declaring war with any other girl whos feeling defiant to step onto the floor$$

Labels (Head to Toe Pandemonium) Winter 2004-2005 Totally done causing havoc. Letting the children know you are the true Women's Label Diva and you're not having it.$$

B.Q. UP IN DRAGS

B.Q. Up in Drags Team Battle - 1 Bangy cunt serving performance, 1 alluring lady selling face, and 1 Town & Country punishing runway

Labels (Head to Toe Pandemonium) Winter 2004/2005 Totally done causing HAVOC. Letting the children know you are the truel label villian, and your not having it $$

Face - An evening at the Black Ball, in a marvelous mask! You are the center of attention, painted in the name of, in a black coctail dress $$

Realness (Bangy vs. Catholic School Girl) The prestige girls will be watching

FEMME QUEENS

Realness - Can you walk through the roughest neighborhood in your city and not be spooked for being a man? If so, bring it in an all new look

Sexy Body - Coming from a Foreign Country (Africa, Japan, Egypt, India, Brazil, Etc..)

New Face - Bring us an Ovah Entrance and a Sickening Exit, this will get you prepared for the big girls

Virgin Runway- You've watched the kids turn it out at the other balls and you've always wanted to walk. With whatever you have on, hit the floor and show us what you've been working on, but you better turn it.

Labels (Battle of the Grand Divas) Winter 2004/2005 is just around the corner and you spent the day shopping in Philadelphia for hottest pieces. Hit the runway in the hi fashion fall designer sportswear you wore shopping, and when you get to our judges panel, give us a peak at your first winter ensemble. (Bags, Tags, and Accessories a must) $$

Ms. Prestige 2004 (Face, Body, & Realness) The Woman of the Year, The Epitome of Style, Elegance, sophisticated glamour at it's best $$

Face of the Year - Make your presence known at the Black Ball, by making a dramatic entrance into the ball room totally done. Declaring war with any other girl who's feeling defiant to step onto the floor $$

Sex Siren (The Ultimate Sex Kitten) Tonight with a cat mask, high heels and satin teddy, seduce the judges. Kittens like milk, don't forget the milk!!

Team Performance - Catwoman and Batwoman have finally put their differences aside, and have decided to team up and bring you the most hell of a performance of a lifetime $100

MINI GRAND 1
$250 Cash & Trophy

HOUSE DISTINCTION

We all know your house names. Now let us know what it stands for! Whether it's face, runway, labels, performance, costumes, hi fashion, realness or just simply being without a doubt ovah. Make the prestige family know it! Creativity and a fab production is a must

MINI GRAND 2
$200 Cash & Trophy

FOOT, EYE, HAT & BELT
(Open to All)

Looking for that well dressed, person, looking for a sickening effect, make us know it as we get into your ovah footweear, your hellraising eyewear, your sickening hat, and your not to be fucked with belt. And bring us a nast secret accessory to make your opponents gag!

GRAND PRIZE
$1,000 Cash & Trophy

ARMAGEDDON
THE RUNWAY RULER IN ALL BLACK W/AN OVAH DRAMATIC ENTRANCE

You are a ballroom superstar, and the children fear you near and far. With a dramatic entrance and dramatic make up effect or an ovah jewel effect dressed in all black show the world that you are the runway ruler, Divas Only! You know who you are, you know exactly what we mean. Wicked effect, immeasurable attitudes, hints of shade, and a nasty walk

FOR MORE INFORMATION & TABLE RESERVATIONS CALL:

Godfather Reno Prestige
Grandmother Matthew Prestige
Father Alvernian Prestige

Email:

realness ultimately signifies the possibility of deception—an enduring illusion—positioned at the crossroads between the Ballroom world and the so-called real world.[32]

Again, realness is a theory of urban performance that emerges from the Ballroom community. The criteria of realness that I have explained are constituted by the ways in which the body is presented and performed within a visual epistemology. This visual epistemology consists of a combination of the performance of race, gender, and sexuality and the interpretations and revisions that members of the Ballroom community deploy. The range of performative gender and sexual identities that are performed at the balls are framed within a discourse of blackness. Mirroring forms of Black gender and sexual performance by means of which members are largely oppressed, the Ballroom community understands that the material realities of their lives (including their safety) are largely contingent on how they are interpellated, how they are *seen* by and within the optic lens of White supremacy on the one hand and Black heteronormativity on the other.

Realness, then, is both an analytic and a guide for understanding the strategic gender performances that members deploy in the urban space in which they live and move daily. Tim'm T. West makes this point about realness best when he describes how some Ballroom kids in the city develop a broader range of performance because of the world in which they live. "A boy rides up to the Bronx on the D train every day, and after a certain street he gotta act like a boy. He turns it on. But after 14th Street, girl, it came right back off! In a certain way, these performances do match a particular reality that people have to live in," he said. Ultimately, Ballroom community members understand that they are seen through a racist and homophobic lens propagated and internalized by multiple sectors of society; therefore, members seek greater agency in shaping how they are viewed by altering and performing their bodies in ways that disguise their gender and sexual nonconformity.

At ball events, one of the categories that best captures the role of realness performance is Realness with a Twist. Realness with a Twist is a competitive category that is a quintessential example of how gender and sexual performativity are deployed by members, as a rehearsal at balls, to prepare for a way of life in the outside world. In this category the performer, who is almost always a Butch Queen, displays both extremes of the masculine-to-feminine spectrum in one performance. At most balls, this category is split into two parts and therefore requires two performances, offering "realness with a twist" part 1 and part 2. This category is most interesting and is executed most effectively when there is only one category and the person changes in the midst of one performance.

During the first part of the category performance, the performer walks down the runway as "thug realness," viewed as one of the most masculine performances in Ballroom culture. As he walks, the DJ plays hip-hop music to underscore his performance. For many in the Ballroom community, hip-hop is inherently associated with masculinity in terms of cultural behaviors and performances. Once he does one walk down the runway, he stops in front of the judges and waits for the music to change. Then the DJ plays "The Ha Dance," the signature song for vogue performance, and the performer "queens out," as we say in the community. He performs vogue femme, the style of "soft and cunt." This demonstrates the skill of the competitor to instantly change his gender performance from "unclockable," unmarking himself as queer, to "clockable," marking himself as queer.[33]

To reiterate my earlier point that gender performance is not about gender alone; rather, it is about sexuality, I extend Wallace's concept of sociovisibility. For Black LGBT people, the race and gender knowledge through which the black body is read marks, often explicitly, sexuality, particularly, position and practice. Community members are well aware of how their sexuality is perceived in light of the sociovisibility through which they are viewed. Onyx, for example, believes that "People assume your sexuality based on your gender presentation. People who don't even know you assume your sexual orientation based solely on your gender presentation." Onyx's point is also evidenced through commentator chants. When, for a Butch Queen Realness category, the commentator chants, "We can't tell who's fucking who," he highlights how one's sexual position and practice are thought to be revealed through gender performance, particularly since being a bottom is associated with femininity and being a top with masculinity. Clearly, Ballroom members expose this as a performative strategy that can create the illusion that one is not the one being fucked but rather the one doing the fucking.

The Limits of Realness

While realness is a necessary strategy and a creative response to the dangers of convergent forms of race, class, gender, and sexual violence, it generates problems that deserve further examination. First, realness is, in part, constituted through tropes of femininity and masculinity.[34] Levin illustrates this point in explaining that she is not ready to walk the Femme Queen Body Realness category because "all I got is my implants now; I gotta get the rest." Later Levin made it clear that, for her, to be successful in a realness body category, "the rest" that is needed is a vagina.[35] In many aspects of the performance criteria in Ballroom culture the terms *cunt, pussy,* and *dick* reflect how body parts—genitalia, breasts and buttocks—are sutured to femininity and masculinity and therefore instantiate one's gender, and sometimes sexual, subjectivity.

An analytic separation between sex, gender, and sexuality is necessary to understand the gender system, yet the conflation of body parts with subjectivity ultimately undermines this analytic separation. At The House of Ford ball in 2001, Jack Givenchy asked a woman competing in a Femme Queen Realness Body category, "Are you real cunt?" He placed his hand between her legs to confirm that she had a "real" vagina, thereby verifying that she was a "real woman." The Woman responded by saying, "It's all real." After telling her that she could not compete in a Femme Queen Body category as a real woman, Jack showed this competitor off to the rest of the participants as a model Femme Queen whom others should aspire to look like. This is a bit of a paradox; on the one hand, the Woman contestant was disqualified from the Femme Queen category because she was a "real"—cisgender—Woman. But, on the other hand, this Woman was presented by Jack as having the "realness" to which Femme Queen contestants should aspire. Hence, within Ballroom culture, realness is at once about authenticity and illusion.

Additionally, a man is often reduced to a penis—a dick—particularly if he is viewed as being well endowed. I have observed competitive performances for categories such as Sex Siren, consisting of masculine Butch Queens or Men, where members of the audience shouted, "You give me dick down boy." Members associate being well endowed with sexual prowess and, in effect, with male-bodied masculinity. Since I do not know of a Sex Siren category that includes Butches, the phrase "you give me dick down boy" refers to masculinity that is ascribed to or performed by a male-bodied man with a flesh-and-blood penis.

Regarding performance, the terms *cunt* and *pussy* refer to ultimate femininity. Members use these terms not only to refer to a particular style of performance, such as "voguing femme soft and cunt," but also to refer to gender categories such as Woman and Femme Queen. For many members of the Ballroom scene, especially Femme Queens and Butch Queens Up in Drag, since achieving "ultimate femininity" is the goal, they welcome such terms when they are conferred on them. Ariel, a Femme Queen and the housemother of the California chapter of The Legendary House of Prestige at the time of my study, explained to me once that she believes members of the community are jealous of her because she is "so pussy." To Ariel being referred to as pussy means that the work she has done with her embodiment (hormonal therapy, implants, etc.) and her performance have paid off. She has achieved "femme realness" because she is seen as such within the community and on the street.

Realness, then, as both a set of criteria and a way in which Ballroom members apply and adhere to these criteria, often conflates anatomic femaleness with womanhood and anatomic maleness with manhood, and these conflations play into performance and presentation. Members fetishize aspects of the body to represent these characteristics in optimum form when they are attached to specific bodies either physically or symbolically, to signify one's achievement of ultimate femininity or masculinity. These cases demonstrate that realness serves as a strategy of resistance to hegemonic gender and sexual norms in terms of the violence to which members are subjected if they do not disguise their gender and sexual nonconformity. Yet, on the other hand, members' enactment of realness ends up reinscribing and relying on these same norms to view and judge each other within the community.

Language and the Ballroom Cultural Context

Indeed, I argue that realness performance is, in part, an attempt by Ballroom members to exercise agency in how they are seen in the urban public sphere by altering and performing their bodies in ways that unmark their gender and sexual nonconformity. But there are issues with the language and meanings that describe realness that also require further consideration. Although in the dominant culture *cunt* and *pussy* are deployed in a derogatory sense toward women and their bodies, and may seem inherently misogynistic, I would offer another, more complicated perspective.

Terms such as *cunt, bitch,* and *pussy* are used often by Black gay men in Black LGBT cultures, and, as some argue, reveal the misogyny and internalized homophobia that exist even in these communities.[36] I agree that internalized homophobia and misogyny exist in Black LGBT communities, just as in the larger society. Yet, when asked about the use of the aforementioned terms, none of my interlocutors expressed any concern. Many members said that these terms are not used with derogatory intent and, as with other terms, such as *nigga*, which have been recuperated in Black culture and are now often used as terms of endearment, *cunt, pussy,* and *bitch* are also used in ways that contrast with their typical usage in the world outside the Ballroom community.

Communities that are marginalized in multiple ways, especially LGBT communities, often construct and use what composition/rhetoric scholar Mark McBeth calls "Gaylect," a form of rhetorical resistance to a dominant heterosexual world.[37] Black LGBT persons who belong to either the Ballroom community or larger LGBT communities constantly create "gay lingo" by constructing new terms and adding new meanings to standard terms in order to build protective boundaries around the marginalized community. As reflected throughout this book, including in the glossary of Ballroom terms that I provide, communities like Ballroom create and use gay lingo as a part of overall performance labor. For example, the names of categories such as Butch Queens and Femme Queens mark an interstitial subjectivity that cannot be easily accounted for in the dominant sex/gender/sexuality system. This performance labor is also the means by which Ballroom members attempt to recuperate putatively derogatory terms and push their limits to create alternative meanings for those terms. Thus, in the Ballroom context, as far as my interlocutors are concerned, *cunt, pussy,* and *bitch* are viewed as criteria and used as a way in which to acknowledge participants' exceptional adherence to those standards established in the community. In this sense, Ballroom members, like members of other marginalized communities, place their community-defined values, terms, and meanings at the center of the culture, deliberately defying the dominant ones by which they are largely oppressed.[38]

The notion that terms like *cunt* and *pussy* are criteria for gender performance in Ballroom, as opposed to being insults or demeaning expletives hurled at female-bodied women or womanness, is best illustrated by the perspectives of Femme Queens like Brianna Cristal. Brianna explained that she realized she could be successful living and competing as a Femme Queen, and thus living as a woman in the outside world, when people began complimenting her on her drag performances (as a Butch Queen Up in Drag). Brianna said, "When I first got into drag, like, a lot of people was telling me about it, saying, you know, 'you look fishy' and 'you look cunt.'" That people conferred on Brianna and her body the terms *fishy* and *cunt,* even before she started taking hormones, meant that she already embodied and performed the level of femininity necessary both to identify as a Femme Queen within the Ballroom scene and to live as a woman (unmarked as a transgender woman) in the world outside of it. Similarly, when Ariel Prestige boasted about being seen as "pussy," she certainly did not view this as a demeaning interpellation within the context of Ballroom culture. Granted, these are examples of male-bodied women, but if one takes seriously the Ballroom challenge to dominant notions of womanhood or manhood, those in the community who use the terms at issue are largely those community members who live as women.

Finally, at The Ford Ball to which I referred earlier, when Jack Givenchy asked the cisgender woman whether she was "real cunt," she did not appear offended at all. Instead, she responded with the affirmative "It's all real," suggesting that such terms signify and serve as criteria for authentic femininity. Moreover, when these terms are used, the speaker does not say, "*You* are a cunt." Markedly, the speaker says, instead, "*Give* me pussy" or "You *look* cunt," meaning "Give me femininity in your performance and self-presentation." These terms are about the desire to achieve femininity, not demean it. Indeed, from outside the Ballroom cultural context, these terms carry a meaning that is much different from what I argue is true within it, but it is important to take seriously the context in which terms are used and the varied meanings they carry for people situated within that context.

Nevertheless, it is worth considering that the uses of these terms in Ballroom may indeed be demeaning regardless of purportedly innocuous intent and the community's embrace. The derogatory nature of such terms as they are deployed in society may coincide after all with the marginal status that female-bodied women, in particular, occupy in the larger Black LGBT community and the Ballroom scene. For some, these aspects of Ballroom culture may undermine the progressive potential of gender and sexual relations within the community.

These cases demonstrate that the productive and subversive aspects of the gender system emerge from a labor of performance, in which new subjectivities are created through the ball events. These new identities are forged out of struggle and contestation. Conversely, the normalization of terms such as *cunt* and *pussy* and the practice of reducing subjectivities to body parts have become inculcated in the culture without any apparent contestation. Members use these terms without taking into account the fact that no matter what the context is, any reappropriation of these terms does not dislodge them entirely from their misogynistic and homophobic meanings. Therefore, joined with Butch Queens' dominance in the community, irrespective of whether it is femininity or masculinity that is being constructed or deconstructed, queered or subjected to scrutiny, the use of *cunt, pussy, bitch,* and similar terms may have the unintended consequence of re-creating within Ballroom culture an essentially masculinist and exclusionary space in which few Women (as defined by the gender system) will feel comfortable participating.

Stunts and Craft

I have argued throughout this chapter that performance labor is a means through which Ballroom members engage in a complex practice of self-fashioning. Through such self-fashioning members experience the pleasure of pushing the limits of normative sex, gender, and sexual identity categories and of what amounts to as a process of transformation. As a community, Ballroom creates and maintains the conditions through which individual members can undertake this self-fashioning. Performance is not only a way for members to engage in pleasure; it is also a necessary strategy for navigating through and surviving the harsh conditions of urban life. Yet a central part of Ballroom members' efforts to reconstitute themselves centers on image and, as they see it, a need to position themselves in ways that give them access to a more livable life. Some pursue more livable lives at any cost, and quite often through nefarious means.

In the Ballroom community these nefarious practices are called *craft* and *stunts.* My aim here is neither to justify nor to indict the Ballroom community as a whole by overburdening it with all the illegal behavior that many believe plagues US society. For my purposes, rather than applying one side or the other of a transgression/unscrupulous criminality binary to Ballroom members, even if only to a degree, I highlight their lived perspective on crafting and stunting. I am most interested in why members take up stunts and craft or benefit from these practices as a form of self-fashioning, while exploring the lengths to which they will go to construct a certain kind of image.

Wider audiences were first exposed to the way Ballroom members—most of whom are poor or working class—acquire goods through illegal means in *Paris Is Burning*. The film highlights a somewhat dated practice called "mopping." Mopping occurs when an individual steals items from retail stores mostly by hiding them on his or her person. Once, while attending a ball in Philadelphia, I went to a mall with some fellow Ballroom members. One of the members needed an item for the outfit he wanted to wear to the ball. As we were walking down an aisle where the item was located, I saw him sweep it into his pocket and leave the store. I had witnessed an example of mopping, which was a common practice in the Ballroom scene before the 1990s. Now what Ballroom members call craft and stunts are forms of illegal acquisition of goods for our more contemporary times. According to Father Al Bvlgari, a Butch Queen, "about 65 percent of the Ballroom community is involved with craft and stunts, and 85–90 percent benefit from it." To Father Al, whether you do it or benefit from it, craft and stunts are wrong.

In general, my interlocutors say craft and stunts are forms of identity theft used to purchase not only clothes and accessories but also hotel rooms, rental cars, plane tickets, and trophies for the ball, as well as to pay cell phone bills. This is an organized, sophisticated system. "There's so many factors in identity theft. It still boils down to the same thing. You have your information seekers and the person that does a lot of the groundwork, who delegates a lot of things. It's like any other organized thing," said Father Al. Diva D Bvlgari explained how information seekers acquire people's personal information: "It hurts my heart that people are this trashy, and they take up this much time. They [information seekers] know when businesses throw away their people's personal information, and they're going to pick it up in the garbage. Some people actually go dumpster hopping and the information is there." Phoenix Manola Blahnik, another Butch Queen, chimed in and said, "Some people don't have to go dumpster hopping; they go to people on the inside, and they can buy six personal profiles for two hundred dollars." Other interlocutors discussed websites where one can purchase personal profiles that can be used to purchase, illegally, all kinds of goods and services. Interestingly, members said that these practices were learned from what they call the straight world. As Prince J Prodigy asserted:

> See, a lot of people think that identity theft and stuff has a lot to do with homosexuals and gay people. What they fail to realize is

that it is something that they have learned and they learned it first from heterosexual people that have been turning stunts for years. A lot of gay stunts and crafting is stuff that has been picked up over a period of time.

There are times when community members are exposed to or confronted with the reality of crafting and stunting even among their fellow house members. For example, one of my interlocutors explained how, while he was a member of a house in Los Angeles, the membership had to travel to participate in the house's national ball in Philadelphia. The housefather asked all members to give him their travel preferences so that he would arrange the flights for about ten members. My interlocutor said that everyone knew that the housefather was "crafting" the plane tickets. As it turned out, the house made it to Philadelphia but ran into some problems with the return flight. Hence, some of the house members, namely, those who could not afford to buy a return plane ticket, had to ride a Greyhound bus from Philadelphia to Los Angeles. While conducting this research, I knew of many crafters and stunters who were caught and arrested and served jail time for these practices.

But why do Ballroom members craft and stunt? Diva D suggested that, of the approximately 65 percent of members who do it, in his view, less than 20 percent actually do it for survival. However, what does survival mean for Black LGBT members of the Ballroom community? Many Ballroom members in Detroit live at home with their parents or cohabitate either because they have been kicked out of their families of origin or because they need to save money while they struggle to live on their own. To reiterate Tim'm T. West's characterization of the house scene as a mostly urban and "lower-class thing," inevitably some Ballroom members have to hustle to make ends meet, often under very difficult conditions, such as homelessness, substance abuse, and other forms of violence and danger that one confronts on the street.

While the Ballroom scene serves as a refuge in some ways, if one is to achieve prominence and recognition in it one has to compete. Hence, to survive in the Ballroom community—and this is perhaps one of the few social spheres to which a Black LGBT person has access—a person has to fashion and maintain a particular kind of self-image, one that usually extends beyond the socioeconomic position in which he or she lives. This image will garner status and popularity in the Ballroom scene. Or, as Diva D put it, "Stunts are used to build up that 'fictitious existence.'" It is useful to reconsider realness within the context of socioeconomic status and consumption among Ballroom members. According to my interlocutors, in addition to all the other functions it serves, realness underpins the creation of a false image, one of socioeconomic affluence. Kali Ford made this point when he said:

> Realness is a false relationship to the economy; it is a [false] image. There are differences between images and reality. In Ballroom, the fear of people seeing weakness and vulnerability becomes an obsession. This aspect of life becomes a protectorate at any cost. In terms of wealth, we are ultimately dealing with people with middle to low class status—some impoverished. Many of these folks don't have jobs at all.

Kali Ford's discussion of realness here suggests a dimension that is somewhat different from what I discussed earlier in this chapter. This form of realness emphasizes an image of higher socioeconomic status and the ability to live a life of relative privilege, or at least a representation thereof in the scene. Self-fashioning and maintaining such an image requires a member to compete and be successful, depending on the category. Often the would-be participant, keen—perhaps desperate—to forge an identity within the community, has to acquire the necessary garments through illegal means. Thus, when Kali Ford talks about an aspect of life that "becomes a protectorate at any cost," he is referring to crafting and stunting. I would argue, however, that many people in the Ballroom scene work and save their money, sometimes forgoing paying rent or making a car payment in order to purchase an outfit that will increase their likelihood of snatching a trophy or winning a cash prize. And cash prize winners can sometimes use the cash to reimburse themselves for purchasing the garments.

Most of my interlocutors were very critical of the crafting and stunting they see as pervasive in Ballroom culture, even as many of them benefit from it. Many Ballroom leaders expressed to me the desire to reduce or eliminate, if possible, the practices of crafting and stunting in the community. Despite the position that many community members take regarding craft and stunts, I offer two points that should be considered regarding these and other illegal practices in the community. First, the practice of crafting and stunting forces a reexamination of what survival means for Black LGBT people in the Ballroom community. Largely excluded from or severely marginalized within the formal economy and labor force in Detroit, for many Ballroom members survival means undertaking a form of self-fashioning that helps to build and maintain the image necessary to achieve prominence in the scene, despite the exclusion and marginalization they endure in the outside world. The Ballroom community allows them to remake themselves, to create a fictitious existence, whether through legal or illegal means.

Second, as my interlocutors intimated many times throughout this study, the overassociation of crafting and stunts with Black LGBT people exposes a societal double standard. Recently, while describing this book project to a colleague at an HIV/AIDS prevention conference, he was incredulous that I was writing a book on "a bunch of Black queens who steal clothes to walk in balls," as he put it. Yet we live in a moment in which corporate theft and greed are the order of the day. Huge corporate scandals and cases of theft or fraud, most to the tune of billions of dollars, like the Enron scandal, and the economic exploitation of low-income people that led to the housing crisis, tend not to be viewed harshly even by other Black LGBT people. Yet the Ballroom community is overburdened with a criminal representation. A truly useful perspective on craft and stunts is one that is as complex as the lives that Ballroom members lead and the conditions under which they live.

Performance undergirds the gender system, the criteria for the competitive categories, and the overall social interaction between members and the roles they play. For these reasons, I see the function of performance in Ballroom culture in somewhat different terms from those in which some critics have heretofore explained it. As one example, there is indeed some truth to the critiques of theorists such as Judith Butler, who asserts in her earlier work that she is ambivalent about drag largely because it reiterates and reinscribes the same norms that it purports to subvert.[39] I argue that performance and the gender system that it undergirds in Ballroom culture offer far more cultural import because they reflect *possibilities* of reconstituting gender and sexual subjectivities, of reconfiguring gender and sexual roles and relations, and of creating ways to survive an often dangerously homophobic, transphobic, and femmephobic public sphere.

Ultimately, in this Black LGBT minoritarian sphere, Black gender and sexual minorities forge lives worth living. Critiques that imply that Ballroom members are obsessed with white femininity and illusions of material wealth discount the actual communal performance labor in which they are constantly engaged to create an alternative existence for themselves within their marginality. Especially with regard to gender and sexual performativity, members challenge the power and consequences of interpellation by assuming greater agency in the dialectic between subjectification and identification. The gender and sexual performativity of Ballroom culture emerges and functions at the interstices of hegemony and transformation to create new forms of self-representation and social relations.[40]

There is much to be learned about gender and sexual nonconformity from the Ballroom community's gender system. In the outside world, community members are required to adhere to the pervasive male/female, masculine/feminine, man/woman, hetero/homo binaries and therefore must behave and identify as one or the other or suffer discrimination, violence, and exclusion throughout their social lives. Even in the larger LGBT community, there is often an expectation that a transgender person must identify as such or that gays, lesbians, and bisexual people must pick one of these limited categories of sexuality. Conversely, in the Ballroom community, members can be, and often are, openly queer in terms of sex, gender, and sexuality, but they are understandably reluctant to make those same queer claims in the world outside of the Ballroom sphere. I argue that these malleable, contingent, and strategic deployments of identity should not always be read as signs of internalized racism, homophobia, or heterosexism, or as nonsubversive for that matter; instead, these practices are strategies deployed by these Black LGBT people to negotiate and survive a sometimes perilous and complex social terrain; communal performance labor and realness are cultural mechanisms through which they can do so. In the next chapter, I demonstrate how the gender system underpins the social relations in houses as I examine the kinship system in Ballroom culture.

THREE

From Home to House

Ballroom Houses, Platonic Parents, and Overlapping Kinship

We queers must make our own family
Blood family tends to desert or oppress us
Waters, Donald and I made a family.
—WAYNE CORBITT *CRYING HOLY*[1]

For the majority of people who entered the house scene when I did
in the late eighties—and of course houses precede me—it is kind of
an alternative social network for those who have been ostracized
from their family or didn't have people in their families or communities who could understand their sexual identity.
—TIM'M T. WEST, FORMER MEMBER OF THE HOUSE OF
NINJA IN NEW YORK CITY[2]

The House of Prestige Domination Ball: Waiting

Each year, The Legendary House of Prestige holds a national anniversary
ball. This gathering is like a family reunion. An anniversary or "Overall Ball" brings together people from the various house chapters to celebrate the year in which their house was founded. The Legendary House
of Prestige was founded in June 1990 in Philadelphia by three Butch
Queens, Carlos, Ali, and Alvernian, and has had as many as thirteen active chapters across the country. In recent years, the anniversary ball has
been held in Philadelphia and New York City. Yet this year, since the
house was expanding throughout the Midwest, Duchess, a Butch Queen
and the housemother of the Detroit chapter, had convinced Father Alvernian to hold the anniversary ball in Detroit. Hence, on June 21, 2003,

The Legendary House of Prestige's thirteenth anniversary ball was held in Detroit for the first time at the Tom Phillip Post Lodge. On this anniversary "overall ball" occasion, members from most of the thirteen chapters came together to commemorate the founding of our house.

I am at the Tom Phillip Post Lodge, which is located on Gratiot Avenue just east of downtown. This is a "spotty" part of town. While on the way to the ball venue, I noticed signs of urban blight on some blocks or streets but also signs of gentrification on others. "The Post," as we call it, is Black owned and Ballroom friendly. As I had been instructed, I arrive early to help decorate. I find myself waiting outside the front entrance in my car with a seventeen-year-old "wanna-be" Ballroom kid. We are the only people there. Since the Detroit chapter is expecting Prestige and other Ballroom members from all over the country, we want to represent the Detroit Ballroom scene in "fierce" fashion. Typically, during the house's anniversary weekend, the members go out to the dance club together the night before the ball to hand out flyers, to show off the house's national members to the locals, and to socialize and enjoy a good time together. Some houses hold cookouts, as well as other preball activities, which explains why Duchess, told everyone, including those who had come from as far away as Buffalo, to get to the hall at two in the afternoon so that we could prepare it for the evening's festivities. He figured this would give people time to sleep in since we all had hung out together until very late the previous night.

This is my debut ball as a member of The Legendary House of Prestige, as well as a member of the overall Ballroom scene, so I am extremely anxious. And the waiting is irritating, to say the least, because not only do I have to help decorate, but I also have to return home before the ball to cut my hair, shave, shower, and put on my suit to walk in the Grand House March. So, yes, I am nervous waiting in the car even though I will not be competing and my housemother and siblings have been telling me that I have nothing to worry about. Still, this will be my first time walking, and during that one-minute strut down the walkway, perfect image and presentation are essential, whether one is competing or not. Such are my thoughts as my coincidental companion and I ponder our fates as we wait for others to arrive. I have already attended balls, so I realize, unlike the young man next to me, that one needs certain attributes to belong to the Ballroom community. One needs patience, for example, because nothing seems to begin or end on time. One experiences a range of emotions, such as the anxiety I now feel, accompanied by excitement and anticipation. After all, I am soon to be meeting, working, and socializing with people to whom I am connected through house membership even though I have never met them. It is all part of the experience of working together to prepare the space for the communal performance ritual, and of the larger work of building and sustaining this community. So, in spite of my anxiety, I am also finding some comfort in the idea that I belong to a community, and that tonight's ball will have something in common with a family reunion. The last time my biological family had a reunion was in the summer of 1992 in Louisville, Kentucky. The virtues of membership in a community or familylike organization are what this chapter is about. Here I explore the day-to-day labor of family and community on which we all depend but too often take for granted.

In chapter 2, I examined the gender and sexual categories of identity (the subjectivities) that constitute the gender system of Ballroom culture. I argued that the gender system serves as the way in which members of the community identify themselves in the scene, forming the basis for the categories in which members compete at balls. The gender identities are constituted, claimed, rehearsed, and concretized in part through the performances enacted at balls. I also suggested that the gender system is expansive yet contradictory in that it is simultaneously fixed and fluid. On the one hand, the gender system reifies gender and sexual norms, but on the other it is also a means through which members subvert these very norms. This point is most clearly evidenced through the Butch Queen, a dominant gender and sexual identity in the Ballroom sphere. Notably, I also examined realness and delineated its function in establishing the gender performance criteria created by the Ballroom community. I argued that realness is a communal standard by which particular racialized gender performances are rendered believable within the Ballroom world. It is a gender-performative strategy used by Ballroom members to unmark their nonnormative genders and sexualities so as to avoid the heterosexist/homophobic and transphobic exclusion, discrimination, and violence they face daily in the larger society.

Keeping the gender system in mind, then, this chapter examines the community-fashioned kinship system and the kin labor associated with the Ballroom community. To explain the context out of which the kinship system of the Ballroom community emerges, I first examine the discourse of Black family that excludes or marginalizes Black LGBT people. Among Black people in the United States, the family is viewed as a primary form of community and cultural belonging. In order to belong, one is expected to adhere to gender and sexual norms within the family as prescribed by a heteropatriarchal discourse. Heteropatriarchy is central to common sense notions—everyday knowledge—of blackness and therefore structures Black cultural membership.[3] Not all Black families reject their LGBT children and siblings, but far too many do. And for those who are rejected, the Black family and the *home* are sites of the acute physical, social, and emotional violence and trauma that such a familial exclusion entails. In other words, within the Black familial sphere, gender and sexual nonconformity positions Black gender and sexual dissidents along the fringes of the putative heteronormative family and community, thus denying Black LGBT people access to Black belonging. What LGBT members of the Ballroom community endure, therefore, makes it necessary to forge alternative kin relations and ties.

Second, I examine the *house,* the kinship unit that is central to the Ballroom community. Through houses Ballroom members challenge conventional notions of marriage, family, and kinship by revising gender relations and redefining gendered labor within the kin unit. Primarily, the house is a social configuration, the principle through which the kin unit is organized. Yet the house can also be a space where the members congregate, and it can be a literal home for Ballroom members. The kin labor, or what I call *housework,* is what Ballroom members undertake to develop and maintain these familylike units. Ballroom members' reconstitution of gender and sexual subjectivities through performance creates alternative gender and sexual relations within the house. While, in some ways, houses reify the gender hierarchies and social arrangements that are characteristic of the biological families from which members have been excluded, these houses also take on the labor of care that the biological kin of Ballroom members often fail to perform. Central to creating new forms of belonging, this housework is undertaken at the balls, in the houses, and throughout all community activities.

Third, in order to enact the labor of care that is necessary to maintain the house, members of the community engage in nonromantic/nonsexual parental partnerships, or what I call *platonic parenting,*[4] which significantly revise putative parental roles and sibling relationships within kinship units. And, finally, since Ballroom culture is a part of a larger Black

LGBT community, many of its members are engaged in multiple kin relations, which mark the interplay between the kinship that is characteristic of Ballroom culture and the kin making that exists within larger Black LGBT community practices. This is what I refer to as *overlapping kinship.*

Housework is, then, necessary to the creation of an alternative familial sphere, which includes creating alternative gender and sexual roles, platonic parenting, and overlapping kinship. These forms of labor are crucial to building and sustaining a community that is otherwise marginalized in a variety of ways. They therefore play out along profound psychological and spiritual, as well as material and social, dimensions.

Black Labor and Family

As I observed in the introduction, during the 1940s—the time of the second Great Migration—numerous Black people, as well as poor Whites, moved from the South to industrial centers in the North seeking a better life.[5] In *"Who Set You Flowin'?" The African-American Migration Narrative,* literary scholar Farah Jasmine Griffin argues that, in industrial cities in the North, Black migrants were confronted with a modern urban power structure that sought to control and contain the migrant body by consistently restricting its mobility, controlling its experience in space and time, and inflicting violence on it.[6] Living in the midst of extreme racial antagonism and under the pressure associated with starting and maintaining a "new life" in a different political, economic, and social environment, gender relations within Black families shifted dramatically from what most had experienced during life in the South. This is not to suggest that life in the South was any less stringent; rather, the demands placed on Black families by labor in the factories were different in the industrialized urban centers of the North.[7]

For instance, after growing up in a small town in Georgia, my grandparents moved the family to Detroit from Fort Lauderdale, Florida, in 1943 when my mother was just four years old. And although my father, who is now deceased, was born in Detroit, his parents had moved their family to the city from Alabama. Like numerous Black people in the South, my family journeyed to the North in the 1940s to gain access to perceived "new opportunities" both economic and social. My grandfather, on my mother's side, worked for Budd Wheel, an automotive manufacturing company, and my grandmother worked at a laundromat. Some of my aunts and uncles worked in auto manufacturing as well. Both my mother and my father retired from General Motors, each having worked there for thirty years.

In the 1940s through to the 1980s, for my family at least, manufacturing jobs in the automotive industry represented possibilities for economic prosperity for Black people as long as they worked tirelessly, remained focused and committed, and stayed in "their place," which too often meant behaving at the expense of their physical, mental, and social health. In the early boom years of the automotive industry, Black migrants were able to earn high wages with no formal education or advanced technical training. While my parents earned really good wages and benefits and in effect raised our quality of life economically through the auto industry, they also found, like many migrant Black families, that these earnings and the relatively comfortable living did not come without enormous costs.

Notwithstanding the extreme forms of racial oppression and violence that Black people were forced to endure, the labor demands in factories had a deleterious impact on Black family life. At first the Ford Motor Company aggressively recruited Black men from the South to work long hours on assembly lines to create products at a faster, more efficient rate. Ford was known as a "man-killing place" because of the difficult demands that working for the company placed on one's life both in and outside the workplace.[8] But building new lives in industrial hubs like Detroit and Chicago was almost impossible on just one income. Therefore, eventually, after many years of struggle against rampant racial and gender exclusion and discrimination, Black women entered the industrial workforce. Typically, both parents worked long hours just to make ends meet.[9]

Working in the factory five to six days a week for at least eight hours a day hindered family members' efforts to build and sustain extended kin relations, relations that were more prevalent in the South.[10] In addition, the burden of domestic work fell disproportionately on women, particularly mothers. Women had to undertake double shifts—working jobs as co–bread winners in addition to undertaking non-market-gendered activities, such as social maintenance and reproductive duties within the household.[11] These gender relations shaped experiences within families for many northern Black children, and they stood as models to emulate. As I argue in this chapter, these familial experiences are significant because, in part, these gender hierarchies and the distribution of kin labor are replicated within Black LGBT kinship yet often assigned to different bodies.

Black Family as Ideology

When I first began my research on the kinship system of Ballroom culture, I wanted to make sense of the ways in which my interlocutors described their experiences with homophobia and exclusion in Detroit as Black LGBT people, and why what most of them described was so similar to my own experiences. The aim here is not to suggest that gender and sexual marginalization is worse among Black communities than it is in other communities or society at large. Rather, Black LGBT people experience these indignities differently, as gender and sexual oppression are compounded by other forms of concurrent marginalization. A useful way to understand the homophobia, violence, and exclusion that Black LGBT people experience in Black families and communities is to conduct an intersectional analysis of race, class, gender, and sexuality. All of these factors shape the realities of Black LGBT people in Detroit in particular and US society in general. Therefore, it is important to examine the social contexts and conditions out of which the alternative kinship practices of Ballroom culture emerge.

In a controversial report, the late sociologist and senator Daniel Patrick Moynihan describes the Black community as a "tangle of pathology" that is plagued by families in disorder marked by and conducive to matriarchy.[12] According to Moynihan, Black families are beset by broken and ineffective males who are dominated by emasculating female heads of households. This so-called matriarchal structure is out of step with an American society in which the man is the dominant figure in the family unit.[13] Moynihan's pathologization of Black families, and by extension Black people, reveals the intersection of race, class, gender, and sexual oppression and the United States' denial of culpability for this oppression, both of which create hostile conditions for Black people in general. Furthermore, while many Black scholars and community leaders expressed outrage about this report, the practical responses to Moynihan's conclusions illustrate the extent to which Black people have deeply internalized his representation of Black families.

This deep internalization is expressed through the propagation of a particularly mythical notion of the Black family that has become a part of everyday ideology or common sense.[14] According to cultural theorist Stuart Hall, "ideology" constitutes the mental frameworks—the languages, concepts, categories, imagery of thought, and systems of representation—that distinct classes and social groups deploy in order to make sense of, figure out, define, and render intelligible the way society works.[15] Part of Black people's response to dominant societal views of Black families, as represented in the Moynihan Report, for example, was an overcompensatory consolidation around a logic of heteropatriarchy. The pervasive discourse of the pathological Black family, one that is outside the so-called norms of families in US society, has and continues to influence politics and social policy, directly structuring the experiences and social practices of Black people. As one consequence, Black homes and the biological family are bound together and undergirded by an ideology that fetishizes a heteropatriarchal (male-dominated) nuclear family structure. And heteronormative gender and sexual relations are the means through which these ideals of Black family are constituted and reproduced. Thus, according to Black common sense, the home is the *place* of "appropriate" reproduction and the maintenance of a heteronormative social order.

Black LGBT people are not necessarily able to rely on, have full access to, or be safe within Black homes. Some of my interlocutors spoke candidly about their experiences as gay men in Detroit, and they view and experience the city as "very homophobic." For instance, because he grew up in a "very religious family," Tino Prestige, a Butch Queen, concluded that "Black people in Detroit are really religious and gay people are put down, so it's like a double whammy where being Black is already a strike against you and gay is the ultimate sin." Tino speaks to the ways in which the Black family ideology—common sense—impacts everyday Black LGBT people. Yet the Black family ideology that I analyze is complex and permeates Black society through a variety of intersecting discourses and venues, in social, political, economic, and religious realms.

One of the common responsive positions regarding the pervasive pathologization of Black families that Black intellectual, political, and religious leaders have taken up is to espouse, as cultural theorist Paul Gilroy argues, a discourse of race as community, and as family, suggesting that the so-called crisis of black politics and social life is a crisis solely of black masculinity.[16] Gilroy further suggests that such discourses instantiate a common sense view that what hinders reproduction of an authentic Black racial nation is the deterioration of heteronormative black masculinity.[17] Therefore, those wishing to affirm the Black nation must begin by reestablishing the heteropatriarchal familial structure.[18]

I do not mean to suggest that Black communities are politically monolithic, nor do I exclude the role that other religious and political ideologies play in shaping the moral and social priorities and interests that permeate Black community discourses. Many political scientists contend that while Black politics is in many ways heterogeneous, it shares common principles that are a product of convergent political and religious ideologies.[19] Furthermore, both civil rights and Black nationalist discourses operated on and continue to rely on an explicit masculinization of the category of race.[20] Thus, Black politics exposes the widespread support for a heteropatriarchal Black familial structure within Black communities. Since nationalism is a means through which groups affiliate, identify, and understand themselves, what cultural theorist Wahneema Lubiano argues makes clear that the consolidation around the heteropatriarchal family is a product of what she calls "non-nation state Black nationalist romanticism," which creates prescriptive and extremely limited options for gender and sexual relations.[21]

Lubiano further argues that nationalism is deeply invested in constructing commonsensical understandings of identity.[22] Common sense prescriptions act as cultural or racial criteria by which one's blackness is deemed authentic and legitimate. Those who fulfill these prescriptions belong to the "nation," whether "real" or imagined. They become rooted and located in a racial/cultural identification. Especially for people who are displaced or rendered, or feel, culturally ambivalent, nationalist narratives based on a shared past and future become a strategy by which to make sense of their subjectivity.

At extraordinary events such as the Million Man March in 1995 in Washington, DC, for example, and within quotidian enactments of Black life, the politics of racial/cultural nationalism includes established gender and sexual practices.[23] Along with family, one's gender and sexual practices are critical sites at which cultural membership codes are formulated and enacted.[24] Since the nation is always conceived in heteronormative terms, heterosexuality is mandatory in the domains of nation, home, and family and is viewed as a prerequisite for "good cultural citizenship."[25] This means that Black gender and sexual minorities encounter cultural membership as a regime of normalization and are thus repressed within blackness as well as outside it. Nationalist ideologies ignore the racial oppression that Black gender and sexual minorities experience in the

United States and compound this oppression because their counternormative genders and sexualities are not allowed in the "cultural house."

Clearly, the stakes involved in cultural belonging are high. Black LGBT people face many challenges as a result of their exclusion from Black families and other forms of belonging that bring attention to the social, psychological, and spiritual ramifications of dislocation. As E. Patrick Johnson points out, since the institutions of Black belonging—home, family, and community—are firmly sutured to common sense notions of nationhood and citizenship, and since the cultural logic of sexual citizenship is lodged in normative sexuality, Black LGBT people suffer severely from the breach committed by the very institutions to which they turn for refuge.[26]

The Black Familial Deal

During my first year of college, my mother and I had one of our increasingly common confrontations about my sexuality. This was a period when my mother seemed to experience her greatest difficulty with my gay sexuality. Although I had not told my mother that I was gay (I did not actually tell her until I was thirty years old), I remember her standing in the doorway of my bedroom when I was home from school on holiday and saying, "If you are what I think you are I'm going to stop all support for you through school." Now, in retrospect, I realize that my mother was struggling to accept my sexuality. She challenged me with an ultimatum: either you stop being gay and be straight or you will lose parental support from me. At that time, my mother was an example of someone with homophobic views that were not based on religious ideology per se—my mother has never been a particularly religious person. Yet I believe it was her common sense belief that homosexuality is just wrong and immoral. In addition, for her, my apparent homosexuality threatened her dreams of having grandchildren and being the matriarch of a heteronormative family.

Like me, other Black LGBT people often experience the home and biofamily as a form of coercion to accept a sometimes explicit or tacit "familial deal" that requires one to hide (suppress) or dispense with one's nonnormative genders or sexualities in order to remain a full-fledged part of the biofamily and the biohome and to benefit from the shelter, clothing, food, and other resources that family and home are believed to provide. For Black LGBT youth in particular, noncompliance, more often than not, results in him or her being forced to live in intolerable and unstable housing conditions or utter homelessness. As a case in point, among the large percentage of LGBT young people who have been in the Child Welfare System in Michigan, most either ran away from or were thrown out of their homes because of their gender and sexual identities. There is no doubt, then, that the prospects of total familial ostracism are real. As the former grandmother of The House of Galliano in Atlanta stated, "Everybody wants to belong; gays are outsiders, so houses are a substitute for the loss of family." The explicit or tacit familial ultimatum is experienced as a kind of social death trap for many Black LGBT people. This runs contrary to the popular notion that home and family are spaces of refuge: love, care, and protection.

Many members of the Ballroom community experience the Black home as a space of confinement imbued with and based on heteropatriarchy and heteronormativity. Noir Prestige, a Butch Queen, described his experiences growing up and grappling with his sexuality within his home and biological family in Detroit.

> It was weird for me because I had so many other issues that [were] making me not want to be gay, be it religion, be it family, or be it how I see other people treat people who were or even how I treated people who were openly gay. And I couldn't talk to anyone in my family except for a cousin who was unfortunately dealing with the same issues. I could only talk to friends and sexual partners. I knew I couldn't bring it up at home because my grandmother who raised me was a very religious woman, so it was like a do-or-die church mentality. She raised me the way she saw fit. I had to be in church; I had to do my schooling. I had rules, and if I broke them, I had to go back to my mom's environment, which was kind of not good at the time because my stepdad, who I thought was my father by the way, was abusive. He got my mom into a drug addiction, so I had to deal with . . . well, do I want to deal with this or do I want to deal with that?

Noir grew up in a household of very modest means. Until he moved in with his partner, Noir lived in a two-family flat on the northwest side of Detroit. He lived with his three siblings; his mother who is addicted to drugs; his elderly but domineering grandmother; and his uncle. Noir's

father was not in his life. Thus, Noir grew up under difficult circumstances, always being pressured by his grandmother and uncle to be
straight. Noir's comments get to the heart of matters confronting numerous Black LGBT people in environments that rely on heteropatriarchal
notions of family and community. These notions are in part drawn from
religious ideology, to discipline Black LGBT family members no matter
the family makeup.

Some of my other interlocutors described circumstances similar to
those of Noir. For instance, Will Ford, a Butch Queen, is close to his
mother but effectively estranged from his father. And Brianna, a Femme
Queen, discussed how her relationship with her father deteriorated, she
believes, because she lives as a transgender woman. "I probably lost the
relationship that I had with my father . . . we were real close. It won't be
like it was," said Brianna. Prince J Prodigy, a Butch Queen, told me that
his father stopped talking to him: "We just stopped speaking." When I
asked Prince J if he thought his sexuality had anything to do with it, he
said, "I think it does." Although Noir, Will, Brianna, and Prince J's stories fall within a diverse range of experiences that my interlocutors described, a common factor is that, for most of the LGBT Ballroom members, their relationships with their families of origin suffered, in some
form or another, due to their nonconforming gender and sexual identities and practices.

Historically, family has been an important cauldron of resistance, a
unit that has sustained Black communities even amid protracted efforts
by US institutions to undermine it.[27] In actual structure and function,
however, Black familial relations have neither coincided with the nuclear
family model touted as the American standard, nor, for that matter, have
the relations in most dominant families. Instead, familial traditions in
the African diaspora define family more expansively than do dominant
representations of family in the United States.[28] While Black families, in
order to survive the assaults constantly waged against them, have drawn
from a variety of kinship traditions, such as surrogacy and extended
families, they have also often fetishized the nuclear family in order not
to appear pathological and antithetical to dominant societal norms.[29]
Therefore, Black family ideology, while purporting to oppose white supremacist assumptions and treatment, is Manichean, maintaining and
reinstituting many of the same structures of oppression that victimize
Black people. Ultimately, the ideology of the Black family does not reflect
the realities of Black people's lives, especially for those who are LGBT.

Redefining Home: Kinship in Black LGBT Communities

In the midst of extremely difficult conditions, only some of which I have delineated, Black LGBT people have endured a long history of undertaking alternative kin practices that redefine home and family. And such practices do not always consolidate around structures of kin and social institutions that replicate dominant society. Recently, there has been a great deal of debate about marriage. This is in large part because heterosexual marriage is in rapid decline and is viewed by many of the national citizenry as an inadequate institution.[30] Many people find it difficult to adhere to the rigid heteronormative constraints associated with marriage, even in the case of same sex marriage. E. Patrick Johnson notes that the pervasive heteronormative logic of marriage sees two loving heterosexuals nesting together, what he calls "homemaking," as the ultimate sign of familial wholeness.[31] Obviously, at least in socioeconomic terms, this dominant logic is inconsistent with the realities of people's lives, whether they are heterosexual or not.[32] Ballroom members, however, forge familial relationships that are not based on conventional constructs such as marriage. Instead, they undertake a labor of kin to create an alternative social and community sphere through a reformulation of kinship. Yet it is important to highlight, from the perspective of history, the relationship between Ballroom houses and other Black LGBT kinship practices.

In his article "A Spectacle in Color: The Lesbian and Gay Subculture of Jazz Age Harlem," the late gay historian Eric Garber describes the large Black migration to northern urban areas like Harlem, at the turn of the twentieth century, as the genesis of an urban underground Black LGBT culture. During this time, Black gays, lesbians, bisexuals, and crossdressers socialized at rent parties, clubs, drag balls and pageants,[33] and it was during the 1920s that a Black LGBT subculture began to take form.[34] This history coincides with my interlocutors' assertions that Harlem is the birthplace of Ballroom culture. The House of LaBeija was one of the first houses of the scene, founded in 1970.[35] Having to negotiate virulent forms of racism imposed by the White ruling classes and homophobia imposed by Black communities, these underground Black transgressive spaces and practices helped to sustain individuals within communities under siege.

One of the only monographs on kinship and community networks among Black gay men is the late anthropologist William G. Hawkeswood's *One of the Children: Gay Black Men in Harlem* (coauthored with

Alex W. Costley), an ethnographic study of Black gay communities in the 1980s. Hawkeswood examined the lives of 193 participants, all of whom resided in Harlem, and investigated how Black gay men refashion an expansive network of friends into family and community. As a result, these Black gay men, not unlike those who now participate in Ballroom culture, redefine what it means to be a family by undertaking the kin labor that family requires.[36] Documenting Black LGBT community practices in Harlem in the 1980s as well, Livingston's *Paris Is Burning* marks similar efforts to redefine family and community among members of the Ballroom community. Both Livingston's documentary and Hawkeswood and Costley's study highlight the importance of Harlem as a site of Black LGBT cultural formation in the late twentieth century.

Sociologist Mignon R. Moore's recent book, *Invisible Families: Gay Identities, Relationships, and Motherhood among Black Women,*[37] is a comprehensive study of the ways in which race, class, gender, and sexuality shape the lives of Black lesbians (or gay women) and the varied and complex family forms these women forge with their same-sex partners, their children, and the larger Black LGBT community in the United States. Moore's book is the only examination of its kind that brings into view Black lesbian kinship forms, which have been largely absent from literatures on LGBT communities, on the one hand, and Black communities on the other.

Here I situate Ballroom community kin practices within a long tradition of LGBT kinship among Black cultures in midwestern cities such as Detroit and Chicago. During the post–World War II period, Black LGBT people who were reared in and lived among largely African American urban communities in the Midwest participated in improvisational but resilient kinship practices and built thriving networks of social/sexual, kinship, and community relations. After the "Roaring Twenties," and throughout the 1940s and 1950s, these Black LGBT social and performance communities expanded far beyond New York City and the urban North and became fixtures in the transgressive gender and sexual underground. As I highlight in chapter 1, the work of Ruth Ellis and Babe Franklin from the mid– to late twentieth century is a testament to the centrality of alternative kinship forms to Black LGBT communities and how they have continued to thrive throughout the country while in the midst of, in some cases, extreme social alienation and deprivation. It is worth repeating that, to date, the Ruth Ellis Center continues to provide housing and social services for LGBT young people, most of whom are Black and members of the Ballroom community in Detroit.

Ballroom Houses: What's in a Name?

Although it can boast of some degree of uniqueness, Ballroom culture did not emerge sui generis. It is truly an amalgam of cultural practices of which the houses are but one example. Ballroom's kinship system resembles the kin-making practices of African diaspora cultures and LGBT cultures in the United States in that it necessarily expands the meaning of family. Typically, Ballroom houses resemble, in structure and function, the familial domains within which Ballroom members live.[38] Yet the Ballroom community has constructed a kinship system that attempts to fulfill the needs, aspirations, and dreams of its members within the context of their lived experiences. In so doing, however, Ballroom members appropriate dominant practices and experiences from which they are largely excluded, reshaping them to fit their own realities.

Most Ballroom houses are named after haute couture designer houses. Famous designer names such as Ford, Galliano, Bvlgari, Givenchy, Chanel, Manolo Blahnik, Mizrahi, Escada, and many more have been adopted as house names. Because of the class position that most Ballroom members occupy, the items that these fashion houses produce usually exceed the economic and social reach of most Ballroom houses. However, some members find other ways to obtain the designer brand items—some legal, others not. Nonetheless, when a house dubs itself with a designer name such as The House of Prada, it has performed an act that is more symbolic than indicative of real purchasing power on the part of house members. Other houses bear names that represent qualities that their founders and parents want their members to emulate, such as Aphrodite or Ninja. For example, Father Alvernian Prestige said that he and his cofounders did not want to follow the trend of naming houses after designers. Instead, he wanted the house to represent success and achievement, so they named the house "Prestige." Phoenix Manolo Blahnik said that naming a house is really up to its founder. He said further that "it is part of their own personal vision, what he or she thinks the house is or some attribute they really admire or really look at."

Because performance is integral to building and sustaining the Ball-room community, especially in terms of the space and occasion of the ball itself, performance is one of the central components of a house. Generally, the fact that there are no houses without balls means that a house has to participate in balls in order to be recognized as a house. Likewise, members' success in performance competitions garners the house status and prestige in the community. With few exceptions, a house is recognized as a house only when its members compete at balls. Houses gain national and local recognition through the individual performances of its members, as well as through collective productions (or "as a house" categories). For example, most houses aspire to be what Prince J Prodigy calls a "power house." Prince J, from The House of Prodigy in Detroit, suggests that a power house is "a house where at least ten of its members have decreed their category, and its members are known to 'slay and snatch trophies' every time they walk." To accomplish this, members are recruited based on their performance abilities and are trained by parents and other house members to compete successfully in particular categories.

Once one joins a house, one has to maintain one's position within it by walking balls. "All members of The Legendary House of Prestige must be walking balls or I will put you out," Father Alvernian once said at a national house meeting. Hence, being approached to join a house, as well as staying in it, is in part based on one's performance labor in terms of preparation and execution. This places an enormous amount of pressure on members to do what it takes to fashion and market themselves appropriately and effectively. Such refashioning is believed to create for them the necessary attention from houses looking to construct a power house. The competitive success, status, and image of a house play a critical role in its creation and maintenance. And although members contribute other important qualities and attributes to a house, performance is a focal point.

Of equal importance are the social relationships and kin labor in which members engage within the house structure. The social relations in Ballroom houses are based on the *gender system* that I examined in chapter 2. The gender system also fosters the flexible gender and sexual arrangements within Ballroom houses. Houses are led by mothers (Butch Queens, Femme Queens, or Women) and fathers (Butch Queens, Butches, or Men) who, regardless of age, provide parental guidance to numerous Black LGBT people who have been devalued and rejected by their blood families, religious institutions of their childhood, and society at large. According to many of my interlocutors in Detroit, the housework in which Ballroom members are involved is especially necessary in a city that they characterize as hostile to Black LGBT people.

Although building kinship ties among Black LGBT communities has been a long-standing practice, according to many of those I interviewed, it was after the release of *Paris Is Burning* that Ballroom houses began to form and function in Detroit, as they do in the documentary. The House of Charles was one of the first known Ballroom houses in Detroit. According to Ballroom enthusiast and photographer Chris "Snaps Monroe" Cushman, the house was cofounded by Albert, a Butch Queen, and Michiee, who identified himself as androgynous, and it was loosely modeled after the houses highlighted in the documentary film. Albert was the housemother, and Brent, another Butch Queen, was the housefather. Although Michiee was a cofounder, he was only a member. Cushman, a White Butch Queen, remembers that Mother Albert's house was a Black gay gathering place, located in a "not very well populated neighborhood right behind the State Fairgrounds" between Eight and Seven Mile Roads on the northwest side. Although mother Albert used to hold "shows" in the huge backyard of his house, The House of Charles was most importantly a means through which Black LGBT participants in this bourgeoning scene could gather, socialize, and do family. As Chris explained, "It [The House of Charles] was a house. They knew enough about the house culture to have a house, to have a housemother and a housefather. It was definitely a family." Interestingly, a former member of The House of Charles, Phoenix Manolo Blahnik, said that The House of Charles organized fundraisers for AIDS awareness; therefore, as early as the 1990s, the Ballroom community was engaged, in some way, in the fight against the epidemic.

In her groundbreaking study of gay and lesbian kinship in the San Francisco Bay Area, anthropologist Kath Weston problematizes what has become a pervasive notion that queer kinship is a form of "fictive kin." For many Black LGBT people, the kin relations they forge and engage in are not viewed or experienced as fictive at all. Weston argues against any notion that gay families and queer kinship are derivatives or a mere passive reflection and imitation of other forms of kinship in US society.[39] Rather, gay families and queer kin are often established out of necessity and on their own terms, while exposing the fallacy of dominant family ideologies by doing the kin labor that many biological families fail to

Fig. 7. A portrait of the House of Charles in Detroit in 1995. Shown in the image are, from left to right, (*back row*) Michael, Michiee, Robert M, and Robert J; (*middle row*) Diva, Albert, and DeAngela; (*front row*) Phoenix and Blue. (Photograph by Chris "Snaps Monroe" Cushman.)

do. Moreover, kinship among Black LGBT communities makes clear that heterosexuality is not the *sine qua non* of family. Instead, family is about and based on the kin labor that members choose to undertake.

The kinship system in the contemporary Ballroom scene comprises a large network of houses that expands and functions throughout North America. Many houses have forged complex national structures that resemble lineages and family trees. This massive kinship structure is the context in which each house is forged. Ballroom houses are performative, much like the expressions of gender and sexual identity that their members deploy. Taking into account the integral role of performance and performativity in the community, I emphasize the labor of family in the community rather than an ideology. This is not to occlude the influence that Black family ideology has on members of the Ballroom community. Instead, my aim here is to highlight the activity, performance, and labor dimensions of the kinship system as I delineate it. Members identify with a house and its name by and through performing the work that sustains it. In other words, because the house is largely a social configuration, its existence depends on its members, the relationships in which they are engaged, and individual and collective performances at the balls.

There are times, however, when these social configurations—houses—consist of members' actually living together in one house or gathering at a parent's house. Mother Albert Charles's house is an example of the latter. And while I was a member of the Detroit chapter of The Legendary House of Prestige, Mother Duchess's small apartment on the west side of the city was a place in which to hold house meetings and gatherings or a location at which members could just hang out. Regarding the former, Mother Goddess, a Butch Queen and the overall mother of The House of Rodeo, mentioned living in a house with other members of the Ballroom scene called Lakewood Estates, located at Lakewood and East Jefferson on the east side of Detroit. In addition, Prada, a Butch Queen from the Detroit chapter of The House of Escada, suggested that, in some cases, houses serve as actual physical shelters in which "those lost souls [can] craft and cohabitate." Even though some houses shun crafting and stunts, as stated earlier, this underground economy permeates all dimensions of the Ballroom community. Nevertheless, primarily, as in the early days in Detroit, kin work is a key factor in any house considered as a social configuration and sometimes within the house as an actual physical space.

Whether or not a "house" is a "home"—a building—house members consider themselves a family and carry out a whole host of activities together to fortify their kin ties, such as taking trips, holding family dinners and reunions, celebrating birthdays, shopping for a ball, bailing each other out of jail, and even fighting with and for one another. Although the ties that bind members together in the Ballroom community are not biological, kin ties are, nonetheless, viewed, undertaken, and experienced as real. Unlike Ballroom members' blood families, emphasis is placed on the labor involved in developing and maintaining relationships that add meaning to the house.

Houses and National Networks of Kin

As stated above, "overall balls" are events akin to family reunions. These family reunions capture the nature of the national house structures. Most houses belong to a larger network of houses throughout the country, akin to an extended kinship structure. The structure and function of these networks combine the virtues of an extended family, on the one hand, and a national organization, similar to a sorority or fraternity, on the other. Houses that have multiple chapters, for instance, function loosely as national organizations with house units located in several cities. For example, in 2004, at a national house meeting in Philadelphia, Father Alvernian proclaimed that there were fifteen chapters of The Legendary House of Prestige. According to him, the chapters were in Milwaukee, Boston, Chicago, New York City, Indianapolis, Louisville, Raleigh/Durham, Philadelphia, Newark, Detroit, Richmond, Cleveland, Buffalo, Baltimore, and Washington, DC. Some of these chapters did not last very long, and many were not fully functional. Yet, these kin units/chapters carry the name and, in most cases, represent an "overall" house organization with a national or home chapter.

Also in 2004 Father Alvernian was approached by Ariel, a Femme Queen, about opening a Prestige chapter in Los Angeles. Alvernian gave Ariel permission to start the chapter, so she brought her kids from another house to form the new chapter, which was called the California chapter. During that same period, I moved from the Detroit chapter to the Los Angeles one while I took up residency in Santa Barbara, about one and a half hours north of LA.

In 2005–7, a San Francisco Bay Area chapter was added to the LA chapter, with Tamia, a Butch Queen, as the mother. The Prestiges from California were known as the West Coast members. Throughout all of these changes, the national house was, and still is, based in Philadelphia where the cofounder and overall father, Alvernian, resides. As I will discuss, "overall parents" are the national overseers of an entire house structure.[40] Overall mothers and fathers open chapters, appoint parents, assign distinct roles to members within a house organization, fire parents, and close chapters. Alvernian closed almost as many chapters as he granted permission to open. During my stint with the house, he closed chapters in New York City, Baltimore, Washington, DC, and Richmond. Other houses dissolved and closed due to inadequate chapter membership or leadership.

In many ways, Ballroom houses are, like biological homes, fluid, fleeting, and fickle. Whenever I was frustrated over not being able to pin down the makeup of a house and its membership; when chapters close, dissolve, or reopen elsewhere; when new houses and chapters pop up out of nowhere; and when parents are removed from or abandon houses, I reflect on similar occurrences in heteronormative families, especially in my own biological family. When I was about eight years old, my mother divorced my father, who was an alcoholic and a batterer. From that time until his death in 2005, he rarely spoke to me. And, beginning in my teens, my siblings and I stopped speaking to one another (and have not spoken for years), while my relationship with my mother has consistently been "on and off."

In my late teens and early twenties, various members of my family began to speculate about my sexuality. After that, rumors about my being gay circulated throughout the family but never to me directly, and everyone distanced themselves from me to the extent that I became estranged from almost all of my immediate family members. I recast my friends as family; I built kinship ties with a diverse community of people, both men and women, gay and straight, and from a variety of racial/ethnic backgrounds in Detroit and throughout the globe. Therefore, what is clearly true in my case and those of other LGBT people I know, not to mention in the Ballroom community, is that kin labor, not biological blood binds or titles that supposedly signify familial roles and entitlements, sustains family or kinship.

The Legendary House of Prestige Domination Ball:
Preparing the Space

There are times when doing family involves actual manual labor. This is usually the case when participants prepare for balls, which I came to understand as I waited outside the Tom Phillip Post Lodge. After waiting for three hours, I finally see cars full of people, most of whom I have never seen before, pulling into the parking lot. As they get out of their cars, the passengers are carrying paper bags from McDonald's and Burger King. "Is Duchess here yet?" several people ask. "Not yet," someone responds. Soon after, Duchess drives up with a car full of other folks, all carrying black plastic bags from the store. "Okay, let's do this, kids," says Duchess.

As the Detroit chapter of The Legendary House of Prestige, we are the hosting house; therefore, it is our responsibility to secure the hall, decorate it, organize the ball, and host the commentators and the out-of-town members of the house. The hosting house also provides the commentators' transportation and lodging and pays their fees. For local commentators the hosting house pays only the fee, for obvious reasons. As soon as we walk into a large, rather old looking hall, Duchess, along with a personal friend who accompanies him, starts delegating duties. "I need someone to set up some tables and chairs and start laying this tile down for the runway," says Duchess. At some point during the process, I stand back and look around to see all of these Butch Queens, Femme Queens, Butch Queens Up in Drag, Butches, Men, and Women laying tile, arranging tables and chairs, cleaning dishes for the bar, decorating the platform and table for the judges, cutting ribbons, lifting tables, hanging streamers, mopping the floor, and cleaning toilets and sinks. Some of us are chatting, laughing, flirting, and just having a good time with one another, even though many of us have not met before. This reflection illustrates the inseparability between ball events and the houses that produce them. In addition, we all work together to prepare the hall for this anniversary/reunion ball, regardless of gender and sexual roles, and even though Duchess delegates duties, he also works. We all indulge in the excitement and pleasure of preparing the space for the ritualized performance event in which we are about to partake in just a few hours. Hence, a house is not only a social configuration; it is also a ritualized set of practices for *housework*.

Kin Labor as Housework

The labor involved in forging kin ties between members is a central activity on which houses are based. In her study of women's "kin lives," anthropologist Micaela di Leonardo suggests that we should analyze kin relations beyond the nuclear household structure and focus attention on the work involved in the conception, maintenance, and rituals of kin ties across households.[41] Leonardo connects women's kin work to housework and child care in order to highlight the centrality of nonmarket activities in sustaining households that women do and men do not do, at least in a heteronormative context. Among the significant differences that distinguish the work that Leonardo discusses and what I am describing here are that LGBT people do the *housework* and an actual home—a building—is not the locus of Ballroom kinship. Instead, because the house is social and not necessarily physical, the *housework* exists within the social relations of the members and emphasizes the activity of creating kin without relying on a fixed space. To conceive of family as labor necessarily involves recognizing and engaging in relationships in a distinctive way.

What happens within the social configuration or the physical space of the house? As a part of the overarching qualities of care, service, competition, and critique that are integral to Ballroom communities, in addition to what I have described, forms of housework that sustain the community are friendship, protection from violence, and parenting. First, by and large, Ballroom houses are convened based on friendship. As Chris "Snaps Monroe" Cushman put it, "Houses are more of a collection or a circle of individuals that see themselves as family." Friendship is a significant relationship in this creation of a house and its quotidian social relations because friends provide social support for each other. For instance, as Kali, a Butch Queen from the now defunct House of Ford, described it:

A house is a clique of friends that got to know each other within the gay life. The establishment of our house was a result of us being friends for six or seven years. Most of us were just a group of friends and then in the year of 1998 decided to become a house. According to my understanding, there were about five of my friends who were coming back from a trip to Atlanta during Black Gay Pride, and they came up with the idea to start a house. We've been together ever since.

An employee at one of the automotive plants in Detroit, Kali sat across the table from me in the kitchen of his new home in a Detroit suburb as he discussed how important the house is to him as a social network, a welcome alternative to the hypermasculine and homophobic environment of the automobile plant. I suspect that this is why he somewhat downplays and disaggregates the kin-making component of the house but foregrounds the role of friendship. Clearly, however, such friendship within the house is an important element in the reconstitution of the experience of kinship even if some Ballroom members do not describe it as such.

While conducting fieldwork in 2003, I typically hung out and met fellow Ballroom members on Friday and Saturday nights at the Woodward Cocktail Bar on Woodward Avenue in the New Center Area in Detroit, just north of downtown.[42] The Woodward is White owned and, in recent years, has become one of the only bars where Black LGBT people can socialize. Many of the friendships integral to houses were forged and, in part, nurtured at the Woodward and at a few other Black LGBT spaces like it. Albeit few in number, in Detroit, such bars and clubs are primary socializing spaces for many in the Ballroom community and other LGBT people. On Friday and Saturday nights, Black LGBT people frequent the Woodward Bar and Grill to drink, dance, play cards and pool, and perform karaoke. Sitting on a barstool—his stoop—at his favorite social venue, Prada Escada links friendship to family in his view of Ballroom culture.

> First of all, a house is a collection of like-minded individuals that share common interests, who for the most part can agree on different issues and ideas . . . or they can just agree to disagree. It is born from groups of good-good friends. The house structure is geared specifically towards the ball scene (particularly in Detroit). As far as its purpose, houses provide a source of family nurturing that oftentimes a lot of kids don't get at home. It gives kids a sense of pride in saying they are a member of such-an-such house or that Miss Thing is my mother, particularly if the house or parent is thought of as sickening in Detroit.

Prada describes houses as going beyond "just a clique of friends" to suggest that they serve multiple functions, including serving as a space not only for friendship but also for nurturing, affirmation, belonging, and conflict. Notwithstanding the integral role of performance in creating a house, Prada points to how Ballroom members recast their friends and comrades as kin as a part of a larger queer community practice.[43]

Furthermore, Lovely, a Femme Queen and housemother of The House of Mohair in Oakland, California, agreed that a house is a place of refuge. She is nevertheless firm in her assertion that a house is about

Fig. 8. Founder and former mother of the Oakland, California, chapter of the House of Mohair, Lovely poses at a ball in Indianapolis in 2011. Lovely is currently Mother Revlon West Coast. (Photograph by Thabiti John Willis.)

more than friendship and access to one's house is contingent on one's commitment and loyalty to it.[44]

> My house is a place of refuge. Here, we do not have a lot of balls. We focus on family, community, and togetherness. . . . Some people jump from house to house to house, but in my house, once you jump out you can't come back. I am not going to play that. That is no respect. . . . So yeah, they jump around here, but I tell them in the beginning, once you leave here, do not think about coming back. And whatever happens don't look for my protection because it was your choice.

An apropos example of what Lovely discusses is Tino and Noir's relationship. Tino Prestige was skeptical of Noir's intentions when they met.

Initially, he thought Noir "might want to get with him." However, as they grew closer, Tino realized how much they had in common in terms of music, entertainment, spirituality, career, activism, and HIV status. Noir brought Tino into the Ballroom scene and The Legendary House of Prestige. At balls, both Tino and Noir walked in Butch realness categories, walking Thug Realness and Schoolboy Realness, respectively. And, as I elaborate in chapter 5, before Noir's untimely death both he and Tino identified openly as gay men living with HIV and devoted their careers and activism to HIV prevention issues. Even though Noir was older, Tino took on the "big brother" role in Noir's life. Their relationship met very specific needs for each: Tino always reminded Noir to take his medications, while Noir helped Tino budget his money. The relationship between Tino and Noir is an example of how two Black gay men can forge a brotherhood through friendship both within and beyond the Ballroom community. "We are truly brothers," Tino said emphatically about Noir and himself.

As is the case for the house, in terms of meaning and function, the emphasis is on the activity and practice of friendship as opposed to the conferral of a title. While their views on houses reflect their individual experiences, expectations, and needs, Kali, Prada, Tino, Noir, Lovely, and others bring into focus the actual work of creating and sustaining a house, in part through friendship.

A Ballroom House Is Like a Gay Gang

In *Paris Is Burning*, the late Icon Dorian Corey describes a house as a "gay gang." Sometimes it is necessary for a house to act like a gang to protect its house members from the violence that can be visited on them because they are perceived to be defenseless against it. Tino, for instance, said that his Thug Realness gender performance enabled him to protect Noir from stalkers, a problem that Noir dealt with often. To take another example, K-C Prestige, a Butch Queen and father of The Legendary House of Prestige's Missouri chapter, who attended the Xstacy Ball in Chicago along with Prestige members from the Richmond, Cleveland, and Philadelphia chapters, described an incident in which he was robbed and violently attacked at a gas station on the South Side of Chicago while attending a ball during the Fourth of July Black Pride weekend in 2003. At 3:00 a.m., the venue at which the Xstacy Ball was held was shut down, and the continuation of the ball was moved to Milan's, an after-hours spot. The attack and robbery happened to K-C and his fellow house members as they stopped at a gas station en route to Milan's. K-C explained it this way.

I was following members from Chicago and Virginia and I wanted to stop at a gas station to refuel when we came upon a semi-well-lit station. I stepped out to pay for the gas and another member [Rico Prestige from Chicago] also got out. As I turned away from the window, a man asked, "Can I pump ya gas?" I said no, I'm fine . . . he then said "well can I get some change from you?" I told him I didn't have any. I walked away and Rico was walking up. I walked up to my car and started to pump the gas. I reached through the driver's window to get or say something and when I turn my back out from the car, there were two men right there in front of me and the one in front hit me on the left side of my ear/face; I was knocked out. When I came to, I was on the other side of the parking lot and all I saw was people circled around Rico holding his head and Father Alvernian holding on to a small wooden bat with blood on it. I looked down and my watch, shirt and earrings were gone. My shirt was missing and I had scars and scratches on both hands and knees. At the same time there just so happened to be a cop coming down the street, so I stopped her and told her what had happened. She radioed an ambulance for Rico. The others told me that, while I was blacked out, when the first guy hit me, Rico noticed something wasn't right and he came over and got him away from me. Guy #2 then hit Rico in the head with a gun, causing him to get six stitches put into the front of his hairline. Father Alvernian noticed what was going on, grabbed a bat out of Jaylen's [from Chicago] car and hit the guy #2 in the back of his head busting it open. The two ended up running off after that along with my jewelry, a necklace and diamond ring from Juan [Chicago].

At the time of the incident, K-C was living in Detroit as an active member of The Legendary House of Prestige there. Throughout my interviews, I was told of similar incidents in which Ballroom members fought off people robbing or attacking other members of their houses.

Houses provide protection not only from random violence on the street but also from violence inflicted on house members by other houses. Sometimes the intense competition between houses at balls leads to violent physical conflicts, when the membership of an entire house will jump on that of another house due to a dispute about the winner of a category. For example, at a ball during the Hotter than July Black Pride event in July 2010, I heard several members of a house, one of whose members lost a category that he believed he should have won, saying, "Wait 'til we get outside; we are going to see who da baddest." And although I have not personally witnessed or been involved in an all-out brawl between houses, I have heard from my interlocutors of incidents in which balls have been shut down because of physical fights between houses.

The Labor of Parenting

There are both important similarities and important distinctions between the construction of gender and sexual roles in Ballroom and similar work in the larger society. As I explore ways in which gender and sexual relations in Ballroom houses adhere to or break with hegemonic societal norms, it is important to situate the role of parents, especially those I call "platonic parents," within the multidimensional context in which many Ballroom members exist. This is helpful in illuminating the subversive potential of houses and kinship in Ballroom culture.

By and large, dominant constructions of family influence how families among minoritized groups are evaluated by society and how family members evaluate themselves. According to ethnographers Linda M. Burton and Carol B. Stack, dominant family models present "family scripts," which are mental representations that shape the roles and performances that family members undertake within and across a range of familial and kinship contexts.[45] As a product of both American and Black culture, Ballroom's kinship system is an outgrowth of both dominant and alternative forms of kinship. One dominant script that is taken on in Ballroom is that masculinity, whether attached to or performed by male, female, or transgender bodies, enjoys privilege within the scene, as it does in the world outside of it. This factor influences whether members choose to be referred to as and play the role of fathers or mothers depending on what "kind" of masculinity or femininity they embody, perform, and represent. In Ballroom, however, male-bodied men (i.e., Butch Queens and Men) are not the sole proprietors of masculinity, and female-bodied women (i.e., Women) are not the sole proprietors of femininity.[46] Therefore, while Ballroom houses do not break entirely from dominant family norms, they find ways to appropriate some and transform other aspects of these norms.[47]

In addition to the central house roles of mothering and fathering, which I delineate explicitly below, the housework of parenting involves several dimensions that extend beyond and redefine parental roles in conventional families. First, house parents are required to be successful ball competitors and recognized as such in the larger Ballroom community. Competition is an integral aspect of the social world of Ballroom culture, so when house parents are known as accomplished competitors throughout the scene, they garner community-defined status. Thus, house parents are typically recognized as icons or legendary performers, achieving this status when they have either "decreed" their category or categories or when they have won a substantial number of trophies nationally. Attaining this status calls for careful preparation and a considerable amount of work. The Ballroom scene rewards this work by recognizing these parents at the balls, mainly during Legend, Statements, and Stars or "shout outs" at the beginning of a ball.

Secondly, in addition to being successful individual competitors, house parents also gain status through the popularity and accomplishments of their houses. Parents recruit free agents, lure members from other houses, and direct their children to recruit members whom they think will fill or add to areas of need in the house. This was made evident to me while attending two national Legendary House of Prestige meetings in 2004, one held in Louisville and the other in Philadelphia. In both meetings, Father Alvernian spoke directly to parents of chapters and instructed them to be mindful of the ball categorical needs at both regional and national levels: "We need more face, body, and sex siren kids in the house, so only recruit for that. Do not recruit anymore Femme Queen vogue or Butch Queens Up in Drag; we got too many of them nationally," said Alvernian.

Third, parenting is not signified by age. Parents are often younger than some of their children. In Ballroom culture, age is not so much about how long one has been on this earth as it is about the length of time one has been in the LGBT or Ballroom scene. For instance, I was older than my former housemother, Duchess, was, in years, but he was older than me in Ballroom years because he had more experience and recognition in the scene. In fact, I was in my mid-to-late thirties while I was a participant. Although I was older than many of the Ballroom members in Detroit, I was considered young in the Ballroom scene. When I interviewed Lovely Mohair during the very early stages of my research, she was only twenty-two years old and was a housemother at one of the largest houses in Oakland. Ballroom parents are appointed or they forge partnerships and engage in the practice of parenting willfully as opposed to assuming mere titles or entitlements based on biological ties or age.

Fourth, in addition to the responsibilities parents have for a chapter, house parents can be and often are "overall" fathers and mothers. For houses that have several chapters throughout the country, overall parents oversee the national structure of the house. In the case of The Legendary House of Prestige, the overall father is the head of all of the chapters, informally supervises all of the parents, and organizes the national house events. The gendered distribution of labor between parents—what mothers do versus what fathers do—undergirds the individual chapters as well as the overall national structure of the house.

Finally, and perhaps most significantly, although the division of labor reinscribes heteronormative gender roles—housemothers as nurturers and housefathers as guides—the members recast which biological body undertakes the labor in the domestic sphere and in the public sphere.[48] A quintessential example of this distinction will be elaborated in my discussion of the various forms of kin labor that mothers and fathers perform. Mothering and fathering are the most salient examples of how housework—as kin labor—is undertaken, and how it is gendered, but also how the duties and roles are assigned to bodies different from those typical of heteronormative families and how this sustains the house.

Housemothers: Butch Queen and Femme
Queen Matriarchs?

Most Ballroom mothers are Butch Queens, although increasingly Femme Queens and Women are parenting houses.[49] Mothering (as socially configured domestic labor) occupies the main work of parenting and thus is an integral aspect of the platonic relationship at the head of Ballroom households. While fetishistic femininity is attached to mothering, the labor is primarily undertaken by biologically male Butch Queens and Femme Queens. Fathering is also socially configured and is linked to fetishized masculinity, but it takes on far fewer and different responsibilities within the house unit. Usually, fathers are Butch Queens or Butches. Generally, masculinity and femininity as conceived of within houses reflect hegemonic norms and, at times, a hierarchy that privileges masculinity over femininity. However, at other times, the qualities and performances are redrawn and attached to different bodies to serve different purposes.

Having said this, I must add that, clearly, mothers do all of the work in the house. For instance, Danny, a Butch Queen in The House of Galliano in Atlanta, discusses what it means to be a housemother: "They are usually into mothering, doing the things that mothers do. If they are good, they are sometimes asked to start other houses in other places. The most important thing for a house to have is a legendary mother." The "mothering" of which he speaks has very specific attributes, which are believed to signify the performance and role of the mother. Similarly, the first mother of The House of Ford in Detroit, Will, a Butch Queen, said that housemothers "walk balls, plan events, organize everything, and delegate responsibilities. Some members view the housemother as an actual mother. He/she is someone the members go to for advice and guidance." When I interviewed Trinity Prestige, a Butch Queen and the last mother of the Detroit chapter of The Legendary House of Prestige, he articulated some of these specific "motherly" qualities when he described his role as the housemother.

MB: What does it mean to be a housemother?
TRINITY: Just being loving, caring, you know, just being able to listen, as well as have people confide in you.
MB: What do you offer that their biological mother doesn't offer?
TRINITY: Something they can't talk to their biological mother about, something that they can talk to me about.
MB: Okay, like what?
TRINITY: Like as far as the lifestyle or as far as relationship problems or whatever, things they just need to talk about that's dealing with the life.
MB: How did you become the housemother?
TRINITY: Because of me being me, people felt like they could open up to me.

Trinity was an empress (akin to an aunt) before Father Alvernian unseated Duchess and appointed him as mother of the Detroit chapter.

Although a variety of responsibilities and expectations accompanies being a housemother, Trinity speaks to the labor of what sociologist Evelyn Nakano Glenn describes as the social, rather than biological, construct of "mothering."[50] The dominant social construction of mothering, combined with an individual member's relationship with the mother or the "mother figures" in his or her life, constitutes the overall social script that housemothers follow. For instance, Will Ford suggested that his understanding of mothering "comes from his mother." A primary component of mothering is a labor of care that every house expects and depends on from its housemothers. Anthropologist Emily Arnold's study of Ballroom houses in the San Francisco Bay Area found that housemothers cooked for their members during house gatherings and meetings, and they monitored their children's diets, and eating and sleeping habits.[51] My interlocutors described housemothers as performing most of the labor of care in a house, acting from desires and expectations that are much like those of their biological mothers.

Housemothers are primary organizers of all facets of the ball events. Duchess played a critical role in helping me prepare to walk in my very first Grand House March at the Domination Ball. He helped me pick out my suit and other accessories for my overall executive realness look. "You look fierce," said Duchess when I emerged from the dressing room at the Banana Republic store at the Somerset Mall just outside of Detroit. I also observed Duchess teaching a young house member the basics of voguing on the dance floor at Club Illusions on the northwest side of the city. He not only organized the ball and nurtured his "kids," but he also helped us prepare for the big ball event. Ultimately, even though most are Butch Queens and Femme Queens, housemothers are seen, and in fact see themselves, as embodying and emulating these socially constructed qualities of mothering.

In his study of home and family life among lesbians and gay men, sociologist Christopher Carrington argues that caring is widely viewed as inherently feminine and intrinsically dwells within the personalities of women.[52] In this sense, even though Butch Queens are gay men, those who take on the role of the housemother are feminized, as opposed to Butch Queens, who take on the role of the housefather. Notably, because Femme Queens live as women, the position of housefather is not available to them. Again, femininity and masculinity are categories that affect how Ballroom members view themselves and how they are viewed by others and, in effect, dictate what roles they assume.

Despite the abiding privilege and power that masculinity enjoys in

Ballroom, many members will say that mothers hold all of the power in the house. "She arranges all of the events and makes most of the decisions," said Danny Galliano. And Mother Goddess, a Butch Queen and the overall mother of The House of Rodeo, speaks for many other Ballroom members when he says, "The mother is the ruler of the house." Goddess is based in Detroit but is responsible for and runs The House of Rodeo's chapters throughout the country.

Hence, some members would concur with Moynihan's thesis about biological Black families by saying that houses are matriarchal. However, in this case, the so-called matriarchal power is situated within a male body, a corporeal site of relative privilege and power in a patriarchal society, even if it is also a feminized Butch Queen's body. Is this not Moynihan with a twist? Consider how Tim'm T. West addresses this question about the role of "male mothering" in Ballroom culture.

> Beyond being just the housemother—and a lot of kids had "real" mothers so this wasn't a supplement for the things that were missing in their lives—it was a deconstruction of what is meant to be a mother. I mean, to be calling a biological man your mother was sort of this radical revision of motherhood. It was really about this is a man who nurtures, who helps to guide us. It is more about the nurturing and not so much about the gender.

What Tim'm underscores is that, even though "a lot of kids" have "real" mothers, they continue to ascribe the labor of mothering, the nurturing and the caring, to their housemothers, who are mostly Butch Queens. And while mothering from a Butch Queen is a "radical revision" of normative gender performance, embodiments, and roles, ultimately, when housework is sutured to femininity, it not only absolves fathers, whether masculine Butch Queens or Butches, from the responsibilities of nurturing and caring, but it also reifies dominant scripts of masculinity. Such family scripts privilege masculinity, whether it is ascribed to or performed by male-bodied or female-bodied men, and this practice hampers the radical potential of the Ballroom houses of which Tim'm speaks.

"I Love My Daddy": Housefathers

While waiting and preparing for a national ball in New York City in November 2003, I was in a hotel room in Newark with Trinity Prestige and some other members of the house. After hanging up the phone follow-ing a brief conversation with Father Alvernian, Trinity said, "I love my daddy." Trinity went on to explain that he believes the conflicts that he and Duchess have are the result of the special relationship he (Trinity) has with the housefather. "It's not my fault that he has always treated me cool," he said. Father Alvernian is one of the only single fathers in the national Ballroom scene. He is the patriarch of the house. The house has never had a national mother. Soon after the Domination Ball in Detroit in the summer of 2003, Father Alvernian removed Duchess as the house-mother and replaced him with Trinity Prestige, the empress at the time.

In my discussion of housemothers, I have not meant to suggest that male privilege within Ballroom keeps housefathers from being fetishized or exploited within the scene. For one thing, the pervasive presence of housefathers in the scene is a rather recent addition to Ballroom culture. This is partly because Ballroom kinship is becoming more sophisticated and evolving into more expansive structures. But while there are differ-ences, housefather roles are still shaped by and subscribe to dominant family scripts. In other words, perceptions of fatherhood within the Ball-room scene are shaped by notions of fatherhood and masculinity in the outside world. Dominant familial scripts in larger society also influence how particular members see themselves as fathers, and the forms of "fa-therly" kin labor they undertake.

Overwhelmingly, Ballroom fathers are Butch Queens, but there are some fathers who are Butches and Men. Although this situation is chang-ing somewhat as Ballroom culture matures, almost all fathers are mas-culine and walk "realness" and male body categories, such as Executive Realness, Thug Realness and Sex Siren. Fathers in the scene approach parenting as guides and concern themselves with the "public sphere" in the scene rather than with the domestic one.[53]

Fathers wield a great deal of power, in some ways typical and in other ways not. Despite their power, however, housefathers are highly sexual-ized and viewed as expendable in some houses, a point consistent with Kali Ford's description: "Housefathers are usually just there to say we have trade in the family. Fathers have big ole muscles and a fierce body. This helps the image of the house, especially if he is a thug, and image is important." Will Ford explained further that fathers perform representa-tional labor for the larger Black LGBT community: "Fathers create an al-ternative representation to the stereotype of Black gay men as feminine." According to many of my interlocutors and the houses I have observed, some housefathers even maintain their positions as husbands or fathers in their biological heterosexual families.

In Lovely Mohair's case, for example, the father of her house, who incidentally was her boyfriend at the time, is, according to her, "outside of gayness." Lovely describes her view of what housefathers should be: "When they walk balls they are usually 'strip trade down.' They are recognized as legendary trade." For Lovely, the father cannot be a Butch Queen or Butch, but must be a Man in accordance with the gender system. His role in the family, as the father, is inextricably linked to his gender performance, how that performance is interpellated, and his sexual practices. Indeed, in Ballroom, house parent relationships are almost exclusively platonic. Thus, in Lovely's boyfriend's case, as a father he is more masculinized and sexualized within Lovely's house than he would be in a typical Ballroom house. Nonetheless, fathers' roles are constructed through a fetishized masculinity that is at the same time sexualized.

In terms of parental labor, some housefathers who are Butch Queens take on more prominent roles in the larger Ballroom scene than within the house. Playing into feminist critiques of the public/private distinction that relegates men to the public sphere (the sphere of politics and power) and women to the so-called domestic one, some Butch Queens are the "overall fathers" and thus are at the helm of the entire structure of the house. I might add that a large number of Ballroom members describe their relationship with their biological fathers as strained or estranged. As is the case with housemothers, members' common sense notions of fathering are in part derived from their relationships with their blood fathers—or the lack thereof. On a recent occasion, for example, Ariel and several other Prestige members expressed dismay with Father Alvernian because they claimed that he was more concerned about and involved in "external" house affairs, such as putting on balls and gaining prominence in the scene, than he was about the hands-on duties of raising and supporting the children in the house. During the meeting I described earlier, Father Alvernian made clear his expectations of house kids to the parents of the chapters. First he emphasized that "everyone needs to have a job." He further insisted, "Next year, starting with the November ball, The Legendary House of Prestige has to be fierce. Next ball is high fashion and ALL BLACK . . . everything." Considering that Father Alvernian is a single overall parent of the house, he is more involved with matters in the public domain of the Ballroom scene than with domestic matters in the house.

Conversely, some fathers are involved in the daily housework of the house, only some of which entails caring for the house children. When they perform such caring, however, they usually assume the role of molding the kids, especially if the kids walk the same categories that they walk. K-C Prestige expressed this when I asked him what values he wants to instill in his children.

> I want my children to stand for the exact same things I stand for, like being an overall good person, basically, put it that way. They should take care of business. I say, be me but be you. Or we'll say it like this, still be yourself, but try to act like me. I want to be able to look at my child and be like, that's *my* child.

In general, both housemothers and housefathers are invested in the house and engage in certain kinds of labor as a couple to maintain them. I would argue, however, that in Ballroom culture, as a microcosm of both the larger Black LGBT community and society in general, caregiving and nurturing as housework are viewed as incompatible with masculinity, even as one benefits from the house labor. This labor is distributed according to gendered divisions based on a masculine/feminine binary and a gendered public/domestic distinction, even though most of the parenting roles are undertaken by Butch Queens.

While acknowledging this conformity, gender relations in the house depart from hegemonic norms especially with regard to the joint efforts of raising house kids. At The Legendary House of Prestige's national meeting in Philadelphia in 2004, Ariel Prestige, a Femme Queen and the housemother of the Los Angeles chapter, and Reno Prestige, a Butch and overall Godfather and father of the Philadelphia chapter, discussed the difficulties involved in parenting.

> ARIEL: Reno, I never knew that being a mother of a house would be this hard, but it is, and when I see that things is going well, it keeps me going and pressing on.
> RENO: Yes, Mother, it is tough being a parent. If I may give some sound advice . . . remember our job is to help the kids learn to help themselves. We are guides, not "getovers." You are a natural nurturer, like a "real mother" should be.

This exchange, along with the gender subjectivities involved, demonstrate how paradoxical Ballroom roles can be. The mother is, as usual, the domestic laborer, even when the role is assumed predominately by a gay man, and yet there are some important exceptions. As a biological male now living as a woman, Ariel is the "mothered" mother, nurturer, caretaker, and socially configured domestic of the house. This is contrary to most Ballroom members' experiences with their blood fathers as biological males. And, as a biological female now living as a man, Reno takes on the role of the "fatherly" adviser—the guide. Such qualities are not typically associated with biological females who are blood mothers. In this case, too, masculinity seems to trump femininity, but this example also demonstrates that gendered relationships in Ballroom culture are nuanced and cannot be reduced in their entirety to a male/female or man/woman binary, even though this binary is embedded in houses. Indeed, both the gender system and the kinship system in Ballroom demonstrate the socially constructed and nonbiological nature of gender.

Gender relations within Ballroom houses and the community at large are flexible and elastic, allowing a space and role for subjectivities that would otherwise be denied such spaces and roles in the outside world.

Platonic Parenting

The reconstitution of gender and parental roles structures relationships between parents in houses. And while many houses are led by single parents, primarily by mothers, in other houses coparenting is nonheteronormative, meaning that the partnership is nonsexual, nonromantically intimate, and nonreproductive. Although they are complex but not always radical, house parent relationships are, overwhelmingly, platonic rather than romantic or sexual. Platonic parenting transgresses the hegemony of the conjugal bioparental configuration of family in society. In some cases, coparents are more like hanging buddies or what Ballroom members call "Judies." Indeed, house parents experience a variety of conflicts; yet intimate/sexual struggles and politics do not dictate their relationship, at least not between each other and not in the same way that they do in families in the outside world.

There are two primary reasons for the platonic nature of parenting in Ballroom culture. First, members become parents either because they decide to or because they are appointed. This outcome is not based on sexual attraction or intimate love for the other parent. Most of the houses involved in my study were headed by a single parent. But even when this is not that case, the parenting role is about running the house, a house

Fig. 9. Godfather Reno at the Legendary House of Prestige national ball, held in Philadelphia. (Photograph by Marlon M. Bailey.)

that is usually already established, consisting of members and children. In other words, the parents of Ballroom houses are not involved in heteronormative reproduction.

The other reason is simply that most coparents do not view themselves as romantically or sexually compatible. The masculine/feminine binary structures desire in Ballroom as it does in the larger Black LGBT community. This is especially obvious when the housemother is a Femme Queen or a Woman and the father is a Butch Queen or a Butch. For example, in The House of Prodigy in Detroit, Cage Prodigy, a masculine Butch Queen, is the housefather, and the housemother is a cisgender woman—a biological female who lives as a woman and is fluid sexually. The two are very close friends, and they behave like sister and brother. Richie Rich, a Butch Queen and housefather of the Detroit chapter of The House of CMB (Cash Money Boys), and Goddess Rodeo both affirm that their relationship with their coparents is based on friendship.

Moreover, the house parents of The House of Galliano had been running the house together, as friends, for six years at the time of the interview. Danny Galliano, now taking on the grandmother role, said that typically parents are not "together," nor do they always reflect a butch/femme binary. Sometimes, both mother and father are Butch Queens and feminine, but this is often not the case.

I want to point out that Lovely Mohair's house situation is the exception to the platonic parenting norm that I describe. Again, this is because, in Lovely's view, her boyfriend is "outside" of gayness, and he is in the Man category in the gender system. As Lovely stated, "My current boyfriend is the father to my house. The men that I mess with are actually trade. They don't do the gay thing, so my children actually see him as a father figure." Thus, the role played by Lovely's boyfriend, the father of The House of Mohair, is almost coincidental insofar as he entered the house and the scene through his relationship with Lovely. This is not to suggest that Lovely and her boyfriend's coparenting is somehow less valuable or valued than the platonic parenting that I focus on here; rather, their relationship provides an important exception to the rule of how parental relationships are forged in Ballroom culture. Nonetheless, parents are generally enmeshed in building and sustaining a house, preparing its members to compete in balls, and ensuring that all the kids are emotionally, morally and, in some cases, spiritually provided for.

Again, being friends does not mean that house and parent relationships are without conflict. Like families, houses are sites of care, support and love, as well as conflict and sometimes violence.[54] Actually, houses are often deeply embroiled in conflict. At The House of Ford ball, the mother of the house, Antawn Ford, dissatisfied with the course the event was taking, ordered the ball to end early, before all of the participants could compete in the remaining categories. The mother snatched the microphone from the commentator and said, "Cut it!" But father Clint Ford immediately rebuffed the mother and said, "No, let them walk. People came here from out of town to walk in this ball. We gon' let them walk." he said. The ball continued against the mother's wishes.

Most houses overcome conflict, but a few do not. Soon after their 2001 ball, the relationship between this housemother and housefather became so contentious that the father ended up leaving. The members of the house described this situation as an ongoing power struggle that finally came to a head. According to Will Ford, both parents are strong minded and their approaches collided. He claimed the father is "people oriented" and the mother is image oriented and those two approaches clashed. Kali Ford disagreed somewhat in suggesting that, on the contrary, the problem was the father's obsession with "image"; he wanted to award very expensive trophies at balls and expected the kids to pay for them out of their pockets. This pressured the kids to participate in crafty behavior to raise the money. Basically, "our housefather left because of his own personal drama with the mother," said Kali Ford. Yet when I asked other members of the house, they informed me that the "house kids" pushed the father out of the house. He subsequently moved to Atlanta and started his own house. The House of Ford ended up closing in 2002 as a result of ongoing irreconcilable conflicts, chiefly between parents and siblings.

Measured against the rigidity of monogamy and the unrealistic nuclear family standards, Black families have struggled against state-sanctioned violence and intrusion, as well as other attempts to undermine them, even as some sectors within Black society collude in these attempts. For the reality is that members of Black communities rely on a variety of kin structures to care for children and themselves in the face of intersecting race, class, gender, and sexual oppression. Consequently, Black people have a vexed relationship with state-sanctioned institutions like marriage. This, of course, is a far different scenario for some White people, especially White men, gay or straight. Thus, in a practical sense, marriage, parenting, and family have meant something very different for Black people than what can be gleaned from current popular discourses about them.[55] Unfortunately, however, these resilient and diverse Black families have failed to support and care for the Black gender and sexual minorities in their midst. And since recasting friends as family is fundamental to Ballroom culture, its kin relations take on the necessary roles and labor of family while operating under the radar of the state and Black moralists, preventing intrusion in the lives of its Black LGBT members, at least temporarily.

Within the Ballroom social sphere, where its members do not enjoy a wide range of intimacy with their biological families, Ballroom houses offer a space for care, service, competition, and critique among people who share similar life experiences. It is important to understand that not only is this bond drawn on characteristics of kin, but it is also based on a common competitive drive to "slay and snatch" trophies for a house as its individual members seek to gain legendary acclaim throughout the Ballroom scene. In other words, the work involved in parenting, bonding, "slaying and snatching," and building a kin unit is central to creating an overall minoritarian sphere.

House Siblings

There are integral nonparental familial relations that constitute houses in Ballroom culture. Siblings are the children and make up the majority of the membership of a house. Sibling ties are forged based on three primary aspects of the community. First, siblings define themselves as kin based on coming out together or joining the Ballroom scene and a house together. As I suggested earlier, age in Ballroom is largely based on how long one has been in the Ballroom scene or how long one has been out in the LGBT world. Thus, siblings determine their relationships to one another and their Ballroom ages to suggest that one is their older sister or younger brother or that they are the same age, no matter how long either has lived.

Second, siblings often walk/compete in the same group of categories at balls. For instance, not only did Noir and Tino Prestige have many things in common, they entered the scene around the same time, and they walked in the same categories: Butch Queen realness categories, such as schoolboy realness and thug realness, respectively. K-C and I forged kin ties within the house in part because we walked executive realness categories. At times we rehearsed our Grand House March routines together. Finally, sibling kin ties are based on friendship. As I pointed out earlier in this chapter, houses are by and large based on members' forging and recasting friend ties as kin ties. Both within the configuration of a house and outside of it, siblings participate in a host of activities together that fortifies their kin relationship.

It is important to point out that, although I argue that parental relationships are generally platonic and nonromantic/sexual, romantic intimacy and sex between siblings and between parents and children are more common than perhaps one would think. Because the conjugal parental relationship is not privileged in Ballroom, it ironically allows for other sociosexual arrangements in the household. Hence, some kin ties in the house are forged through sex, meaning that couples enter houses together as siblings/lovers and on other occasions become a couple or sexual partners after or by virtue of entering the house. Ariel and Pokka established a rule for the L.A. chapter by writing into the house bylaws a prohibition of sex between house members unless they are in a monogamous relationship. In addition, couples that enter into a house must have been together at least a year in order to be in the house and have sex with one another while members of the house. These provisions were put into the bylaws, perceivably, to curtail what was viewed as rampant "incest" in houses in the scene.

In the Detroit chapter, Duchess Prestige and K-C Prestige had a romantic/sexual relationship for several months while Duchess was the mother and K-C was one of the kids. This relationship was kept secret for most of the time that it was happening, mainly because Duchess did not want the other children to know. In other houses, rumors always circulated about parents having recruited members so they could have sex with them. There were particular houses in Detroit that had parents who were notorious for recruiting some of the most attractive Butch Queens in the city's scene and having sex with them. As Noir Prestige once put it, "in order to get into certain houses, you had to have sex with the parent." Noir identifies a common problem when some house parents use their prominence and power in the scene to lure new and less-established members to their house for sex. Yet, Ariel and Pokka placed a partial injunction against "incest" among siblings, a prohibition that undergirds the heteronormative family. But there is no biological basis of the kin relations in the house; therefore, there is no real incest involved. Thus, while Ballroom members engage in a radical revision of the heteronormative bio-family in some ways, its members simultaneously reinscribe and uphold that very heteronormativity in other ways.

Finally, parents give titles to their children to signify older siblings that are not based on age but rather on experience. These names are designed to reflect kids in the house that are leaders among the children much like big brothers and big sisters in the members' families of origin. The Prince is similar to an elder brother and the Princess is similar to an elder sister. These titles and roles are also a way of distributing housework throughout a house among its kids. Princes and Princesses help to prepare for balls and carry out other duties assigned by the parent(s). These elder siblings, as it were, provide parents with assistance with running a house, particularly when a house is headed by a single parent.

Overlapping Kinship

"Pokka is my gay son. His parents went through shenanigans when they found out he was gay, so I helped put him through school," said Ariel.

From 2004–5, Pokka, a Butch Queen, and Ariel, a Femme Queen, were platonic parents of the Los Angeles chapter of The Legendary House of Prestige. When I spoke with Pokka, now in his late thirties, he described their relationship in a slightly different way.

> Ariel didn't put me through school literally, but she was my gay mother and she guided me through the gay life. She played a motherly figure. She kept me out of trouble by helping with who to date and who not to date. We had conversations that I couldn't have with my biological mother. My parents knew about me, but Ariel got me through the gay lifestyle.

Prior to joining the Ballroom scene, joining a house, and taking on the role of a house parent, Ariel was Pokka's "gay mother." Upon joining The Legendary House of Prestige, this relationship included platonic parenting over other LGBT people in the Ballroom scene, but the previous gay parent and child dynamics remained a part of their interactions.

Ariel and Pokka exemplify how the kinship system and the labor undertaken among Ballroom members are part of a web of kin relations that function in larger Black LGBT communities in the United States. Regardless of age, social position, and, in some cases, even gender and sexual identification, Ballroom members are part of a complex kinship network that layers and overlaps kin relations within the Ballroom house structure. There are house chapter mothers and fathers, overall (national) mothers and fathers, grandmothers and grandfathers, God-mothers and God-fathers, Emperors and Empresses, and Princes and Princesses who all function within the Ballroom scene.[56] In addition, however, members may have gay mothers, fathers, and siblings. Although when one joins a house that person inherits parents, siblings, and often an entire lineage, gay parents are chosen. For example, here Richie Rich explains why he chose Goddess as his gay mother.

> My mother is someone I am looking to become. I feel that you should pick your parents in the likeness of what they do and who they are and what you want to become in the Ballroom scene. A lot of people don't pick their mothers like that. And sometimes a lot of people realize that their choice is not the choice that they want and they end up choosing another. That's why some people have several different ones.

Goddess interjects:

> But there is a big difference between a house parent as far as the
> Ballroom scene [is concerned] and a gay parent. There's a totally
> big difference. A house parent has more duties than just being a
> regular parent. A housemother has to uphold the house, and it's
> real stressful. A lot of people believe that being a housemother
> is easy, but they rely on you for things like traveling, getting pre-
> pared for balls, or they may even need a place to stay.

As is the case with housemothers, gay mothers play a more focal role
within gay kinship structures than gay fathers do. As in Ballroom culture and gay kinship, the father is less involved in the day-to-day raising of the children but is more concerned with overseeing the kin unit
and assumes the roles associated with the public sphere rather than
the domestic one. The house parent and gay parent roles differ, but for
the most part they overlap, especially for the housemother. Like Richie
Rich, Nurse CMB, forty years old and the overall mother of The House
of CMB, models his "mothering" after his gay mother: "I model myself
after my gay mother who happens to be a heterosexual woman, as far
as how I run my house. I teach my kids that knowledge is power, and I
push them to go as far as they can because being Black and gay is double
jeopardy."

House parents and gay parents look after, nurture, and shape their
children, whether in the gay world or the Ballroom world. And while the
reification of kinship norms expresses melancholia or a deep longing for
the heteronormative biological home and the gendered structures that it
entails on one end, there is a strong practice of surrogacy, an undertaking of the labor of care that has been lost on the other. Black feminist
theorist Stanlie James refers to this surrogacy as "othermothering" and
argues that an entire community is responsible for the cultural work of
nurturing and caring to ensure its present and future.[57] And in Ballroom
and larger Black LGBT communities, housefathers and gay fathers take
on key "parental" responsibilities as well, albeit that they are different
roles. This practice has been fundamental to Black families throughout
the African diaspora, the Ballroom scene, and the Black LGBT world in
general. Drawing from different resources of kin, clearly Ballroom members do not totally sever ties with their biological kin, but, in their recasting of the terms of kin, they are able to achieve greater agency in building

a family of their choosing or, at the very least, a kin unit whose members share certain collective identities, experiences, desires, and challenges.

The Grand House March

Back at the Domination Ball, after all the waiting and the preparation, the anxiously awaited moment has arrived: the Grand House March. This is the moment when the labor of performance and housework coalesce to create community at the ball. "Let's make some noise for the Midwest chapters of The Legendary House of Prestige," says Frank Revlon, the commentator. "First to the runway, C A N I C . . . Can I see that De-troit? I wanna see that De-troit. I wanna see the Di-vas. I wanna see that De-troit. I wanna see professah. I wanna see professah," Frank Revlon chants. I walk Executive Realness, the first "realness kid" to step on the runway. As I make my way down the runway, I hear my house members chanting, "You wanna be a capital P—R E S T I G E." "P—R—O—P R O D I G Y," members from The House of Prodigy shout in an attempt to compete with the Prestige members.

At this moment, I am on the runway and all eyes are on every aspect of me. I strut down the runway, pretending that I know what I am doing. I stop in front of the judges' platform, make a quick pivot, look at my watch as though to check the time, and walk back in the direction from which I came. As I turn, the crowd acknowledges my "looking at the watch move" with a roar. My heart soars. I am relieved that the terrifying moment is over, and I have made it through unscathed—for the time be-ing. As we do for every member of The Legendary House of Prestige who walks down the runway that night, we celebrate each other, the house, and the overall community.

Prada Escada captures what I believe many people feel when they walk down the runway encouraged by the support of their house members.

> Even when a person gets their props and kudos from the com-munity at large, no other feeling is greater than knowing that you have succeeded on behalf of your house. It is this process of con-gratulating and advising one another on our various specialties that begins the bonding process for us from individuals to family members. . . . Once you walk, even if there is shade thrown at you,

you can always look to your other family members to be there to support you—even sometimes ready to fight on your behalf. Sometimes it's more theatrics than it is a family bond, but nine times outta ten it is because you genuinely have begun to care for these people on a deeper level. Just as [in a] real family, you are not going to get along with every member, every time. But the balls always give us a chance to put all that down—if only for an evening.

Prada emphasizes the interrelationship between performance at the balls and the way in which members of the Ballroom scene experience themselves as agents in the creation of kinship and community.[58] This aspect is also exemplified at the end of the Grand House March.

Frank Revlon looks over all the members of The Legendary House of Prestige and says, "DJ, cut the music. Cut the music please. Do you see this?"—gesturing across the room—"Do you see this? They are sixty odd deep; this is Ballroom evolution. Now, we need to take this from state to muthafuckin' state to muthafuckin' state to muthafuckin' state!"

At that point it was evident that this ritualized performance is central to the maintenance of this community and adds meaning to the lives of at least some of the people there. For, especially in this case, the work of world-making requires a productive relationship between the queer quotidian lives of Ballroom members *and* the in-the-moment creative, expressive, and transformative social sphere that is always open to revision.[59]

As participants in the production of a new social sphere, one that provides the kind of support, recognition, and critique that many members do not enjoy in the outside world, Ballroom members are always marking and reconciling the difference between being just a member of a house and distinguishing themselves from others within a house through commitment and deeds. All of my interlocutors' explanations rest on the notion that Ballroom house members, for whatever reason, decide to participate in the "doing of family."[60] Thus, in deciding to be family, one has to commit to and engage in what the doing of family entails. This is an indictment of biological families for failing to perform the labor that the concept *family* signifies. Ultimately, in Ballroom, a house exists only as long as the members do the work to fortify it.

Ballroom exemplifies the transformative nature of culture and illustrates that the tasks of self-fashioning, creating, and sustaining social configurations such as houses, and of building a community, is ongoing. Even when this cultural labor is steeped in the structures of oppression that it purports to resist, possibilities and hope may be found in the productive space between full hegemony and full transformation, in the interstices. Ballroom houses offer an alternative perspective on the same-sex marriage debate—if its members were ever to be asked—that takes into account the very complex realities that structure Black LGBT lives. I do not mean to suggest that Ballroom members can overhaul the conditions under which they live; I argue instead that they "make do" with what they have in order to survive. In the next chapter, I examine the ways in which the gender system and ritualized performance are core dimensions of ball events.

FOUR

"It's Gonna Get *Severe* Up in *Here*"
Ball Events, Ritualized Performance, and Black Queer Space

I don't wanna see just spinning; I don't wanna see just dipping.
Bitches vogue! This is performance.
(SELVIN KAHN, BALLROOM COMMENTATOR)[1]

I wanna see a nasty battle
at the front line on a horse's saddle
girls get ready, get ready attack
let's go to war like we're in Iraq.
(NEIMAN MARCUS ESCADA, BALLROOM COMMENTATOR)[2]

The House of Ford Ball

The members of The House of Ford are very excited about their ball at the Detroit Masonic Temple. Located on Temple Avenue between Cass and Second Avenues in the Cass Corridor area, near downtown, the Detroit Masonic Temple is a massive fourteen-story building with over 1037 rooms/units, including a 4404-seat Masonic Temple Theatre and a 1,600-seat Cathedral Theatre.[3] Housemother Antawn Ford had urged me not to miss this House of Ford Ball. The Rich and Famous Ball, slated for this evening, Sunday, February 18, 2001, is scheduled to begin earlier than usual because the management of the building is requiring patrons to vacate the premises by 4:00 a.m. As he did for The House of Supreme International's Anniolation Ball a month earlier, Kali Ford, along with some other members, has invited me to sit at The House of Ford table. So, anticipating a large crowd, I arrive at about 11:00 p.m. so I can talk to the members of The House of Ford before the ball begins in earnest. Most important, I want to make sure I claim the seat at the host table that

Kali Ford has promised me. Besides, the Detroit Masonic Temple is considered "high class" by Detroit Ballroom standards, especially since balls are usually held at places far less expensive to rent. I figure that the "kids" are so excited about this special venue that this will be an extremely well attended event.

As I enter the huge lobby, I remember when, as a child, my mother would bring me to the Detroit Masonic Temple to see musical theatre productions that came to town. It is odd being in this space for a gay ball after having come here so many times as a child to see gospel musicals. But the ball is not being held in the theater; instead, it will take place in the Crystal Ballroom, where a balcony overlooks the main floor. This immaculate room is decorated in an Italianate style with murals painted all over the walls and ceiling. I note the two large chandeliers in the room and the electric candelabras ensconced on the walls throughout the space. Although wedding receptions and other, more formal gatherings are held in the Crystal Ballroom, this seems like a perfect space for a ball.

I count thirty tables with chairs organized in two rows with fifteen on each side. Each table is decorated with a white tablecloth and a red rose in the middle. There are ball flyers scattered about on all of the tables. On top of a hardwood floor I see the somewhat makeshift runway, consisting of a red rug situated between the two rows of tables that extend the length of the room. Slightly elevated, the seating for the panel of judges is positioned at the end of one side of the runway. The judges are to occupy seven chairs distributed along two tables. Each table is covered with a white cloth and a black skirt. A vase of tulips is placed in front of each chair. The DJ's table is just above the panel of judges, where DJ Cent (a Black lesbian who is one of the most prominent DJs in Detroit) is wearing headphones and turning records on the turntables. The trophy table is to the immediate right of the panel of judges, and a table with cheese, crackers, and fruit is to the left. Having attended only a few balls prior to this one, it surprises me that the setup for this ball is so similar to those I have seen at other balls. Yet, as I would later reflect after having attended numerous balls, the standard ball floor plan and the logics behind it are clear to me. Since balls are held at a variety of places, the hosting house has to perform the labor of transforming the chosen venue into an appropriate space for a ball event. The spatial arrangement at a ball is an integral part of the event itself, so at every ball, the hosting house takes great care to see that the space is organized in accordance with accepted Ballroom practice.

On this night the house music beats are pumping so loudly that I can feel the vibrations rippling through the wooden floor. After walking around the hall a bit, I head toward The House of Ford's table. While I bob my head to the beat (it is about midnight), I notice the ballroom is almost full, with a diverse array of people, and more are still coming in. From what I can observe, there are only Black people here, a circumstance that reflects the Ballroom community in Detroit. There are men, women, and transgender men and women (both Femme Queens and Butches), and Butch Queens Up in Drag. There are people here from a range of age groups. There are fat and thin people and light- and dark-skinned people. The outfits people have on range from street wear to huge flowing gowns in an array of rich colors and creative styles. Some are wearing leather and fur coats, with lots of glistening gold and silver jewelry, hats, and a profusion of other accessories. Some Femme Queens and Butch Queens are scantily clad, revealing with pride the results of their body work. Femme Queens competing in body categories have come to the ball unabashedly exposing their rounded butts and voluptuous breasts, made so with implants or hormones. And some Butch Queens competing in Sex Siren categories are shirtless, showing off their perfectly chiseled torsos over a variety of stylish pants and shorts, many with fishnet backsides. The vast diversity among the crowd emblematizes the egalitarian nature of the community. Clearly, these participants are prepared to compete in categories that emphasize, playfully, specific parts of the body. For in Ballroom there is a category, a space, and a niche for just about everyone.

Typically, before a ball begins, members socialize, catch up on the new "tees," flirt, and make their presence known to the community. At this time, usually, prominent members of the scene will let the commentator know that they are present so he can "call them out" onto the floor during Legends, Statements, and Stars, the moment of the ball when particular members are recognized and celebrated. I suspect that the several people who have approached me to say hello have done so because I have my video camera with me. A few people have ducked away from the camera to avoid being captured on tape, which seems odd since video and still cameras are commonly used at balls. The notorious Mother Dutch of The House of Dutch has come to say hello. I have also seen the Legendary Eriq Christian Bazaar and many other nationally prominent members of the Ballroom scene.[4] And now, to my surprise, Kali Ford calls me over and says, "I want you to meet my grandmother." True enough, his grandmother is sitting at one of The House of Ford's tables, which has been partitioned with a red velvet rope. Minutes later Clint Ford, a Butch Queen and the housefather, introduces me to his grandmother, his grandfather, and his boyfriend, who is just a spectator. As I watch performers practice their voguing routines and organize their clothing and other materials while others drink cocktails and greet each other, I can feel the excitement spreading throughout the room. All of sudden I hear Jack Givenchy approach the mic and say, "Brrrrrrrr kat-kat, it's gonna get *severe* up in here." The "nasty battle" is about to begin.

In previous chapters, I have described the core dimensions of the cultural labor that members of the Ballroom community undertake. Thus far I have examined the ways in which this cultural labor consists of Ballroom's reconstitution of gender and sexual subjectivities, and its creation of an elaborate, overlapping kinship structure. Yet, in Ballroom culture, there are no houses without balls, and there are no balls without houses. These aforementioned practices are inextricably associated with Ballroom members' creation of an alternative world through ritualized performance and practices at ball events. Balls and houses are mutually constitutive. This interconnection between kinship and performance creates the conditions for the twin labor—kinship and performance— that builds and sustains the community.

To demonstrate the inseparability of houses and balls, my analysis alternates between these two domains even as I focus on ball events in this chapter. Here I examine how a ball becomes a space and an occasion for Ballroom members to engage in the work of individual and collective self-fashioning, a crucial strategy of life for multiply marginalized communities. I am primarily concerned with performance as enacted by members of the Ballroom community and the spaces they create in which to enact it. By and large, in the Ballroom scene, space is socially produced for and through forms of performance at balls. I suggest that these, mostly ritualized, forms of performance are the discursive means through which Ballroom members reconstitute their world. In other words, what I refer to as performance labor at balls helps to create an alternative world for Black LGBT people, one that is affirming, celebratory, competitive, and critical. I view Ballroom performance as a form of labor, of work, that members of the community undertake to forge their minoritarian social sphere.

There are three main parts to my examination of the performance labor of Ballroom culture. As I mention earlier in this book, the various performance dimensions of Ballroom culture, as known today, have emerged from earlier performance traditions in clandestine—safe—spaces carved out by Black LGBT communities. These underground spaces enabled Black LGBT people to engage in nonnormative gender and sexual practices. Likewise, in the first section, I highlight briefly how in speakeasies, buffet flats, and people's private homes, Black LGBT people used performance as a way to create and participate in transgressive forms of gender and sexual expression and to develop new performance styles. Throughout this chapter, I argue that contemporary Ballroom performance forms are an amalgam of early and other ongoing Black LGBT cultural practices from across the African diaspora in general and Detroit in particular.

Second, I delineate, in ethnographic detail, what actually happens at balls, the events for which underground Black queer spaces are created by Ballroom members. This section is, in part, based on several balls in which I participated before, during, and after my stint as a member of The House of Prestige's Detroit, Los Angeles, and Oakland chapters.

After illustrating what constitutes a ball and what members do at them, in the final section I offer an analysis of Ballroom performance. Here I examine the performance labor in which members participate, emphasizing its ritualized dimensions. The ritualized dimensions of balls consist of members transforming rented halls and ballrooms into a ball space, or what I term Black queer space, as well as the performance system that undergirds the overall ball event. Balls rely on ritualized performance and a relationship between the music/DJ, the commentator, the audience, and the performers engaged in the competitive runway categories. I call this relationship the performance system of Ballroom culture. Again, much of the ritualized and other performance forms I highlight emerge out of an amalgamation of both traditional and contemporary African diasporic forms. Ballroom members marshal these performance forms to create a Black LGBT culture and an alternative world.

Ballroom Performance: Some Early Practices

Although Ballroom has morphed into a complex, distinct, and expansive culture, ball performance has emerged out of a wide variety of Black LGBT performance traditions. Earlier I discussed briefly the history of kin making in Black LBGT communities in New York City, where Ballroom culture began, and in Detroit. In these earlier subcultures, although they are similar to Ballroom culture in important ways, kinship has been defined in different terms and has served a variety of purposes that differ from its use in houses in Ballroom culture. Black LGBT people forged networks and spaces of kinship to escape the twin oppressions of racism and homophobia. Likewise, historically, performance has contributed to the development of Black LGBT social and sexual networks. A history of Black LGBT performance is too expansive to elucidate here; nevertheless, I want to highlight some key performance forms and practices that are inheritances of Ballroom culture. In this sense, it is important to understand the role of Black LGBT performance historically in order to situate the performance of Ballroom culture in its appropriate social and cultural context.

Barred from White social spaces and forced to suppress their nonnormative gender and sexual identities in heterosexual spaces, Black LGBT people created their own spaces in which to express themselves through performance at alternative locales. At the turn of the twentieth century, the Black LGBT people who migrated to northern cities, whether in search of improved economic opportunities or kin or communities that were more socially liberal, all came expecting a better life. Many were disappointed. Racial oppression structured the often harsh socioeconomic conditions that greeted Black people in the North. Moreover, those who openly transgressed hegemonic gender and sexual norms were often shunned and surveilled. For many Black LGBT people, race, class, gender, and sexual hegemony was rampant in urban cities in the North during the 1920s and 1930s. In chapter 3, I also elaborated on the effects that these conditions had on Black family and kinship formations in the North and, more specifically, in Detroit, which forced Black LGBT people to forge alternative kinship structures akin to those in Ballroom culture. In this section of this chapter, however, I want to consider how, due to the realities of multivalenced forms of oppression, Black LGBT people negotiated opportunities to convene and express themselves creatively, in the midst of hostile conditions, in local and extended communities. It was within this context that many Black LGBT performance traditions evolved.

The Harlem community in New York City may have been something of an exception in this respect. For this community was more fluid than those in many other northern locales in terms of gender and sexuality, and at times more tolerant of homosexuals who openly expressed their nonconformity.[5] In Harlem many Black LGBT people frequented establishments with a predominantly heterosexual, often White, but progressive patronage. Although these venues fostered some social interaction across gender and sexual boundaries, and at times racial ones, performance was the catalyst for such interactions. And it is evident that drag queens were relegated to spectacle, meaning that their racialized, gendered, and sexualized bodies were often included primarily for the purpose of entertainment and heteronormative spectacularization of queer identities, expressions, and bodies.[6]

This heteronormative spectacularization and objectification of their bodies and identities provoked many Black LGBT people to construct social networks and performance spaces of their own in which they could explore gender and sexuality unhampered by the exploitation and objectification of the heteronormative gaze. Some spaces were more private and discreet than others, so increasingly social and sexual interaction between Black LGBT people occurred in places other than where they would perform; some of these performances, as noted, were attended largely by White heterosexuals.[7]

Performance, of some sort, was usually a feature of the evening in the variety of places where Black LGBT people gathered, such as private parties, speakeasies, and nightclubs. Costume balls in Harlem, for example, featured some of the best-known Black LGBT performances. Thus, members of the Ballroom scene today reference the balls in Harlem as the birth of the contemporary Ballroom scene. "The Ballroom scene has existed for more than one hundred years, and the balls have primarily been about cross-dressing," said Junior LaBeija, a Butch Queen and Icon of the Ballroom scene.[8] People from all over the city, gay and straight, White and Black, came to see these balls in Harlem. According to gay historian Eric Garber, drag queens such as Charles Anderson and "Gloria Swanson" were among the notable performers in the early days.[9] And, while researchers have tended to place greater emphasis on male-to-female (MTF) drag performance, there is a long history of female-to-male drag performance as well. In some cases, women, mostly lesbian, performers did not always do drag king performance per se. Rather, as artists, they unabashedly dressed in a more "boyish" or masculine fashion. For instance, Gladys Bentley, a popular musician of her time, was openly lesbian and often wore men's attire.[10] The same performances that transgressed dominant gender and sexual norms in terms of comportment, embodiment, desire, and practice in the early days have been codified into more discreet gender and sexual identities and subjectivities today. Hence, drag performance and other kinds of gender-bending have been and continue to be forms of performance that are fundamental to Black LGBT cultures. Increasingly, as in the case of Harlem, and over time, performance forms such as drag became an integral part of the social fabric of Black LGBT communities in general and became associated more specifically with Ballroom culture.

In other northern cities, like Chicago, drag performance was (and still is) a consistent part of performance cultures, particularly in clubs that Black LGBT people attended.[11] In Detroit, race and class dynamics influenced how drag was performed and the locations in which it was performed. Drag shows were popular during regular club nights or clubs would allocate one night during the week solely for a drag show. Because Detroit was and is a city that in general is predominantly segregated by race and class, gay communities are segregated in a similar way. Black LGBT people and Black heterosexuals do not patronize the same clubs, at least not at the same time. Clubs or club nights are demarcated, explicitly or implicitly, as either gay or straight in order to capitalize on the patronage of specific audiences. Spatial separation between social/sexual groups has always been a palpable reality in Detroit.[12] As far back as I can remember while going to clubs and bars in Detroit, rarely have I been in a nightclub that had a mixed patronage of straight and gay. This structured separation of social space sustains a heteronormative social/sexual order by preventing groups from mixing and blurring sexual boundaries.

Nonetheless, the Detroit club scene has always had its share of drag queen divas. These were drag queens who impersonated Black divas in the popular music industry, such as Diana Ross, Patti Labelle, Melba Moore, Donna Summer, Stephanie Mills, Whitney Houston, and Aretha Franklin.[13] Black drag performers performed exclusively for Black LGBT audiences, and these performances continue to this day. Since Black drag queens are a part of the larger Black LGBT community, their impersonations of R&B divas filtered into Ballroom culture. For example, Diva, a Butch Queen Up in Drag member of the Ballroom community, is one of the most successful and longtime MTF drag performers in Detroit who impersonates Black R&B divas exclusively. Diva is one of the few drag performers who makes a living at it. "I perform almost every day now because I have to pay the bills," said Diva, when, in August 2000, I interviewed him during one of his performance nights at the Rainbow

Room Club, an LGBT bar on East Eight Mile Road. Diva has remained in Detroit throughout his career and has helped to build the contemporary drag scene in the city.

Contrary to what was presented in *Paris Is Burning,* and on which many critics commented, Black drag traditions have almost exclusively emphasized Black women singers rather than White women.[14] This is the case, in part, because Black drag performance, MTF, is associated with Black popular music. Since drag performance involves lip-syncing, a drag performer's impersonation of R&B divas is focused on how effectively his physical appearance, facial expressions, body language, and gestures can emulate a known Black woman entertainer. Here Diva further elaborates on this point.

> I like older music, and I like the divas like Chaka, Patti. Aretha, and Anita Baker. I make my own clothes, and while I'm making the clothes I learn the song. I do my homework; I watch their videos to try to get a feel for the singer. For example, I don't look like Chaka, but I can give you big hair like her.

Perhaps the most important point about Black drag is that the performance and all of the qualities thereof have to be recognizable to the spectators in the community in order for them to be appreciated. According to my interlocutors and from my own experiences as a spectator at numerous drag performances, the impersonations of R&B divas are enjoyed because they are recognized and loved among Black working-class LGBT communities in Detroit.

Another type of performance relevant to today's Ballroom culture that I observed in Detroit's Black LGBT club scene and other midwestern cities during the 1980s is the phenomenon of the "kickin' queens." Kickin' queens were those who deployed high or roundhouse kicks in an acrobatic style while performing their dance routines. Kickin' is a well-known vernacular form of performance in Black LGBT communities. Black gay poet Marvin K. White describes the performance in his poem "The Children": "hitch kick and bitch kick, remind the butch queens just how high children."[15] Kicks by kickin' queens normally commanded a lot of space on the dance floor, with their creatively improvised movements, which seemed, at once, wild and reckless and yet composed. It was not so much the kicking as it was the reactions the dancers elicited from those dancing around them. My friends and I sometimes avoided dancing next to kickin' queens for fear that they might eventually kick us. Conversely, others would gather and form a circle around them to watch this performance/competition. Almost automatically, a kicking competition would develop within the circle as dancers vied with each other to see who could outkick whom. Several years later, when I returned to these clubs, I observed a similar practice happening inside a circle of onlookers and participants, now known as the dance art of voguing.

This kicking performance form is deeply rooted in Black vernacular dance in the African diaspora.[16] According to the choreographer and dance professor Darrell Jones, kickin' queens perform a dance that is similar to the *gumboot dance,* a South African mine worker dance of resistance that involves high kicks and vigorous stepping. In my interview with Jones, who teaches voguing along with other vernacular dance forms of the African diaspora at Columbia College in Chicago, he suggested that the gumboot dance allowed South African mine workers to "exhibit resistance to intolerable conditions in the diamond mines through a dance form." But what is most apropos about this example for Ballroom culture is Jones's claim that the kicking maneuvers that Black LGBT people enact on the club dance floor, especially those by Femme Queens, are used to "assert their authority" or enact an "intimidating movement" to deter those who would attempt to harm them.

Among Black LGBT communities, kicking, as a creative and embodied form of resistance, is referred to as *vopping* or the *vop.* According to Jones, "*vop* is a vernacular term that refers to a high kick with a vigorous quality." The term is from the French word *vattement,* which is defined as a kick movement. Furthermore, Jones pointed out that, among the dancers of the Alvin Ailey Dance Theater, this term is used to describe a very dynamic high kick, and because Alvin Ailey dancers are very competitive, the vop is a competitive dance move in which participants see how high they can kick. "Ooh, that girl was vopping!" many of the dancers would say, according to Jones. I take notice of the linkage between the kickin' queens and the club and bar patrons that encircle them and these vop performances deployed among Black dance communities. Whereas once upon a time the people within the circles kicked, they have now turned to voguing, incorporating spins and dips, reminiscent, perhaps, of earlier kicking maneuvers.

Vopping, drag, and other performance traditions and practices in Black LGBT culture, performed at private parties, at costume balls, in gay clubs and bars, or on the street, have contributed, in large part, to the performances of Ballroom culture. As the father of The House of Infiniti in Detroit reiterated, "Ballroom dates back to the sixties, and during that time they were mostly drag balls. But during the seventies, the performance categories expanded to allow for more 'types' of people to compete." In fact, it was during the 1960s that the relationship between the house balls of Ballroom culture and Black LGBT performance traditions coalesced.[17] This joining together of a variety of disparate Black LGBT cultural practices has developed over time and perceivably, in part, led to the emergence of contemporary Ballroom culture in Detroit.

While there were only a handful of spaces in which Black LGBT people could congregate in Detroit, one such space was the after-hours house music spot, Club Heavens, which was located on the northwest side, where many of the early Ballroom members in Detroit started voguing, as well as participating in other dance forms.[18] Many of the voguing circles that were created every Saturday after midnight in the 1990s were led by members of a nascent Ballroom community at the time. For example, The House of Charles organized balls in Detroit according to my interlocutors. The housemother, Albert Charles, organized these balls at his residence. As Chris "Snaps Monroe" Cushman recalled:

> He [Albert] had a big backyard and some of their earlier shows used to be out in the backyard with curtains made from bedsheets, literally, a built-up stage in the backyard where they would invite all these people to come and charge them at the back gate of the backyard. . . . [H]e was a window dresser at Hudson's Department Store. He was very creative and so he would find all kinds of window-dressing stuff that he would bring to the shows. There would be all these pillars and columns and just really wild stuff, and it was great.

Over the years, balls have been transformed from performance competitions on a makeshift stage to multifaceted, extravagant, and euphoric events. Many members rhapsodized effusively about the intense pleasure they get from participating in balls. Balls do not happen with frequent regularity, so when they do, members anxiously await and look forward to them and revel in the competitive performance opportunities they offer. As Father Al Bvlgari attested, "It feels like Mardi Gras. It is just so much going on, and it is just so entertaining." Phoenix Manolo Blahnik aptly described balls as "a wonderful outlet for people that definitely need that space and that time to vent their creativity. It's also a stress reliever. I have been to a lot of balls, and it is fascinating to me. It's just amazing. I think what I got most out of it is just the creativity." Thus, not only do Ballroom members gain pleasure from individual and collective self-fashioning using performance, altering the body, and donning designer garments, but balls also serve as a means through which members can express their creativity in order to cope with the daily stresses of life in the world outside of Ballroom.

In 1997, The House of Escada held the first official ball in Detroit, and houses continue to open and organize balls to create an expansive Ballroom scene. And Black LGBT performance forms enacted at various sites throughout the city, from bars and clubs to parties and balls, at Albert Charles's house and others, have contributed to this contemporary Ballroom scene. Hence, the contemporary Ballroom scene encompasses a variety of performance categories, and the competition is open to an ever-broadening range of gender and sexual subjectivities. Contemporary Ballroom culture is a product of the necessary and distinct convergence of performance and kinship on which its members thrive. Ultimately, Ballroom culture has joined drag performance, other forms of gender and sexual performativity, and a litany of performance categories with a sophisticated kinship network to develop an entire community practice and a minoritarian social sphere.

Similarly, as dance ethnographer Jonathon David Jackson notes, the world of Ballroom and its ball events provide the space and occasion for community members to embrace their own gendered and sexual meanings freely.[19] In the scenes that follow I resume my illustration of this performance labor that members take up to create the space, occasion, and practices that building this alternative sphere entails.

Legends, Statements, and Stars

By 12:30 a.m., the ball is getting ready to start, exactly an hour and a half after I arrived. I see Frank Revlon, the commentator, walking around the room with a flyer in his hand.[20] The ball does not actually start until almost 1 a.m. As is the case with all balls, the actual event begins when the commentator takes the microphone. "One, two, whatchu gonna do," he says after blowing into the mic. He stands at the head of the runway in front of the panel of judges with a handheld microphone. "Okay, let's get this ball started 'cuz chile I ain't gon' be here all night. Bring me your flyers so I can announce your upcoming balls." Several people walk up to Frank and hand him their flyers. "Okay, we got The House of Ebony Awards Ball in Atlanta, Georgia, on June 28th. The Rodeos are having their ball in Los Angeles; okay girls, you betta turn it in Miss LA on July 6th. The House of Escada Ball will be held right here in Detroit during the Black Gay Pride weekend on July 27th, so you know that ball is going to be 'ovah.'" Frank Revlon announces several balls and reads a brief description from each flyer to encourage people to attend. "Announcements" are the primary means through which information about events in the Ballroom community is disseminated.[21]

"DJ, cut the music," Frank now says. "I want a moment of silence for all of the Immortal Icons and Legends in the Ballroom community who have passed on. 'Cuz without them, none of us would be here today walking this runway." Everyone observes a moment of silence. "For those of you who don't know Immortal Icon Miss Dorian Corey or Angie Xtravaganza, go rent *Paris Is Burning*," he admonishes the audience. Commentators often take time at the beginning of a ball to remember the ancestors of Ballroom culture, to commemorate them, as well as to teach the legacy of Ballroom culture to the young kids in the scene, and I'm witnessing such an introduction now.

"Legends, Statements and Stars" is the moment of the ball when the commentator recognizes the prominent and up-and-coming people in the room by calling them to the floor to do their thing. In Ballroom culture, value and recognition are inscribed in what I call a community order. Each position is arranged in order of importance: Immortal Icons (founders of the Ballroom scene), Icons (Ballroom history makers), Legends (multitrophy winners with Ballroom histories or those viewed as veterans), Stars (up-and-coming Legends), and Statements (up-and-coming Stars). "DJ, gimme a beat," says Frank Revlon. DJ Cent plays the Ballroom runway song, "Fly Life."[22] "Brrrrrrrrrrrrrrrrrr ka-kat. Brrrrrrrrrrrrrrrr ka-kat," he says as he bounces his head to the beat and paces up and down the runway.[23] All of a sudden he stops, turns to the crowd to the left, puts his hand on his hip, and says, "I know we ain't had a ball in a while, but don't act like you don't know how it works; let's make some noise. C-A-N-I-C, I wanna see my sista. I wanna see Miss Liquid. I wanna see that vogue femme, I wanna see that dainty femme, that dainty very cunty femme. I wanna see Miss L-I-Q-U-I-D," Frank chants as the crowd roars. Liquid Escada, a Butch Queen, emerges from the crowd and walks the runway toward the panel of judges with his hands on his hips, swishing his hips, glamorously, from side to side. When he reaches the end of the runway, he performs two half-circle pivots to show off his outfit (red shirt and black slacks). The crowd claps along with the beat, and Frank keeps chanting in rhythm with Liquid's walk. "What's her name?" Frank calls out to the audience. "Escada!" they respond. "Who is this?" he calls out again and gestures to Liquid. "Escada!" they yell in response. "A little bit louder!" he yells. "Escada!" the crowd responds. "Alright, werk," says Frank.

Next Frank Revlon looks around and spots someone else he wants to call out. "There she is. The diva of all muthafuckin' divas in this city of Detroit. She slayed Butch Queen Up in Drag in muthafuckin' everything, honey. Y'all know it's been a long time since she's been at a ball but, uh, we gon' make some noise tonight for her, honey. She needs no introduction, capital D capital I capital V capital A, Miss Diva . . . the Diva!" says Frank. Diva, a Butch Queen Up in Drag, walks onto the runway from within the crowd on the right side, to roaring applause. It is well known in the community that Diva makes her own clothes, so everyone focuses on her outfit. She is wearing an all-black two-piece with matching pumps. Her fishnet top is draped over her left shoulder. She wears a necklace with a silver cross with silver bangles on each wrist. Basically she is "accessoried-down," as we say, with rings, and a black purse, all topped off with sunglasses tilted just above her forehead. People stand up and throw snaps at her.[24] "The D-I-V-A, the Diva. What's her name? Diva, the runway . . . Diva." Diva asks Frank Revlon for the microphone to make an announcement. "Hey ya'll; well, this is my last ball as mother Chaos [Detroit Chapter], but I am now the Midwest housemother of The House of Chaos, so just call me 'Mother.'" Frank Revlon calls out several other people during Legends, Statements, and Stars. This portion of the ball continues for about an hour.

Soon after, Frank Revlon introduces his cocommentator, Jack, one of the most prominent commentators in the Ballroom scene. Jack is a Butch Queen from The House of Givenchy in New York City. Jack steps onto the runway next to Frank with a microphone. "Wait a minute, goddammit, get up and make some muthafuckin' noise. Rrrrrrrrrrrrrr cha-cha. It's gonna get *severe* up in *here!*" shouts Jack. The crowd lets out an exuberant roar. "Alright, the Armanis are here! The Chanels are here! The Ebonys are here! The Rodeos are here! The Blahniks are in the muthafuckin' house tonight! Brrrrrrrrrrrr. It's gonna get severe up in here . . .

ooh cha-cha-cha-cha-cha. Okay houses, what's your name?" The crowd responds with a litany of names. Who is in the house? Who's gonna take it tonight?" (People are shouting their house names and holding up signs displaying their house symbols). Then Jack says, "Everybody from the Midwest hit the floor goddammit: Chicago, Ohio, Milwaukee, Indianapolis, and Detroit." After that, a long line of people marches down the runway toward the panel of judges and everyone strikes a pose. One of the roles of the commentator(s) is to get the crowd revved up and excited for the competition, and Jack and Frank are two of the best at performing this task. The room is pulsating with excitement. And more than that, many members are recognized for their accomplishments in performance and the houses to which they belong, as well as the labor they have contributed to the community, which has helped to develop and sustain it.

The Grand House March

After raising the energy in the crowd to this rousing crescendo, Frank Revlon asks for the lights to be dimmed. The music changes from house to an R&B ballad. One of the most important ceremonial aspects of balls is the Grand House March. This is the opportunity for the hosting house to show off its members and some of their performances, and to demonstrate the standards of the categories for the evening. As the music plays, Frank reads a brief statement from The House of Ford that describes its history and the goals and values that its members seek to emulate. Then, one by one, he calls the names of the eleven members of The House of Ford as each walks the runway. Each member is dressed to the hilt in a black tuxedo with a white shirt and red tie. Antawn Ford, the housemother, and Clint Ford, the housefather, are the last members called. No other members perform as they walk down the runway. The House of Ford is an entirely Butch Queen house and is known as a "labels" house. This means that their members walk in runway and labels categories such as Foot, Eyewear, and Belt or High-Fashion Street-Wear (each item has to be made by a haute couture fashion house). "The F is for fabulous; the O is for ovahness; the R is for ravishing, and the D is for distinguished. Put those together and you have The House of Ford," says Frank as the eleven Butch Queens in black tuxedos stand in a straight line in front of the panel of judges. Antawn and Clint sit in large high-backed chairs in the middle of the line of house members. Clint thanks the crowd for coming and wishes everyone luck in their categories.

Immediately after Clint Ford's speech, Jack introduces seven judges (two women, one Femme Queen, and four Butch Queens), and the competition begins. Typically, the panel of judges consists of no less than six people and can have as many as nine. Judges are supposed to be prominent figures who are accomplished ball performers in their respective categories. The parents of the house sponsoring the ball select the judges for the evening. Each judge has "chop" power, meaning that one judge can single out a contestant and eliminate that person from the category. To avoid improper or biased use of chopping, Ballroom rules do not allow members of the hosting house to compete in the ball. This is an attempt to reduce the potential for bias in the judging. This is one example of the protocol used to maintain fair rules of engagement and to reduce conflict. Of course, this is not a foolproof system. Contestants and houses always complain about and fight over judging, accusing the judges of inappropriately chopping members from competing houses. Since members of the houses to which a judge belongs can compete in the ball, sometimes judges use their positions to give an upper hand to their house or to punish other houses.

Jack stands in front of the panel of judges and says, "Okay, judges, you remember that I am known to clear the whole panel. The only person allowed to be shady here tonight is me. When someone is walking a category and you see it then say yes, but if you don't, chop them quickly. We will not tolerate anybody around here looking like dog shit. If you look horrible we will tell you." The music starts, and the categories begin. The commentators run the ball, facilitating each category from beginning to end. Judges decide the winners in each category. Because commentators ideally are in the most neutral position, they wield considerable power at balls. For instance, if there is a conflict or discrepancy in a category, the commentator can override a judge's decision. He can also dissolve the judges' panel if he finds that its members are ineffective or explicitly biased against a particular house. Still, the house parents of the hosting house have absolute decision-making power because they have written the criteria for each category and it is their ball. Make no mistake, power struggles are a constant feature of ball events, and they serve as occasions during which the power dynamics in the broader scene are brought to bear.

As required, Jack and Frank call the categories in the order listed on the flyer. "Anybody best dressed in the house tonight?" he says. A critical role of the commentators is to keep the ball flowing, so when they call a category, and no one appears at the back of the runway, the commentators begin a countdown: "Who's walking best dressed? Ten, nine, eight, seven, six, five, four, three, two, one, category closed; next category." Throughout the night Frank and Jack move quickly through the categories and work the crowd as a team.

Close to an hour into the competitive portion of the ball, I hear the song "Nasty Girl" by Vanity 6.[25] This song is played for the Femme Queen Body category. "Anybody walking body—body, body, body?" says Jack. "Body, body, body—anybody walking body?—Body, body, body?" He repeats. As he calls the category, a very attractive woman with a well-shaped body approaches the walkway in a brown and cream bathing suit. Apparently, she does not realize that the category is for Femme Queens only. "Are you real cunt?" says Jack as he puts his hands between her legs. "Yes, it's all real," she responds. "Chile, this is for Femme Queens; you can't walk in this category." Then he turns her toward the crowd and says to the audience, "If you wanna see what a Femme Queen is supposed to look like with body, DJ pump the beat, this is the Legendary Sanaa Ebony."[26]

Jack calls the category again as a true Femme Queen approaches, "Bodacious body, luscious body, body, body; ten body, nine body, eight body, seven body, big body." As the Femme Queen comes into view across the crowd, everyone stands up, claps, and yells with excitement. Jack reels off a string of body-related adjectives to describe the Femme Queen. "Luscious body, big booty body, tits body, hips body, body, body," Jack chants. A strikingly beautiful Femme Queen with caramel brown skin and shoulder-length hair (it is a weave) stands in front of the panel of judges in a tight-fitting burgundy dress with a black corset on the outside. She appears to be full figured and well shaped with voluptuous breasts, big hips, and a round butt. She turns to the judges and wiggles her butt. This is a body category, so the Femme Queen contestants know that competitive emphasis is placed on displaying and highlighting particular parts of the body, especially the buttocks, hips, and breasts. The commentator signifies this emphasis in his chant. "Okay honey, all the way from Jersey this is mother Chanel; judges score her," instructs Jack. "Tens across the board; okay, stand to the side," he directs her. "Anybody walking body—body, body, body," he continues. Suddenly, I could feel the crowd's energy rise. Someone has stepped out, but I cannot see her at the moment. Everybody is on their feet, and some stand on their chairs. People are throwing snaps and jumping up and down with excitement. "E-bo-ne, E-bo-ne," members of The House of Ebony chant. "Here she is," says Jack. A moment later, a tall Femme Queen appears from behind the crowd at the back of the runway. "Body, body, body; here is a sexy body; body, body, body; do you see the body? Body, body, body," Jack chants with the music. She walks in rhythm down the runway, stopping to shake her very large breasts. Her chest is scantily covered, and as she shakes her breasts they fall out of the small top that she wears. She has on a tight, low-cut pair of jeans that rests on her hips and reveals part of her butt and her perfect curves. She receives tens across the board. The two contestants stand in front of the judges. "Which one do you see judges?" implores Jack. Members of the contestants' respective houses are chanting their house names. "E-bo-ne; Chanel, E-bo-ne; Chanel," members of the crowd yelled. The first judge points to Ebony. "Ebony one; Ebony two; Chanel one, Ebony three; Chanel two; Chanel three," Jack counts the votes one by one. It is tied three to three, and the crowd goes into a frenzy. "E-bo-ne; E-bo-ne; Chanel," they repeat. "Come on Miss Thing, which one do you see? Either you see it or you don't," Jack says impatiently. "Ebony four; Ebony wins." The next few categories bring us to the end of the first half, and it is already 3:00 a.m.[27]

One of the high points of the second half of the ball is the "Butch Queen Voguing Femme" battle. Battles take place when vogue performers challenge one another or when a commentator pits two well-known performers in the same category against each other to see who the best is or simply to entertain the audience. Battles also serve as tiebreakers within any category to determine who wins the trophy, the cash prize, or both.[28]

As I examine in greater detail later in this chapter, there are two primary categories of vogue: Old Way Vogue and New Way Vogue. This is to be a New Way Vogue category. In general vogue categories attract numerous competitors, and this aspect of the event is usually very long, sometimes running as long as half an hour. As with most categories, many people step to the runway in response to the initial call. When they walk they receive "tens across the board" or they are chopped—either because they do not meet the basic criteria of the category or because members of the judging panel simply do not like them or their performance. After the initial chop there are twelve competitors left for the battle.

Jack Givenchy joins Frank Revlon to do the commentary for this category. Frank starts off by giving instructions to the participants. He emphasizes to the crowd that they must keep the runway clear, and he tells the performers that he will disqualify them if they move off the runway. To get the crowd going, Jack starts a chant: "Here we go loop de loo, here we loop de li," and Frank joins in, "here we go loop de loo ka-kat, here we go loop de li ka-kat," and then they join in together, "all on a Ballroom night." As the category continues, they riff on this chant: "Here we go loop de ka-ka-ka-ka-ka-ka ow, here we go loop de li, ow, here we go loop de loo, all on a Ballroom night." The crowd, including me, joins in the chant, saying "ow, that's hot." Eventually the entire crowd learns to recite this chant.

During battles, especially voguing battles, the crowd gradually encircles the performers, blocking the view of the judges and other people in the room. Even though it seems to happen impulsively, this unnerves commentators. In response, commentators often admonish the participants and the crowd, instructing them on proper etiquette at balls. Each of the battles consists of one contestant against another until the competitors are pared down to six sets of competitors (one against one). After six battles, the number of competitors for this category has been trimmed to three final competitors. The most climactic battle is between Diva D Bvlgari and a member of The House of Ebony. Bvlgari and Ebony are the fifth set to battle. The DJ plays "The Ha Dance," a house music mix that is the signature song for voguing.[29] Both tall and lean Butch Queens, Diva D Bvlgari and the member of The House of Ebony stroll down the runway toward the judges, performing one of the basic elements of New Way Vogue: "soft and cunt arm control." When they get to the judges, the "nasty battle" begins, marked by the commentator's chant, "Brrrrrrrrrrrrrrrrrrr ow." The two voguers spin around and drop on the count of one. They perform what Ballroom members call a "Machiavelli," a dramatic spin and dip that is executed on the beat of the music and on Frank's and the crowd's "ow." "Pitty pat, pitty pat, pitty pat, ow," Frank chants as the two voguers perform another spin-and-dip combination simultaneously. The goal for each performer is to execute the elements of vogue in a fashion that distinguishes him from his opponent for the judges. During the contest, Ebony and Bvlgari "throw shade" at one another, using stylized arm motions and feigned gestures at the other's face.

After they perform a series of spin-and-dip combinations, the commentator signals for the competitors to wind their performances down and get ready to end on a pose on a count of three. Ebony and Bvlgari stand in front of the judges and gradually minimize their performances to very fluid but precise arm/hand gestures. "One, pitty pat, pitty pat, pitty pat, two pitty pat, pitty pat, pitty pat, three, pitty pat, pitty pat pitty pat, and hold . . . that . . . pose," says Frank. Diva D does a final slow dip and ends his performance. Both performers have been exemplary in their voguing skills. They have mixed "soft and cunt" with "dramatics." In voguing, dramatics involves hard, fast, and aggressive execution. "Judges, who do you see, who do you want?" asks Frank in a musical rhythm. Diva D Bvlgari wins the contest, but he loses the category finale in which he competes against another member of The House of Ebony and a member from The House of Chanel. The member from the House of Ebony wins the overall battle. The contestants congratulate each other and slip back into the crowd.

By the time the ball ends at 4:30 a.m., we have run the gamut of exciting categories, overextended our time in the rented building, and emptied the table, once filled with food and several trophies. Plates, cups, and flyers are scattered all over the room like confetti. People quickly gather their belongings and banter in anticipation of the next upcoming ball. As I file out of the building with the others, I can hear excitement and anticipation in the voices of some members: "Wait until the Escada ball in July bitch" and "It's going to be war at the Prodigy Ball because those judges were shady tonight." This incredible ball has ended—until next time.

Ritualized Performance at Ball Events

The ball event that I have described demonstrates the centrality of performance in Ballroom culture. Of course, far more takes place at balls than space allows me to delineate here. Indeed, balls are multifaceted events that reflect the complicated lives of their participants, who are marginalized by race, class, gender, and sexuality. Yet this investigation seeks to uncover the cultural labor of performance that members of the Ballroom community undertake both to fortify their community and to withstand the difficult conditions under which they live. Therefore, I ask, what can this performance labor offer toward a better understanding of what building an alternative minoritarian community and practice entails? I address this central question in the pages that follow.

Throughout this chapter, I argue that there is a core ritualized performance dimension to balls. I am not suggesting that the ball itself is a ritual; instead, I argue that there are particular aspects of the ball that are, indeed, ritualized. At this point it is important to offer a point of clarification: depending on the culture, rituals range widely in form and practice. Rituals serve a range of purposes for the people who create and participate in them.[30] Rather than attempting to advance a universal definition of *ritual*, I am most concerned with the forms of performance labor in which members of Ballroom culture engage that are ritualized. I am interested in the role that this performance labor plays at the ball, as well as in how it impacts the overall culture. In addition, I highlight connections between performance forms in Ballroom culture and "infectious"[31] forms of Black performance to demonstrate how members of this community draw from Black cultural traditions and participate in creating new ones.

In "Communal Space and Performance in Africa" the theatre scholar L. Dale Byam explains *ritual* as follows:

> Ritual is the event that draws the community together, reaffirms it and highlights the connection between man and god. The communal quality of ritual creates an implicit space central to the community's ethic. . . . Such space was indeed a marketplace of community culture, brandished to ensure the preservation of a way of life.[32]

For Ballroom members, balls are akin to rituals in that these events concretize and affirm values that strengthen and protect this vulnerable community.[33] Yet, perhaps even more critically, the performances and other practices in which participants engage at balls bring the community together to enact a politics of social, cultural, and spiritual renewal. As the cultural anthropologist Victor W. Turner argues, rituals are occasions during which performances reflect the values and worldviews of particular cultures. At the same time, rituals are transformative in that they expose the contradictions and openness of a culture.[34] For rituals are a means of maintaining the status quo while making transformation possible.[35] Taken together, for members of the Ballroom community, ritual performance instantiates the values and practices of the culture, and it creates new meanings (new categories and roles, for instance) that reflect the increasingly complex lives of the members. The ball and particularly the performances enacted at them are a primary means through which Ballroom members forge an alternative social sphere.

At balls, members of the Ballroom community draw from existing traditions of performance in the African diaspora to reconstitute themselves and in effect create this alternative world, at least for a time.[36] The ritualized performances in which Ballroom members engage at balls constitute what the performance theorist Barbara Browning calls an "infectious form of Black performance" that emerges from a continuous history of "African diasporic community-defining practices."[37] Notably, the essential role that ritual performance plays in the production of more expansive notions and practices of gender and sexuality in Ballroom culture resembles other ways in which performance is put to use throughout the African diaspora. More specifically, according to Browning, balls bear striking similarities to other diasporic rituals of performance, both secular and religious, in which members revise and expand the possibilities of gender and sexuality as a counterhegemonic practice.[38] Furthermore, Browning suggests that there are more obvious similarities between performance in Ballroom culture and "the less public, more discreet practices of diasporic religions," such as candomblé, santeria, and voudou.[39] I elaborate on the similarities between ritualized performances engaged in voudou ceremonies and those at balls later in my analysis.

The two primary components of ritual practice at balls are the creation of Black queer space and the performance system. These two inextricable elements are fundamental to all balls. I view these elements, along with the other aspects of the ball, as the fundamental social, discursive, and psychic building blocks of the Ballroom community, which serve as the nexus between the performance labor and the realities of members' lives in the outside world.

Creating Black Queer Space

An essential aspect of Ballroom practices is the creation of an appropriate space in which to hold and participate in balls. In the Ballroom scene, space is socially produced. In various cities throughout the United States, Black LGBT people face homophobia at straight Black bars and clubs and racism at White gay ones. Black LGBT people have a vexed relationship with space (built environments), particularly social space.

In Detroit, few, if any, bars or clubs are owned by or welcoming to Black LGBT people. And this scarcity of welcoming social spaces is also typically the case for Black LGBT people throughout the country.[40] Thus, I am interested in how the members of the Ballroom community in Detroit enact social practices to create Black queer space. Extending Judith Halberstam's notion of queer space, I define Black queer space as the place-making practices that Black LGBT people undertake to affirm and support their non-normative sexual identities, embodiments, and community values and practices.[41]

Since it is standard practice to hold balls at separate venues, Ballroom houses take great care to transform the chosen place, the building, into an appropriate space for the ball. This is chiefly the responsibility of the hosting house. In Detroit, the Black LGBT community has not been able to mobilize the resources to secure a consistent space in which to socialize, let alone to hold a ball. There are, however, a couple of places that are rented by houses there—one of the most labor-intensive tasks that Ballroom houses have to undertake is locating a space in which to hold a ball. In The House of Ford's case, they raised the money among themselves to pay the high costs of renting the Masonic Temple because they expected this grand building to entice more people to come. Houses pay the rent for the hall mainly through raising money from the house membership to pay the deposit and then use the money they make at the door to pay the rental fee, as well as the other costs of the ball. It is worth noting that halls, lodges, and community centers typically charge cheaper rates on Sunday nights because the hall would otherwise not be in use. Overall, the fact that balls are held mostly on late Sunday nights somewhat mitigates the difficulty houses have in locating spaces that are both available and affordable.

Balls are both public and private events. They are public because anybody can attend. As long as one pays the entry fee (usually twenty-five to thirty-five dollars) one can attend as an observer, a participant, or both.[42] Balls are private, however, insofar as they are publicized solely through "word of mouth," on Ballroom websites, or at other balls. Therefore, one needs to belong to the general Ballroom community or the Black LGBT community in order to learn when and where they will take place. Differing from the grandiose costume balls of old, these ball events are, in some respects, an intragroup phenomenon in that one has to be a part of the "magic circle" of Ballroom to access them.

Once a ball location is secured, transforming the spatial arrangement is essential to the overall ball ritual. Standards for the spatial arrangements of balls are well known throughout the Ballroom community. As with most Ballroom practices, these standards are not written anywhere; instead, they are just known. These arrangements are indispensable to the ritual performance enacted at the balls. I began this chapter by describing what I saw at the Masonic Temple in which The House of Ford held its ball in 2001, noting how its members had to rearrange the Crystal Ballroom in the Temple dramatically to make it look and feel like the proper space for a ball. The Masonic Temple is known as a multipurpose venue largely because it is such a huge building. Although it hosts many types of events because of its size and multiple interior spaces, when it is rented for local community gatherings those gatherings are most often heteronormative events, namely, weddings or religious ceremonies. It was thus quite ironic but necessary that The House of Ford work creatively to rearrange and transform the space in preparation for its ball, which demonstrates that balls can be held practically anywhere as long as the space is transformed appropriately.

Central to this transformation is the designation of a T-formation to order audiences and performances. As dance ethnography Jonathon David Jackson observes, balls are spatially organized in the shape of a *T*, and the performer's runway is a narrowly demarcated area that is positioned between the spaces allocated to the audience on both sides.[43] Runways can be constructed in a variety of ways. They can be configured as an elevated platform, a colorful rug, or a design etched into the floor. Such an arrangement is intended to resemble the runway that professional models use; it is elevated and runs into the audience space so designers and other onlookers can get a full view of the models in their clothing. In Ballroom the performances on the runway occur between audience members on both sides, while other members are scattered throughout the room. More often than not, this spatial arrangement changes at various moments during the ball. Members often surround the runway on three sides with the panel of judges at the front end of the runway (see fig. 10).

The panel of judges, occupying no less than six seats, is positioned at the front of the runway on one side, allowing the judges to face the performers directly. All performances are oriented in the direction of the judges. The panel of judges is often elevated slightly to give the judges the best visual perspective. The panel is arranged in this way, in part, because there are several categories that require the judges to scrutinize the lower

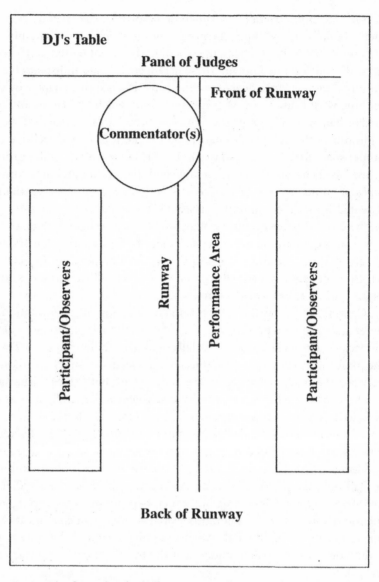

Fig. 10. The floor plan for ball events in Ballroom culture. (Illustration by Marlon M. Bailey.)

portion of a performer's body, and some categories include floor performance. The table for the DJ is positioned either just above the panel of judges or to the right or left of it. Contestants and crowd members stand at the back end of the runway, the area directly facing the panel of judges. All of the space outside the arrangement of the *T* is a general area where members of the crowd stand or sit to view the performances. This is also the area from which participants emerge.

Some ritual performances can be adapted to variations in locale, but Ballroom's spatial organization, as well as the labor involved in creating it, directly informs the dimensions of the performance ritual. For example, the runway is a site where recognition and affirmation are conferred, but it is also the space in which competition and critique are vigorously enacted in the presence of many other members of the community. The runway is the focal point, the place of spectacle, that emblematizes the interrelationship among the onlookers/participants, commentator, judges, and DJ. It is the place where all these actors intersect insofar as it is the blend of their energies that converges in and spurs on the performer on the runway—an interaction that is similar in many respects to the manner in which call-and-response techniques converge to render a song. When they prepare the space for the ball, house members adhere to the traditions and social dynamics of Ballroom culture to help ensure that their ball will be memorable. House parents, especially, are aware of what it takes to host an "ovah" ball, so they arrange the space carefully to create the environment for a transformative experience.

Spatial arrangements signify, facilitate, and maintain a social hierarchy in Ballroom culture. For instance, judges are usually prominent participants in the Ballroom scene. Their location in the *T* and their role in the ball are a testament to this fact. During the ball, while sitting on the panel, judges do not participate in the actual performance, whereas the audience, commentator, and DJ do; nonetheless, they wield a lot of power. They also have to perform the task of judging under extreme pressure from competing interests, mainly the other houses. When I was a member of the San Francisco Bay Area chapter of The House of Prestige in 2006, Tamia, the housemother of the chapter, asked me to take her place as one of the judges at a ball while she took a break. As I sat at the judges' panel, for about thirty minutes, I became keenly aware of the difficulty and pressure involved in judging performers who competed on the runway before me. In one sense, I did not feel worthy to judge, since I was not well known in the Bay Area scene. I was afraid to chop anyone for fear of being rebuked by the members of the performer's house. It was the spatial position that judges occupy, which is supposed to be commensurate with one's social position in the scene, that made me feel enormous pressure. Overall, however, the experience, albeit brief, was not as bad as I thought it would be. Fortunately, most of my judgments were in line with those of my fellow judges.

Most important, judges are supposed to be neutral—at least the role requires them to be—but it is difficult for such prominent players in Ballroom culture to remain so. As I have noted, no judges at balls come from host houses, a regulation intended to ensure that they judge participants—their peers—impartially, but because the judges are usually house members themselves, they often fail to be nonbiased. Yet, in spite of the judges' powerful role, and despite the hierarchical social and spatial arrangements in Ballroom culture, no position holds ultimate power in and of itself. Instead, power is always negotiable and relational.

The spatial location of the members enforces a balance of power between judges and the commentator, for example, by situating the commentator between the judges and the performers, while the crowd of Ballroom members ends up surrounding both parties. This is specifically the case regarding the commentator's role as the facilitator of each category. Of course, a single judge can chop—eliminate—a participant from a category; however, the commentator is positioned such that he can impact a judge's decision and, in more extreme cases, override a chop. Some commentators flex the power that they have attained through their popularity in the scene. For instance, Jack Givenchy was "flexing" when he stood in front of the judges and reminded them that he had "cleared the panel" at another ball. In other words, he told the judges to remove themselves from the panel if they were not up to the task or they should expect to be replaced with new ones. Jack is extremely popular in the scene, so he enjoys the latitude needed to take such actions as he deems necessary. But such latitude, importantly, is something that the audience and the community confer on commentators, based on their stature and reputation. Hence, most commentators use their veto power sparingly and with discretion because they know they have to answer to the parents of the hosting house, as well as to the community in general.

I use this example to argue that the positions of the judges, the commentator, and the other actors that make up the spatial arrangement as a whole coincide with the status of the actors in the ball, their roles and performances, and the social dynamics in the Ballroom community. The

space and the social dynamics that play out during the ball are hierarchical yet flexible and work to reinforce the social organization of Ballroom
culture that is accepted widely by its members.

Ballroom spatial arrangements must meet specific criteria, but the
configuration does not remain fixed throughout the duration of a ball.
The role of the spectator is active and transitive; spectators are expected
to "help out" with the performances. There are times when the spatial
arrangements conflict with the role of the spectator. Spectators feel confined during climactic moments. During many performances, the audience becomes so excited that the *T* configuration is transformed when
audience members move onto the runway and encircle the performer(s)
and the commentator. In other words, with the performers in the middle,
audience members get "caught up" in the moment and surround the performers and, in effect, end up obstructing the view of the judges. Echoing
another common element of performance traditions in the African diaspora, the *circle* appears often in Ballroom performance, even when the
spatial arrangement is not originally configured in such a way.[44] French
theorist Henri Lefebvre argues that space is a product of social interaction, deeply rooted in a dialectic between space and the transformative
practices of social subjects.[45] Thus, the spatial arrangements that are codified within Ballroom culture and implemented at all balls, no matter the
location, are what Lefebvre calls "spatial practices."[46] Because Ballroom
members create a social sphere betwixt and between domains that are
replete with racism, elitism, sexism, and homophobia, they exist within
a liminal zone. Therefore, the socially reconfigured Black queer space of
the ball is where the members convene to create continuity, new identities, and new strategies for adaptation and survival.[47]

The Performance System of Ballroom Culture

It is important to note that no space is ready for a ball event until the
participants arrive and play their roles. The participants are the finishing
touch to any ball space. And, irrespective of the spatial arrangements, the
space is not complete until the house music is playing, people are talking and socializing, participants are practicing their voguing and runway
skills, the smell of cigarette smoke and alcohol are in the atmosphere,
the runway is clear, and the commentator takes the microphone. Thus,
the spatial practices, the combination of people, performances, practices,

and place, produce the space for the ball. Spatial practices, then, are the creative work that is undertaken by Ballroom members.

Music/DJ: House Music

An essential element of the performance system in Black culture is the music and the DJ who mixes and spins the records on a turntable to create the sound that underscores the runway performances at balls. Although this is not the most spectacular aspect of the performance system, the joint function of the music/DJ is yet another indispensable part of the system and thus the ball event. The central function of the music/DJ is regularly signified by the commentator when he says, "DJ, pump that muthafuckin' beat," or "DJ, give me a beat," before every runway category. This is the primary means through which the music/DJ is recognized and comes into focus, although limited attention is paid to this crucial role.

The "beat" to which the commentators refer has changed over the many years that that balls and Ballroom culture have existed. The music played at balls has been consistent with trends in popular music consumption among larger Black LGBT communities. During the early years of Ballroom culture, disco, club, and house music were the primary music forms consumed in the community, which, in many cases, also reflected the musical tastes of Black LGBT communities. It is important to reiterate that musical taste is racialized, gendered (some music forms are feminized and masculinized), and sexualized, and this is often brought to bear in the club through the race and sexual identities that patrons claim, how these patrons congregate, and their motivations for socializing in a particular musical space.[48] Over the past three decades, musical taste and consumption among Black LGBT communities have shifted from primarily house music to mainly hip-hop. Although this shift is not total, it is exhibited in Ballroom culture in the increased variety of music played at balls, which includes not only house music but also hip-hop and R&B. This increased musical variety or the expanded notion of "the beat" the commentator requests has also impacted the performances, their execution, and the criteria by which they are judged.

I have participated in balls in which the DJ played R&B songs to underscore Sex Siren categories for Butch Queens, Femme Queens, or female figured participants. Because of their sensual, smooth, and sexy sound, R&B songs like "Love Hangover," recorded by Diana Ross, an iconic figure for Ballroom members, and "Nasty Girl" by Vanity 6 are frequently played. Another song that continues to maintain popularity is "Love Is the Message," by MFSB, a tune from the early Black gay club scene in Chicago.[49] This has become the signature song for Old Way Vogue. These are a few examples of how the addition of various popular Black music forms, including early house music, have provided and continue to provide the beats for many categories in the Ballroom scene.

Yet I want to highlight the beats of house music because of how important it is to New Way Vogue performance, a dance form and competitive category that best exemplifies the crucial function of the performance system and its actors and the ritualized practices that undergird this system at ball events. House music was created mostly by, and to appeal to, poor or working-class Black LGBT people.[50] Yet this music form's Black LGBT roots have caused it to be associated with femininity. Even in some sectors of Black LGBT communities it is referred to as "sissy music," exactly contrary to the masculinized rap and hip-hop music forms. As a result, house music is one of the most understudied and underappreciated forms of Black music. Even as socially progressive Black heterosexuals have recently been consuming house music more frequently and enthusiastically, the music's Black LGBT roots are largely ignored.[51] Ultimately, outside of the Ballroom scene, house music is consumed by audiences that are largely segregated by race and sexuality.

Like other performance traditions from which Ballroom culture draws, house music has not only Black LGBT but also African roots. Among the many types of house music—from Chicago house and New York garage to Detroit techno—the common traits are that the music is always 120 beats per minute (bpm) or faster, and, owing to its African roots, the rhythm—the beat—is the most important dimension of the music.[52] Even as house music's prominence in the Ballroom scene in Detroit declines, there are still songs that are played to underscore specific categories at balls. For example, "Fly Life" by Basement Jaxx is the signature song for categories that require the "runway walk," which is a particular kind of walk/performance that calls for the competitor to stylistically prance down the runway emulating a professional high fashion model. "Fly Life" underscores categories, such as High-Fashion Runway, High-Fashion Street-Wear, and European Runway. Many of my interlocutors said that the prominence and repetition of the beat in house music guides their performance, putting them in a zone that enables them to block everything out of their minds and focus on their walk while still feeling and hearing the beat and the support from their fellow Ballroom members on the sidelines.

"The Ha Dance" by Masters at Work is a song that is always played for New Way Voguing categories. When the commentator calls for the beat, the DJ starts the song, and the competitors begin their journey down the runway synchronizing their duckwalks, catwalks, and hand performances to the beat of the song. The DJ plays the song until the competitors arrive at the panel of judges or until the commentator says, "DJ, cut the beat." Once the next competitor is ready, the DJ starts the music again and repeats this process throughout the entire category. For my interlocutors, particularly those who compete in New Way Vogue categories, this song enhances that performance because its polyrhythms force the performers to create movements that go with the beat while also adhering to the criteria of the category. "The Ha Dance" and how it should impact the performance are well known by all of the participants-observers at the ball. I have not seen a New Way Vogue category that was not underscored by "The Ha Dance."

For the Black LGBT members of the Ballroom scene, the drums and percussions directly shape the movements the performers execute on the runway. Drawing from author John Chernoff's work on African music and aesthetics, writer Anthony Thomas makes two crucial points to suggest that the rhythm in house music emerges from African music traditions.[53] In turn, I suggest that this linkage between house and African music is also reflected through house music's function in the performance system of Ballroom culture. First, Thomas suggests that rhythm and repetition capture the dancer in the groove of the house music.[54] It is the repetition that, among other aspects of the environment in which the music is being played, such as the other dancing bodies, the dimmed lights, and the moans and groans made by the others in the space, coproduces a hypnotic, "getting-caught-up" state among the dancers.

Second, as is the case with African music, in house music the power and creative potential lie in the gaps between the notes or beats. This is what Ballroom members refer to as the "backbeat." As I describe in greater detail below, the backbeat is the moment and the means through which performers, chiefly voguers, can be more free and creative with their movements in ways that enable them to perform beyond the perceived limitations of their own bodies. The repetition of the rhythm and the backbeats that lie within it, along with the vocal accompaniment from the commentator and the other participants/observers, helps to create what I refer to as the epiphanic moment, particularly during vogue performance categories. Thomas's two points explain how rhythm helps to create the conditions for the epiphany that members experience as a result of the ritualized performances they enact.

Just as audiences that consume house music are segregated based on race and sexuality, so is the community of DJs who create and play house music in Detroit. There is a small group of DJs in the Detroit house music scene, and now most of them are heterosexual and spin records for mostly heterosexual audiences. Out of the roughly twenty house music DJs, all but three are known to be heterosexual and spin for heterosexual audiences exclusively. Yet, again, the decline of "house-heads" in Detroit,[55] which might be attributable to the rapid drop in the city's population, has forced these DJs to take on gigs mostly outside of the United States in Canada, Europe, and Asia where Detroit's techno house sound has become extremely popular. As a consequence, these DJs spin for mostly non-Black and sometimes more sexually diverse audiences abroad and almost exclusively heterosexual clubgoers in the United States. Black straight DJs typically do not spin at Black LGBT events in Detroit.

In the Black LGBT community in Detroit, the late Ken Collier, who was a Black gay DJ often referred to as a legend of Detroit house music and its distinct techno sound, helped to usher in an era for Black LGBT people in Detroit. As the resident DJ for Club Heavens, Ken played for the kids some of the original beats that are now used to underscore Ballroom categories. Other important Black gay DJs in Detroit who were pioneers of the Black gay house music scene include Alan Ester, Melvin Hill, and Ken Collier's younger brother Greg Collier, who for a time was the resident DJ at the once popular but now closed Todd's dance club. Stacy "Hotwaxx" Hale and DJ Cent are the only known Black lesbian DJs that spin for Black LGBT clubgoers.

DJ Cent did not belong to a house of which I am aware; nonetheless, she is the most prominent and respected DJ in the Ballroom scene in Detroit. She spun for nearly all the balls in which I participated in Detroit. Unlike commentators, Ballroom DJs are usually local, and they are secured and paid by the sponsoring house of the ball. That DJ Cent is the most prominent house music DJ in the Ballroom scene signifies that she knows Ballroom culture, meaning she knows which songs are to be played for a given category. Furthermore, DJ Cent knows the uniqueness of the Detroit scene. The role of the music/DJ is inextricable from the other elements of the performance system. At balls there must be a music/DJ aspect in order to enact the ritualized performances as a part of the performance system.

The Commentator

One of the most important actors in the Ballroom performance system is the commentator. Referred to by Ballroom members as the "master of ceremonies," the commentator serves an invaluable function in ball events, and his intermediary spatial positioning during the performances, as one who moves between the participants and the panel of judges, reflects the multipurpose role he plays and the power he can wield. From my experiences as a participant in balls, and according to all of my interlocutors, the commentator can either make or break a performance and even an entire ball. As Kodak Kandinsky, a Butch Queen, who was the most popular commentator in Detroit, stated, "The commentator is the life of the ball." It is the commentator who incites the crowd and performers: "He makes you want to walk."

This very essential role is played by a very small group of commentators who are prominent in the Ballroom scene. In the course of my research, I found that there is a two-tiered system that organizes the pool of commentators in the Ballroom community, comprising national commentators and local/regional commentators. National commentators are hired to commentate at balls all over the country. Currently, there is an elite group within the scene. From what I have gathered, there are only seven commentators who commentate at balls regularly, nationally, and they are all Butch Queens. I have seen all but one of these commentators perform, and I have seen most of them several times. These commentators are Jack Givenchy, Selvin "Koolaid" Givenchy (now a member of The House of Kahn), and the late Eriq Christian Bazaar, who are all from New York City; Jay Blahnik and Alvernian Prestige, both from Philadelphia; Neiman Marcus Escada from Chicago; and Kodak Kandinsky from Detroit. There are also local commentators who perform at balls in their respective cities or sometimes throughout a region. In Detroit the local commentator was Frank Revlon. I have been told that there is a commentator who is a Butch in Los Angeles, but to date I have neither met him nor observed him commentate. Tiffany, a local commentator in New York City featured in *The Aggressives,* is the only female-bodied woman commentator of which I am aware in the Ballroom scene.[56] In general the near exclusivity of Butch Queens as commentators is one of many examples of how Butch Queens dominate Ballroom culture, and there does not appear to be any movement afoot to change this dominance.

A commentator's orchestration is pivotal, not only to the actual ritual performance but also to broader community traditions. The commentator recognizes and commemorates the Immortal Icons and Legends in the culture. As demonstrated at The House of Ford Ball, commentators call for moments of silence to commemorate Immortal Ballroom Icons and Legends who have passed on. After Immortal Icon Pepper Labeija passed away in June 2003, commentators all over the country held moments of silence to commemorate her as a pioneer of the contemporary Ballroom community. Thus, commentators celebrate and teach the legacy of Ballroom to novices in the scene.

Some commentators use their chanting skills to employ critiques of social inequality. In one of his most famous chants, given below, Neiman Marcus Escada uses the art of chanting to criticize the US government's lackluster HIV/AIDS prevention efforts.

What's goin on in the U.S.A?
George Bush got us in a disarray
We got soldiers in Baghdad
We should be fightin' AIDS instead

I argue elsewhere that Neiman Marcus Escada's chant is an astute critique of the Bush administration's overemphasis on fighting a war in Iraq, as a priority of national security, as opposed to aggressively waging a war on HIV/AIDS here at home. As an influential figure in the Ballroom scene, Escada helps to create a social epistemology of HIV/AIDS that offers creative and critical ways in which to examine and withstand the epidemic's deleterious impact on the community.[57]

Sometimes using harsh language and tone, commentators instruct participants on the standards of Ballroom performance and practice. My point here is evidenced in part by the epigraph that begins this chapter. At the official ball for the Hotter Than July Black Pride Celebration in Detroit in 2010, commentator Selvin Kahn screamed into the microphone, after a few competitors had performed in a Vogue category, "DJ, cut the

Fig. 11. Selvin Kahn commentates a ball in Detroit during the Hotter Than July Black Pride ball in 2010. (Photograph by Mireille Miller Young.)

music! Look bitches, I don't wanna see just spinning; I don't wanna see just dipping. Bitches vogue! This is performance!" Implicit in Selvin's rant is a concern that voguing among this new generation focuses too much on the Machiavelli and not enough on basic vogue performance, which includes hand performance, catwalks, and duckwalks, in addition to spins and dips. The kids just want to "slam themselves on the floor," said Father Al Bvlgari, as opposed to including all the elements of vogue to create the overall performance. Commentators believe they need to protect these dimensions of the art form of vogue and make sure the novice performers adhere to these basic elements before they commence to "cutting and mixing" to create new forms.

The commentator's function and reach of influence extend beyond the ball event into the overall world of Ballroom culture. He or she is the keeper of cultural traditions. Yet out of the multiplicity of functions the commentator performs, I want to focus the crux of my analysis on his role as the interlocutor, a traditional role in Black performance throughout the African diaspora. In this capacity, the commentator is paramount to the survival of Ballroom culture and its ritualized performance practices.

According to Black theatre scholars Carlton and Barbara Molette, in the original minstrel traditions of enslaved African Americans,[58] the interlocutor was the "man in the middle" who imitated the White master within his performance rituals of critique and resistance.[59] By definition, the interlocutor is the speaker or performer who is positioned between others. He is the agitator and facilitator. I view the Ballroom commentator as an interlocutor for two primary reasons: (1) He is positioned between the performers and the judges and is often surrounded by the crowd; 2) he uses call-and-response techniques and chants to establish the pace, to complement each performance, and to incite the crowd. Most importantly, the commentator facilitates the various forces in the performance ritual, such as the performers, the music, and the crowd.

Let me briefly illustrate my point by providing some examples. At the beginning of the ball, Frank Revlon spent a considerable amount of time energizing the crowd. This is an important aspect of the role of the commentator not only at the beginning of the ball but throughout it as well. However, as Kodak explained, many balls have hosts in addition to commentators. The host gets to the ball first and gets the crowd going. Legends, Statements, and Stars is the primary vehicle for getting the crowd excited by acknowledging prominent members of the community in a theatrical fashion. "C-A-N-I-C, I wanna see my sista," said Frank

Revlon in rhythm with the music. Once the commentator "calls out" a prominent member of the community, that member performs on the runway to receive recognition and accolades from the crowd.

The commentator uses repetition and "call-and-response" to raise the energy of the crowd. Furthermore, he employs these techniques in conjunction with the audience and the performers. For instance, when Diva came onto the floor, Frank said, "What's her name?" Then, Diva stopped her sashay abruptly in the middle of the runway. She put her hands on her hips and waited for the crowd to respond. The crowd shouted, "Diva!" Hence, Diva and Frank engaged in a mutual and complimentary act of performance along with the crowd. Diva's movements accompanied Frank's call, and she anticipated the crowd's rousing response, which she received. The interaction between them thus took place on a verbal and nonverbal level.

The linguist Geneva Smitherman insists that "call-and-response," as well as other rhetorical techniques, are typical modes of Black discourse, techniques that are also used in other African American cultural traditions.[60] Smitherman maintains that "'call-and-response' is the spontaneous verbal and nonverbal interaction between speaker and listener in which all of the speaker's statements ('calls') are punctuated by expressions ('responses') from the listener."[61] In many Black churches, for example, when the preacher performs a call to the congregation, the congregation typically responds with a verbal "amen" or an "ummm hmmm" and others nod their heads or raise their hands in the air as non-verbal forms of testifying. Likewise, the commentator plays a key role in the modes of discourse in Ballroom culture. He both reinforces established values and norms within the culture and creates new meaning. In the case of the ball, the commentator calls out, the performer responds with a gesture or a particular move, and some audience members respond by saying "werk Miss Thing," or "ha," while others throw snaps to encourage the performer. In other words, the commentator, the performer, the audience, and the DJ (through the music), collectively help out with the performative acts and the performances deployed at the ball. This foursome, as it were, is integral to the full realization of the ritualized performance, but it is the commentator who orchestrates the activity of affirmation and validation, as he is positioned between the runway performer and the judges. They all contribute to these efforts that affirm and celebrate, while transforming the discursive terrain of Ballroom culture each time the performance ritual is enacted.

Chanting is another very important technique that commentators use. Commentators have to be experts on and skilled in using terms that enjoy currency in Black LGBT communities, but they must also be proficient in broader Black vernacular modes of communication. Moreover, commentators must be masters of improvisation. As Kodak attests, "You have to be able to come up with something off of the top of your head in the moment." According to other commentators I have observed, chanting is like rap or a mode of expression they call "talking mess." "Chanting is . . . fast-paced. You have to come up with something and keep repeating it until it falls with the beat," said Kodak. Chants that commentators use fall primarily into three categories: (1) sounds that imitate a rhythm or what members call "the beat," (2) stock chants associated with the various categories, and (3) what I call the "mantras" of the evening.

Like a scat singer in jazz, the commentator imitates rhythms or beats using a variety of sounds. This is an improvisational technique that requires commentators to have keen senses, precise vocal skills, and exceptional coordination. Unlike the jazz singer, the commentator imitates the beat as opposed to matching other instruments, yet, much like the jazz singer, the commentator can move between musical beats. For instance, the commentator needs to listen to the music and imitate the rhythm, watch the performers and anticipate their movements, and improvise the sounds, all at the same time. When Frank Revlon chants, "Ka-ka-ka-ka-ka-ka-ka ow," each enunciation imitates the sound of the rhythm while it marks precisely the movements of the performer. With his chant, the commentator can push the performer to "hit her marks and feel it." Yet he can also make it difficult for the performer by reducing the enthusiasm in his chant or by holding back, causing the performer to have to work much harder on the runway. In these cases, the performer loses focus because instead of allowing herself to get caught up or taken over by the energy generated by the commentator, the crowd, and the music, she is forced to focus on the lack of help she is getting from the commentator. However, if she is creative, meeting this challenge can attest to her ultimate skill at improvisation. More often than not, the commentator's "ka-ka-ka-ka-ka-ka-ka" serves as a guide. He is letting the performer know when to break, to spin, or to dip because the movement, whatever it is, has to coincide with and end on the beat.

The deeply bound performance relationship between the commentator, the runway performer, the audience, and the DJ (the music) is similar to the relationship between the drummer and the dancer in many

African dance rituals. Performance ethnographer Margaret Thompson Drewal's work on performance in Yoruba rituals is apropos here. In her discussion of the improvisational style of African rituals, Thompson Drewal suggests that:

> Improvisation is transformational, often participatory and com-petitive, in which case it constitutes a multidimensional process of argumentation. Dancers and drummers, for example, negotiate rhythmically with each other, maintaining a competitive interre-latedness. This is particularly critical because of the close concep-tual and formal link between music and dance in Africa.[62]

This is also the case in Ballroom culture, as the commentator energizes the relationship between the runway performer and other participants in the performance ritual. Especially in vogue performances, the commen-tator's chants help shape and accentuate the competitor's body motions as his voice highlights the competitor's physical and rhythmic skills. This role is similar in many respects to that of the interlocutor in voudou rit-ual practices I observed and in which I participated during my research in Accra, Ghana, and Lomé, Togo, in the summers of 1995–98. In these rituals, all of the participants gathered in a circle. This circle consisted of drummers, members who played other rhythm instruments, and par-ticipants/observers, who sang and performed the ritual dance intermit-tently. Notably, no one was allowed merely to observe the ritual or remain apart. Everyone was expected to participate. The drummers were located on the periphery, while others danced in the middle of the circle. Most important, a person in the middle, an interlocutor, facilitated the labor of performance that everyone contributed to the ritual. He moved quickly around the circle, coaxing the drummers to play with greater intensity, coaching the singers to stay in rhythm, and monitoring the dancers to ensure he would catch them in the event they collapsed into a frenzy of spiritual possession. At times the interlocutor single-handedly managed the pace and intensity of all the forces of performance in that space.

The stock chant is another significant part of the commentator's ar-senal. Stock chants are important tools that enhance the relationship be-tween the commentator and the performer. These chants are developed and evolve over time, as do the categories they describe. Furthermore, stock chants are known and used by all commentators, and they are fa-miliar to all members. All members at the balls are included in the performance because they have inside knowledge of these chants and the ways in which they mark the performances. In general, commentators draw from a repository of stock chants. When a commentator looks at a given category on the flyer, he recites the chants that are commonly used to alert the performer to what will be expected of him or her on the runway. I will explain the function of flyers and the categories they describe in greater detail later, but here, for the sake of illustration, let me return to a popular category that is always accompanied by a stock chant.

As I argued in chapter 2, Realness with a Twist is one of the most subversive categories of performance in Ballroom culture. This competitive category requires a stock chant on the part of the commentator. As the competitor runs through his two-part performance, one part thug and one part queen, the commentator simultaneously marks his performance with a chant: "Realness, realness with a twist, these are boys that twist their wrist; these are the boys that twist like this, that's realness, realness, realness. Realness, realness with a twist, a little bit of that, a little bit of this; it's realness, realness, realness, realness." Another variation of this chant runs "Realness, realness with a twist; this is a bitch who bends like this; this is the bitch who can pop like this; it's realness, realness, realness." The commentator repeats this chant throughout the performance. The chant reminds everyone of the goal of the category: to demonstrate how performance can be deployed, skillfully by one body, for the purpose of disguise, on call.

In the course of playing their productive role within Black LGBT modes of discourse, commentators often create new chants or mantras of the evening. This occurs most often when commentators vibe together during the performance, meaning that new phrases are created out of the spontaneous performance relationship between two masters of wordplay. For instance, Kodak said that he loves commentating with Jack Givenchy because he is a master of words and they work off of each other: "I can offset whatever he says and go with it, and it's all spontaneous." Kodak brings into focus the necessary performance relationship that the commentators have to build and maintain between themselves to contribute to the overall success of the ritual. Moreover, Kodak's statements confirm that the performance relationship between commentators evolves in the moment. He also pointed out that there are times when two commentators come together and are so in sync that the effect is magical: "When I commentated with Selvin Givenchy [now Kahn], it was just there. We looked at each other, and we were like 'wow,'" Kodak recalled. During the House of Ford ball, Frank Revlon and Jack Givenchy constructed a mantra together, which they used throughout the second half of the ball. Their rendition of "here we go loop de loo, here we go loop de li, ka-kat; here we go loop de loo, all on a Ballroom night," began as a spontaneous chant that gradually spread throughout the ballroom, illustrating that the role of the commentator is about a process of innovation and creativity. Most of all, commentators take the lead in cultivating this innovation and creativity, which members of the community as a whole come to the ritual to practice.

The Audience/Participants

As demonstrated in The House of Ford Ball, what my interlocutors refer to as "spectators" are indispensable, not only to the performance system but also to the entire ball event. Since most ball events draw very large and diverse crowds of mostly Black LGBT people from, usually, various cities across North America, these spectators bring remarkable energy and excitement to the ball event. Phoenix Manolo Blahnik emphasized this point.

> Without spectators there would be no ball scene. And I think that is a fact of the Ballroom scene that really goes understated. No one really mentions the spectatorship of the ball. There are a lot of people that are interested in the Ballroom scene but don't participate in the Ballroom scene. They just like to go and view and watch.

Phoenix's point is well taken, but I would suggest, instead, that at ball events there is no such role as a *mere* spectator, even if the person is not a "member" of the Ballroom scene. One of the most significant similarities between balls and ritual performance in the African diaspora is that spectators are always simultaneously participants because they contribute to and ultimately cocreate the performances that are being enacted.

In his salient essay "The Aesthetic of Modern Black Drama: From Mimesis to Methexis," the theatre and performance theorist Kimberly W. Benston argues that, because of its deep roots within the sociopolitical actions of the community, Black performance facilitates an interplay between drama and ritual. Black performance minimizes the illusionary divide between spectator and performer, self and other, and viewing and participation. Benston calls this *methexis* or a communal *helping out* by all people assembled to view a particular performance.[63] *Helping out* necessitates direct participation and investment in not only the actual dissident performances but also the various attendant communal strategies in which minoritarian people are engaged. Within the performance situation and space, the members in attendance participate in an exchange of energy, voices, and bodies, creating a dialogic and dialectic form of community affirmation.

Throughout The House of Ford Ball, and as I have highlighted in the subsequent analysis, the audience/participants cocreated or helped out with the chants, assisted with marking the beat (which is so important in the performance), rooted for members of their houses during the performance, created a cacophony of houses chanting and celebrating their names, and praised the judges for decisions with which they agreed and scorned those with which they did not. This is essential to the performance system at the ball, and such exchanges are dynamically enacted during the performance. Yet such exchanges are relative and situational based on the distinct qualities and skills that individuals bring to the collective.

Ballroom Competitive Categories

Again, considering The House of Ford Ball, as well as the other balls that I have described, it should be clear that the main allure of the ball is competition. This is made evident not only through the excitement and intensity of the social interaction and performances that take place but also through the nature and function of the ball event itself. In fact, throughout all of the elements at balls that I have discussed, competition stands as a key aspect of a ball that brings people to the performance space. For most the objective is to "snatch the trophy" and the cash prizes, which can range from five hundred to well over a thousand dollars, but it is also about gaining recognition and status within the Ballroom world. Successful participation in the competitive aspects of the ball demands an enormous amount of labor in terms of preparation and execution, but for many members, far beyond the trophies and the cash prizes, the symbolic, social, and psychological benefits exceed the costs.

The competition at balls is organized around categories. Although there are standard categories, new categories continue to develop as Ballroom culture expands. My discussion here is not exhaustive, mainly because categories based on body presentation, performative gender and sexuality, and theatrical productions abound in Ballroom. Nonetheless, this is a brief overview of some of the competitive categories highlighted in the House of Ford Ball.

As I observed while explaining the gender system in chapter 2, it is important to understand that, while this system forms the basis of the competitive categories, these two systems do not coincide completely. The gender system is its own entity, and its functions extend beyond balls. However, for the members, the competitive categories are the raison d'être of balls. Categories are typically listed and described in detail on Ballroom flyers. These flyers provide basic information about the ball such as the hosting house, the theme or title of the ball (e.g., The Domination Ball), the date, time, and place. As noted before, flyers created by the various houses are read during the Announcements time at the beginning of the ball. The most important function of the flyer is, however, to provide the criteria for each category. This is why people need to obtain a copy of the flyer prior to a ball in order to prepare for categories and the ways in which they will walk (see figs. 3–6, which show the flyer for The Legendary House of Prestige's Black Ball II in chapter 2).

As demonstrated in the flyer, most categories that are listed are arranged based on the gender system. Each component of the system constitutes a main set of categories.[64] Hence, most flyers list the categories based on particular subjectivities. The largest numbers of categories are constructed around the Butch Queen. Categories such as Butch Queen Up in Pumps, Butch Queen Realness, Butch Queen Realness with a Twist, and Butch Queen Voguing Femme are all attached to the subjectivity of the Butch Queen, to then create another performance. Despite this emphasis on Butch Queens, the primary purpose of structuring the categories based on the gender system is to ensure that members are required to compete in categories with others of their own gender. For example, as we have seen, when a cisgender woman tried to walk in the Femme Queen Body category, Jack Givenchy disqualified her because she is a "real woman" as opposed to a Femme Queen. Ballroom members have developed rules and regulations to ensure fairness even though these safeguards fail at times.

There are, however, categories that are not limited to the gender system. Category headings such as Open to All (OTA) or Best Dressed Spectator encourage participation from members of the Ballroom community, as well as from those who do not belong to a house or might be attending a ball for the first time. A reliable way to recruit new participants in the Ballroom community is to allow a space for nonmembers to experience walking in a ball and possibly winning. House parents are always looking for new members who can fill vacancies in their houses to strengthen their units.

Last, the As a House and production categories are designed for participants to compete in a group within a category. Productions usually include more elaborate performances, which consist of props, sets, and costumes that adhere to a theme outlined in the flyer. As a House and production categories also call for a greater diversity of skills in performance, meaning that the house needs to be able to execute, in exceptional fashion, a range of performances such as Runway, Voguing (Old and New Way), and Hand Performance, for example.

Under most main category headings, there are a series of subheadings. For instance, within the Femme Queen category, the flyer lists three or four common categories such as Femme Queen Body, Femme Queen Face, or Femme Queen Sex Siren. Most of these categories are based on "realness." As I have argued, realness relies heavily on a visual epistemology that members in the Ballroom scene adopt because they understand that it influences how members are "seen" in society at large.

But realness is not the only basis on which criteria for categories are drawn. Other categories call for effective presentation of physical attributes that one is assumed to inherently embody, such as Face and Sex Siren. For example, in Face categories, the competitor must learn to *present* his or her face as opposed to *performing* it. This requirement is exemplified in what I heard Selvin say at a ball during Black Pride weekend in 2010 in Detroit: "No clumps, no lumps, no bumps," he intoned into the microphone as he pranced up and down the runway during a Butch Queen Face category. Thus, what undergirds the criteria for this category is the belief that if one is beautiful naturally, with no clumps, lumps or bumps, one does not have to perform; instead, the beauty or flawlessness is self-evident. Therefore, in this category, competitors approach the judges by drawing focus to the face and by using their hands to guide the eyes of the judges toward the head. They smile and show their teeth.

Fig. 12. Butch Queens contesting in a Bazaar category at a ball in Detroit in 2010. Contestants in Bazaar categories usually make their own garments. (Photograph by Mireille Miller-Young.)

They tilt their heads slightly upward to highlight the contours and shape of the face, nose, and chin. Most of all, competitors in this category must demonstrate that they are not "painted" and do not have blemishes or "bad skin."

Conversely, there are categories called "Bazaar" (sometimes referred to as "Bazaar Bazaar"), in which the competitor has to do more *performing* of the physical attributes than *presenting* them. In this category, which is linked to the face, the performer is supposed to be creative with his or her face and work with and highlight the uniqueness of an overall look. Bazaar categories also call for competitors to create and present zany and outlandish outfits based on a given theme (see figs. 12–13). Face over Thirty and Face over Forty are popular categories that take aging into account within the general Face criteria. Although such categories, and the ways in which judges approach them, can seem superficial and harsh—and indeed some are—the commentator, house parents, and other members of the community who have more experience in the scene typically are very generous with advice and help prepare fellow members to present or perform effectively in these categories. And, frankly, there are some categories in which members will not be competitive no matter what they do. Some Ballroom members, like me, cannot vogue, for example, but because there are so many distinct categories, a person who cannot vogue, more often than not, possesses other attributes that make him or her competitive in other categories.

Body categories are similar in this respect. Although, especially for Femme Queens, body categories are, in part, about realness, they are also about *presenting* the body, showing body parts such as voluptuous breasts or a large, round, and meaty butt. These are often the objectives of realness body categories, whether explicitly or implicitly expressed. Again, and at times problematically, Ballroom relies on certain features of the body to instantiate sex and gender authenticity. At the Ford ball, the Femme Queens were either scantily dressed or wore form-fitting outfits. They shook their body parts in front of the panel of judges to show the flexibility and elasticity of these parts, and in many cases, to show that they are attached firmly to the body. This signifies realness for the body category. For Butch Queens or Men, the aim is to present a muscular and perfectly chiseled body with no fat in "the wrong places." But for men who walk in the Sex Siren category, the focus is very much about the penis. The men are dressed in swimsuits, shorts, or underwear, and if they are well endowed, and, better yet, if the penis can be seen, either

Fig. 13. A Butch Queen competes in a Bazaar category at a ball in Detroit in 2010. (Photograph by Mireille Miller-Young.)

in a see-through outfit or if a portion of it hangs out of the clothing, this adds to the effect of the presentation of the male body.

Sex Siren is a particular body category that emphasizes the physical sexual appeal of the participants, mostly Butch Queens, Butches, and Men. This is a quintessential body category and is very popular. Prince J Prodigy described Sex Siren this way.

> Basically it's sexy; you know what I'm saying? It doesn't necessarily mean sexy with your clothes off, but it's just something that's got a natural sexy feel. It's like, you know, I've got the ten and a half, meaning that you've got that perfect body and then some, you know. You've got the face; you've got the body; you've got the moves, everything. You're just sexy. You just exude sex.

To digress slightly on the theme of Prince J's description, Sex Siren is one of the most popular categories mainly because it indeed shows flesh. I must admit that wherever I am in the ball space, I try to position myself in a way that allows me to see everything the competitors are willing to show during the Sex Siren category, no matter if they are Butch Queens, Femme Queens, or Butches. Especially for Butch Queens, the more flesh they show, the better, and particularly if the crotch and buttocks are perceived as what Prince J would call "perfect." This way, they are more likely to excite the crowd and the judges and win the category.

Even though body categories such as Femme Queen Body or Sex Siren are based on notions of physical perfection and very rigid ideas about what that actually looks like, there are other categories that are more diverse and inclusive. Again, in Ballroom culture, body categories abound. For example, there are Big Women's Body, Thick Butch Queen's' Body, Big Boy Body, Full Figure Girl, and a variety of other categories. As the categories I mention proliferate, it should be clear that I have not come close to introducing all the possible categories at ball events. It suffices to say that, while on the one hand categories are rigid and exclusionary and stringently policed, on the other hand I have also observed a great deal of fluidity and diversity among the categories in which participants can compete. Balls feature many performances and presentations, but most of all they are opportunities in which all people can fit in somewhere and demonstrate their skills and attributes.

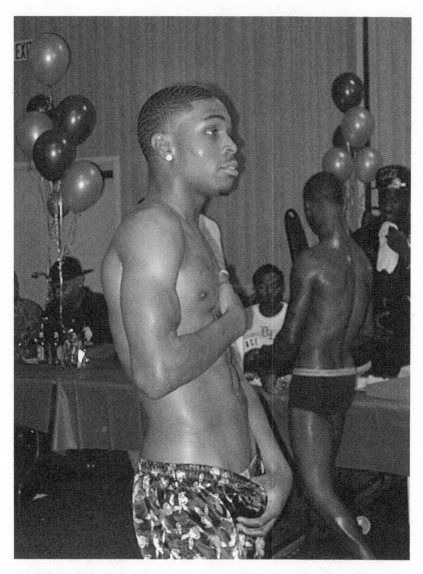

Fig. 14. A Butch Queen competing in a Sex Siren category at a ball during the Hotter than July Black Pride festivities in Detroit in 2010. (Photograph by Mireille Miller-Young.)

Vogue Performance

The centrality of competition is evidenced most prominently in vogue performance categories. Based on my description of The House of Ford Ball, vogue competitions also capture best the epiphanic experience that the performance system induces during a ball event. Voguing brings the forces of performance together in a way that is profound but ephemeral. It is a primary aspect of the overall structure of the competition at balls. Therefore, in the final portion of this chapter, I return to voguing in order to situate it in the context of the ritualized performances at balls. To explicate vogue performance at this juncture helps to bring into focus the function of the performance system during the ritualized aspects of the ball.

Although it draws from a variety of African diasporic dance practices, in its contemporary form vogue performance is solely a creation of Ballroom culture. The name of the dance form was coined after *Vogue*, the international fashion and lifestyles magazine.[65] Distinct from all other competitive categories, voguing is a dance form that involves an engagement of the entire body in the performance.[66] The picturesque hand and body movements that are most familiar to the public, especially through Madonna's music video *Vogue* (1990), form the basis of vogue performance in Ballroom culture. There are two overarching categories of vogue: Old Way and New Way. Duchess Prestige explained that "arm control, body movement, beat knowledge and rhythm, and syncopation" are essential to all techniques of vogue. As I detail shortly, whether it is Old Way or New Way, each form demands a command of the aforementioned skills, which are nevertheless enacted differently depending on the form.

First, Old Way Vogue emerged in the 1960s, 1970s, and 1980s when Immortal Icons of Ballroom culture, mostly from New York City, such as Paris Dupree, Kevin Ultra Omni, Hector Xtravaganza, Willie Ninja, and others developed the performance. My interlocutors in Detroit associate Old Way with *Paris Is Burning*, in which this version of vogue is elaborated extensively. With "Love Is the Message" as musical accompaniment, Old Way Vogue incorporates many of the dance and movement forms of the African diaspora, some of which became popular in the United States during the 1970s and 1980s, namely, break dancing, martial arts, and Capoeira. Old Way style also reflects some influence of disco music. In some ways, vogue performance coheres with the shifting popularity of distinctive music forms among Black LGBT communities because performers shape and adapt the movements to music.[67]

Diva D and Father Al Bvlgari agreed that there are two distinct styles of Old Way Vogue. "There is a smooth fluid style, and then there is a pop and rock type of Old Way. A lot of people don't do that [pop and rock] type of vogue anymore," said Diva D. Likewise, Ballroom community historian Father Aaron Enigma from Chicago suggests that Old Way style is also characterized by "freeze-frame poses and fluid hand and arm movements."[68] On the one hand, executing the freeze-frame poses and smooth fluid style requires close attention to clean and precise lines; using arm, hand, and leg motions; and creating lines with the entire body, especially when one is doing floor performance. On the other hand, the pop and rock style is less fluid and is more of a combination of freeze-frame poses, mostly performed by Femme Queens, Butch Queens Up in Drag, and Women, and the floor maneuvers enacted by break-dancers performed by more masculine Butch Queens or Men. While Father Enigma suggests that the freeze-frame poses and smooth fluid style have historically been a Femme Queen technique, I would add that this Old Way pop and rock style was exemplified by the late Immortal Icon Willie Ninja, particularly in his vogue performance featured in *Paris Is Burning*. Hence, over time, especially among Ballroom members in the Midwest, Butch Queen participants have sought to masculinize a form that was previously feminine or a Femme Queen technique of Old Way Vogue.

Regardless of style, what is essential is the kind of adherence to rhythm that Old Way requires in order for the movement to exhibit a performer's creativity while staying true to the basic techniques of vogue—mainly "beat knowledge," as Duchess said. Accordingly, Father Al insisted that Old Way style, both fluid and smooth and pop and rock, is underpinned by a beat-to-beat motif. He went on to say, "It's a beat-to-beat-to-beat type thing; if it's not on beat, it's very choppable," meaning, as we have seen, that the performer will be eliminated from the category. Indeed, in recent years, Old Way Vogue performance has been overtaken by New Way; many of my interlocutors say that none of the new voguers perform Old Way anymore. Yet Old Way Vogue style has an indelible place in the development of vogue performance.

New Way Vogue exhibits African diasporic dance traditions also, but it involves more prominent contemporary forms of popular music and dance, as well as more of the other aspects of the performance system in the Ballroom community such as the commentator's chants. In this sense, New Way Vogue exemplifies best the creative developments and potentials of performance in the Ballroom scene in recent times.[69] The New Way form of vogue has been shaped by house music, and these rhythms are deeply embedded in the execution of the movement. In addition, my interlocutors say that hip-hop has undoubtedly impacted New Way Vogue, due, in part, to the influence of hip-hop on Black LGBT and performance cultures in general. However, the impact of house music on the execution of vogue performance has been far more salient. According to Diva D Bvlgari, whereas the Old Way emphasizes clean lines and precision on the beat with a "beat-to-beat" motif, New Way requires the performer to catch the inner beats, or what Father Al Bvlgari called the "backbeat, the inner beat versus the main one," which is an important feature of the polyrhythms of house music. "A true [New Way] vogue performer should be able to listen and hear that beat and go on from that, not the main beat," said Father Al.

There are five elements that apply to both Old Way Vogue and New Way Vogue: duckwalks, catwalks, spins, dips, and hand performance. Creative variations on these elements are most effectively exhibited in a subcategory of vogue called Vogue Femme. Furthermore, as performance in Ballroom culture expands, more distinctions and categories are created. For example, within the subcategories, there are three styles of New Way Vogue that apply to Vogue Femme performances. These three styles are "soft and cunt," dramatics, and performance (a combination of soft and cunt and dramatics). Diva D delineated the distinctions among the three styles. "'Soft and cunt,' consists of clean, soft, and smooth hand/arm movements in a fluid and flowing way. 'Dramatics' are choppy, jerky, and spasmic movements with an energetic edge. 'Performance' uses a combination of both to tell a story with your hands/arms and the entire body." Diva D explained how this form of vogue combines the "rough and tumble," with "pussy and dainty." These forms of vogue performance are primarily meant for Butch Queens, who aim to represent the shifting interplay between masculinity and femininity. But Diva D also illustrates that members of the Ballroom community are always "cutting and mixing" to create new forms that are innovative and relevant.

Despite such diversity in style, any performance of vogue is expected to include all of the elements while adhering to the accepted standards of each form. More specifically, there are three primary aesthetic criteria by which the performances are judged: (1) each performer has to include the five elements of vogue in his or her performance; (2) each element has to be performed within the rhythm established by the music, the commentator's chant, and the audience;[70] and (3) performers must distinguish themselves by demonstrating intensity (with a physical crescendo at precise moments), exhibiting skills that are exceptional and adding a special touch that reflects the performer's personality. Typically, the performer who exemplifies these attributes in the most effective fashion snatches the trophy and the prize and the respect of the Ballroom community, particularly with regard to the vogue category.

The first two elements, duckwalks and catwalks, involve forward movement in small steps with the body in a midlevel or low-level squat (almost touching the ground).[71] As the name implies, when duckwalking, the performer's feet are parallel and advance in small steps. In Vogue Femme categories, the catwalk is used more commonly for locomotion. In the battle of New Way Vogue I witnessed at The House of Ford Ball, Diva D and Ebony began the battle by proceeding down the runway and performing a catwalk in the direction of the judges. The catwalk was accompanied by hand and arm gestures that were controlled, precise, and synchronized with the rhythm of the commentator's vocalized accompaniment and the house music beats. While voguing, femme performers often accentuate the duckwalk or catwalk with arm and hand performances. To display arm and hand control in performance, one gesticulates with the arms and hands in conjunction with the torso in an asymmetrical antiphony to the lower part of the body.[72] As the performer approaches the panel of judges, these standard elements are mandatory and constitute the foundational movements of vogue on which performers build to distinguish their performances from those of their competitors.

Once Diva D and Ebony arrived directly in front of the judges, both of them immediately performed a combination of the next two elements, the spin and the dip. Spins and dips are the intermittent apex of the vogue performance. This spin-and-dip combination is often called a Machiavelli or "falling out." The choreographer and dance professor Darrell Jones explained that in Black vernacular dance circles, this dip is called a Kamikaze. Whether it is referred to as a Machiavelli, falling out, or Kamikaze, the spin-and-dip combination represents, within the context of intense competition during a vogue battle, the participants' willingness to put their bodies on the line and take ruthless measures to win. In other words, the spin-and-dip combination is what participants are working toward, what the commentator is coordinating with his voice and the music, and what the audience is eagerly anticipating. And performers seek to enact

Fig. 15. Ninja Prestige catwalks his way down the runway in a Butch Queen Vogue category at the Love Is the Message Ball in Los Angeles in 2005. (Photograph by Marlon M. Bailey.)

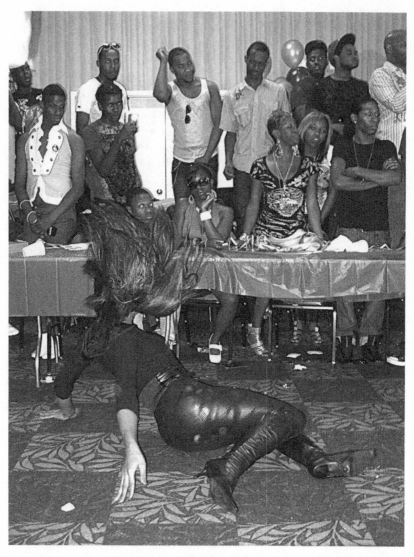

Fig. 16. A Femme Queen contestant performs a Machiavelli in front of the panel of judges during a vogue category at a ball in Indianapolis in 2011. (Photograph by Thabiti John Willis.)

Fig. 17. Two Butch Queens engaged in a vogue battle at a ball in Indianapolis in 2011. (Photograph by Thabiti John Willis.)

the most efficient culmination of the vogue performance in order to "slay
the competitor and snatch the trophy," as it is termed in Ballroom communities. Diva D and Ebony performed variations on these elements and
repeated them throughout their performances. Another Ebony house
member ended up winning the final battle, and Diva D conceded that he
was eventually outperformed. No matter who wins the battle, it is clear
that, for members, vogue is one dance form that captures the power of
performance in Ballroom culture and the ways in which this artistic labor
affirms the values and practices created by and within the community.

Ballroom Icon R. R. Chanel, a Butch Queen from New York City, captures the importance of balls not only to the Ballroom community but
also to people in larger LGBT communities of color who frequent them:
"Balls are the only places where queens come together and do something
and feel accepted and wanted for who they are and what they do."[73] Not
only is the ball a space and occasion for "queens to come together"; it
also allows for and depends on the participation of a very diverse array

Fig. 18. A Butch Queen voguing at a ball in Indianapolis in 2011. (Photograph by Thabiti John Willis.)

of mostly, but not exclusively, Black LGBT people who come together and "live" in ways that are not allowed in the outside world, if only for just one evening.

In general ball events constitute the culturally productive domain of Ballroom culture. I cannot emphasize enough the critical role of performance as the glue that holds this discursive domain of the world of Ballroom together. Ballroom members create alternative spaces to the White queer or Black heteronormative spaces (social and material) from which Black LGBT people are excluded. Performance undergirds the gender system and the criteria for the competitive categories, but the system in which it is enacted also provides a means though which the many elements of the ball event come together to create moments of epiphany for all participants. In so doing, through social and spatial practices, Ballroom members create a collective realm, a betwixt and between place, a liminal space, where such transformation is at least possible in ways in which it is not believed to be in the larger heteronormative world in which Black LGBT members live. Ultimately—a point to which R. R. Chanel attests—such potentials explain why members of the community persistently participate in balls and undertake the performance labor required to vigorously compete in performance categories. As it is the nexus between the ball events and the kinship system in Ballroom culture, performance labor assumes a prominent place in the overall cultural work that sustains the community. In chapter 5, I investigate how Ballroom members, through performance and kinship, meet the challenges of the disproportionate impact of the HIV/AIDS epidemic on its members.

FIVE

"They Want Us Sick"

Ballroom Culture and the Politics of HIV/AIDS

I see Ballroom as an artistic community that can connect with
youth on issues of HIV/AIDS prevention, and the relationship
between drugs and unsafe sex.
WOLFGANG BUSCH, DIRECTOR, *HOW DO I LOOK*[1]

What's Your Intervention?

After three days of driving from Oakland, California, my ex-partner and
I arrived in Detroit in January 2003. Fortunately, a buddy of mine from
college who is now a Detroit police officer allowed me to stay with him
and his girlfriend, free of charge, for the duration of this eight-month
stint of fieldwork. This was perfect because not only was I low on funds
but his three-bedroom house was only a five-minute drive from the
building where I was going to be working. He lives off of Six Mile Road
about five blocks west of Telegraph, a usually congested major road on
the far west side of the city bordering the western suburbs. Much like
the neighborhood east of downtown described in chapter 3, this side of
town is "spotty." The farther west of Telegraph one travels, the more upper class and White it is. My friend's neighborhood consists of working-
class Black and White families, one of the only mixed neighborhoods I
am familiar with in Detroit.

The afternoon after my arrival, I attend a meeting at the facility occupied
by the Men of Color Motivational Group, Inc. (MOC), an agency that
touts itself as the only Black gay HIV/AIDS organization in Michigan
that primarily targets Black LGBT populations in its efforts to prevent
the occurrence and spread of socially communicable diseases. I had met
the executive director during Detroit's annual Black Pride Celebration

in July 2002.[2] At that time I arranged to work at MOC as a consultant because it had a unique and expansive Ballroom program, funded by the Centers for Disease Control, designed to work with Ballroom members to reduce the spread of HIV/AIDS within the community.

As I leave my new temporary home, I head east down McNichols (Six Mile Road) for about half a mile, from Telegraph Road to Grand River, another major artery that extends from downtown, diagonally, through the western part of the city. As I approach Grand River, going east, I start to see more and more Black people. In general, this is a lower-middle-class Black area. I see several sidewalk shops and fast-food restaurants on both sides of the street. I have been told that MOC will be on my left at the corner of McNichols and Grand River just before the Subway sandwich shop. Directly across the street from MOC is Redford High School, a predominantly Black school, on the right side of McNichols. Embedded in a Black community at the edge of the city, I see the building I was looking for on the corner of this highly trafficked intersection. And immediately above the entrance, I am somewhat surprised to see a very conspicuous sign that reads "MEN OF COLOR MOTIVATIONAL GROUP, INC.," in large letters.

I park my car in front of the main entrance and ring the doorbell. A man comes down a set of stairs to let me in, and after I tell him that I have a meeting scheduled with the executive director, he escorts me up the stairs to the reception area in the main office. As I reach the top of the stairs, I immediately see the executive director talking to one of the employees, and I overhear him say, "Yeah that sounds good, but what is your intervention?" I introduce myself, and we go into his office. Throughout the summer this would be his mantra: "What is your intervention?" He would say this to us whenever we came to him with prevention ideas and strategies. Before, and often instead of, reading or listening to our proposals, he would cut us off and says this. If a proposal or the idea did not have a very clear-cut, specifically marked target population with measurable outcomes, he always said, "Okay, but what is your intervention?"

Even in the early stages of working there, I began to question the extent to which this organization was sincerely willing to break from the existing approaches to HIV/AIDS "prevention" that are imposed on Black LGBT communities by public health agencies and work toward intraventive approaches, strategies that emerge from among the members of

those communities. Since I had worked for HIV/AIDS prevention organizations before, I wondered what would be different about MOC, given
the distinctive sociopolitical environment in which it exists. I was not
sure that this organization's leadership genuinely cared about the unique
qualities and character of Ballroom culture, ostensibly one of the reasons
the organization claimed to be interested in this Black LGBT community.
Or was MOC concerned only about statistical outcomes, irrespective of
whether or not its organizational strategies were culturally appropriate,
sensitive, and effective in enhancing the quality of life of Ballroom members, a precondition for reducing the spread of HIV in the community, as
opposed to focusing solely on sexual behavioral change?

In chapter 4, I examined the ritualized performances at ball events,
the cultural-productive domain of Ballroom culture. I argued that Ballroom members, like other marginalized communities throughout the
African diaspora, use ritualized performance as a form of cultural labor
to create an alternative, more egalitarian, social existence. As a source
of celebration, affirmation, competition, and critique, Ballroom performance provides the discursive, social, and psychic means through which
Ballroom members refashion themselves in order to navigate the hegemonic gender and sexual norms in the majoritarian society, the realm
of society in which they are oppressed and from which they are by and
large excluded.

Therefore, in this chapter I discern whether Ballroom can meet the
most extreme social, political, psychological, spiritual, and communal
challenges: its members' struggle against the scourge of the HIV/AIDS
epidemic in the United States. How does Ballroom confront the challenges of the HIV/AIDS crisis as a community at a time when the prevention and treatment efforts of most public health and community-based
organizations (CBOs) have been ineffective in reducing infection rates
and the overall devastation caused by the epidemic in Black communities?[3] Literally, Ballroom's Black LGBT members are fighting for their
lives.

As a community whose members are affected disproportionately by
the HIV/AIDS epidemic, Ballroom uses performance as a means of creating a new social sphere that critiques and revises dominant institutional
practices. Recognizing the cultural currency of Ballroom, several public
health organizations have focused their prevention efforts there. However, while these organizations appropriate the *culture* they disregard its
members. And, as a result, Ballroom members forge new strategies that

are tailored to their community practices and needs. Nevertheless, just as popular discourses on HIV/AIDS ignore the daily life struggles that Black LGBT people face, dominant representations of the epidemic dismiss the forms of cultural critique that Black LGBT communities such as Ballroom employ to contend with the social perils of the disease. A close examination of Ballroom culture reveals the more subtle, but no less important, defenses against the spread of the virus that emerge from within the community itself.

Throughout this book, I emphasize both the forms of marginalization that members of the Ballroom community experience and the alternative social, performative, and communal practices members undertake to withstand such oppressive conditions. In the first part of this chapter I add HIV infection and the "risks thereof" to the already oppressive conditions under which Black LGBT people live, an added condition that further excludes them from cultural belonging. For Black LGBT people, blackness, nonnormative genders or sexualities, socioeconomic marginalization, and disease equate to social exclusion from national, cultural, and communal forms of belonging. Thus, social factors such as HIV/AIDS form the basis of social, political, economic, and spiritual marginalization for Ballroom members in the United States.

Second, through an ethnographic account of my experiences working at MOC, I suggest that the prevention methods endorsed and funded by public health agencies or CBOs are ill-conceived and ineffective because they are fraught with racism, sexism, and homophobia. In fact, from the perspective of those in the Ballroom community, MOC operates much as Western nongovernmental organizations (NGOs) operate in the struggle against the pandemic across the globe, as viewed by many African and Caribbean people. When explicit and implicit forms of discrimination operate within organizational cultures, public agencies designed to fight HIV/AIDS end up exacerbating its disastrous effects on marginalized communities.[4] My aim is to provide concrete examples that reflect the theoretical claims I offer about Ballroom and HIV/AIDS. Therefore, my experience from *within* MOC brings a firsthand perspective to bear on the multitude of problems with HIV/AIDS prevention that resonate throughout Black communities in the United States in particular and the Black world in general.

Third, I examine how the nonmarket values that sustain Ballroom culture (care, service, competition, and critique)—the *housework*, the creation of and participation in prevention houses and balls—help to hold back increasing infection and the debilitating consequences of HIV/AIDS. I also discuss the contentious debates within the Ballroom community over what to do about the HIV problem and who should be doing it. I conclude this chapter on a sobering note by considering how, despite the cultural labor that Ballroom members undertake and the hopeful potential for its structures of care, service, competition, and critique, some members continue to contract and die from complications of HIV or AIDS.

Considered broadly, reconstituting gender and sexual subjectivities, creating an expansive kinship structure, and using performance as a means and occasion to affirm, celebrate, and critique its members should be understood as key aspects of Ballroom's creative response to HIV/ AIDS. Undoubtedly, the intervention of Ballroom culture in the spread of this disease reflects the difficult work of forging a community. In short I show how this complex labor of community remaking undertaken by Ballroom members mitigates the harsh realities of HIV/AIDS and provides a viable communal response to this epidemic.

Ballroom Culture and HIV/AIDS: Intersectional Marginalization

I have argued that the multiple forms of marginalization that Black LGBT people experience are due in part to their racially minoritized status in US society. Black poor and working-class people are by and large excluded from or oppressed by majoritarian sectors of our society. In other words, whiteness carries power and privilege that many Black people desire but to which only few have access, especially among LGBT communities. Furthermore, Ballroom members are simultaneously excluded from or marginalized within forms of Black belonging. The exclusion and marginalization are a result of multiple social factors, but chief among them are their gender and sexual nonconformity. Drawing from ethnographer Michele Tracy Berger's work on stigmatized women of color with HIV/ AIDS in Detroit, I employ the concept of *intersectional marginalization* to theorize the multiple and intersecting forms of marginalization and exclusion that Ballroom members endure.[5] Intersectional marginalization helps elucidate the social locations that members of the Ballroom community occupy prior and in addition to direct or indirect encounters with the HIV/AIDS epidemic. These intersecting social locations are then exacerbated by the deleterious treatment of those who are infected with HIV/AIDS or at risk thereof.[6] Hence, Black LGBT people who are working-class or poor members of the Ballroom community live under simultaneously oppressive conditions. In order to accurately explicate the experiences of Ballroom members, I add HIV/AIDS infection, and the risk thereof, to this matrix of marginalization and exclusion to demonstrate how the epidemic affects this community differently from how it affects other, similarly situated communities.

To date very little scholarship has investigated the impact of the HIV/AIDS epidemic on Ballroom communities in the United States.[7] Given the disproportionate impact of HIV/AIDS on Black communities across the country, and its particular devastation of Black people in Detroit, and given that the Ballroom community is embedded in Black communities in the city, it is necessary to consider HIV/AIDS and its effects on Ballroom communities as an instructive case study. In the Ballroom community, HIV/AIDS and the attendant bureaucracies that disseminate, facilitate, and manage a whole range of public and private resources for prevention and treatment are measured by and entangled in a set of larger, more complicated, institutional practices and controls. In other words, invariably, the interlocking oppressions of race, class, gender, and sexuality shape Black LGBT people's experiences even as they exacerbate the suffering of marginalized groups at the hands of the virus.[8]

The epidemiological profile of HIV/AIDS makes clear the severity of the epidemic's impact on African Americans. Since the beginning of the HIV/AIDS epidemic in the 1980s, African Americans have been disproportionately represented. During the last twenty years, the overrepresentation of African Americans in the epidemic has gone on unabated and, indeed, has increased in severity. In the United States, African Americans comprise, according to recent statistics, almost half of both people living with HIV and all new diagnoses (46 and 45 percent, respectively) while constituting nearly 14 percent of the population.[9] The perilous impact of the epidemic is starkly clear among Black men who have sex with men (hereafter MSM) who,[10] in 2006, accounted for 63 percent of new infections among all Black men and 35 percent among all MSM.[11] This national overrepresentation of African Americans in the epidemic is vividly reflected in the State of Michigan and in Detroit in particular. African Americans comprise only 14 percent of the total population of Michigan but a staggering 58 percent of all HIV/AIDS cases in the state. In 2003, the year I began exploring the HIV/AIDS dimension of my fieldwork, there were 11,047 reported cases of HIV/AIDS. In Michigan, Black men made up 53 percent of all cases among men, 49 percent of whom were MSM,[12] and Black women made up 73 percent of all cases among women.

Like many other cities with large Black populations, Detroit is among the places hit hardest by the disease.[13] As the largest city in the state, Detroit has the lion's share of HIV/AIDS cases, but the public health establishment has not been successful in decreasing infection rates in the city. For instance, in 2003, Detroit had 4,540 reported cases of people living with HIV or AIDS.[14] That same year Black people comprised 70 percent of all new HIV diagnoses, with Black men accounting for 51 percent of cases among men and Black women comprising 19 percent of cases among women.[15] It is estimated that Black MSM accounted for the most HIV/AIDS cases among all men in Detroit. Based on HIV/AIDS epidemiological data from Michigan in 2008, Black MSM suffered disproportionately increasing rates of new cases of HIV/AIDS, and Detroit had the highest prevalence of HIV/AIDS in the state.[16] Infection rates, particularly among Black MSM, remained consistently high from at least 2003 to 2008.[17]

To discuss the impact of HIV/AIDS on Ballroom seriously we must examine the processes of exclusion and marginalization that function *within* already marginalized communities. Therefore, this section hinges on two essential questions: whose bodies and well-being are valued and considered worth saving and on what basis is such value determined? My interlocutors describe what I refer to as institutional forms of homophobia/heterosexism, which influence how HIV/AIDS is addressed in the greater society, among Black communities, and within Black LGBT communities. I use *institutional homophobia/heterosexism* to describe both these practices and their underlying logics, which marginalize homosexuality and naturalize and privilege heterosexuality within sociocultural institutions. It is important to note that my interlocutors do not always describe homophobia/heterosexism as something done *to* them, such as a verbal or physical assault or a decision to exclude them from a job or club. Instead, the concept of institutional homophobia/heterosexism, like that of institutional racism as theorized by African American Studies scholars, brings into focus the ways in which Black sociocultural institutions such as home/family, churches, education, and discourses about HIV/AIDS in Black communities are structured and function based on a priori marginalization or exclusion of Black LGBT people. This is the case particularly regarding the HIV/AIDS epidemic. It is within these Black cultural institutions that Ballroom members explain how their lives are disregarded when it comes to addressing the HIV/AIDS epidemic.

A very thin and frail Noir Prestige began one of our many interviews by excusing himself to go to the bathroom, apparently to throw up. "Excuse me, I just started new meds; this shit is horrible, but I shall survive," said Noir in the living room of his small, tidy apartment in the Wayne State University area, which he shared with his boyfriend of eight years. Well into our discussion, Noir reflected on some of the factors that had led to his own seroconversion. He believed that his family's homophobia and his family's prohibition of open discussions about sex made it difficult for him to deal with his homosexuality. When I asked him whether he could even talk about sex, let alone his homosexuality, with his family he said:

> No, not at all, especially not with my grandmother. We [me and my siblings] weren't having sex as far as she was concerned and if you were you ought to repent because it's a sin, especially if I'm not married and we going to deal with it like that. And then eventually you better have sex because you'll be married and there's a beautiful relationship, do what you need to do, procreate. . . . So, my life was about alternative resources, party lines, sneaking out to the clubs, but I could never deal with me wholly. My lifestyle was secret. I knew about and was aware of HIV/AIDS just from being in the lifestyle. But, I was naive about the disease and the possibility of me getting it.

Noir went on to suggest that his family's homophobia and mandatory silence about sexuality prevented him from being able to seek guidance on dating and sex from his family. In his view such guidance could have encouraged him to become better informed about HIV, which might have prevented him from seroconverting.

Not only was Noir a member of the Legendary House of Prestige; he was an HIV/AIDS caseworker at the Horizons Project in Detroit. The Horizons Project is an HIV/AIDS prevention and services organization located on the east side of Detroit. Noir indicated that, from this particular vantage point, for many people, religion—the church—is integral to defining whose lives are valued in Detroit, chiefly determining who gains access to social support, care, and information about HIV/AIDS issues. Homophobia/heterosexism produced, in part, by religious ideology structures access to and the quality of information about HIV/AIDS and sex.

This point was reiterated by Tino Prestige. In the conference room of the Horizons Project on the first floor of a very old, abandoned-looking school building, Tino sat directly across from me and discussed why the HIV/AIDS problem is so severe among Black men.

> The spread of the virus is increasing among Black men because, I believe, [he pauses to find the right word] of a lack of information and sexual responsibility. There's a lack of information in the school system, *no* discussion of sexuality, no discussion of how to be sexually responsible even if you are heterosexual. People have a whole lot of ignorance about LGBT issues, and people still think that it's wrong, and this is attributed to religious views.

Similarly, Noir described how once, when he worked for MOC, as he moved among schools to do presentations for students on HIV/AIDS, school administrators told him to make sure he did not "encourage the homosexuality aspect" of his topic. Here, on the one hand, HIV/AIDS is linked to homosexuality to displace it from heterosexuality. For this reason, Noir reiterated the need to "de-gay" HIV/AIDS in order for people to take the problem seriously. Yet, on the other hand, public discussion of HIV/AIDS, especially among young people, requires a delinking of homosexuality and AIDS to ease the homophobic fear that merely talking about homosexuality will lead young people to "adopt" it. Consequently, homosexuality and the Black homosexual subject are rendered invisible vectors of HIV/AIDS, someone and something that no one may talk about openly but is assumed to be the culprit nonetheless. Overall, attributing the lack of information about the virus to the problematic linkage of homosexuality to HIV/AIDS resonates with the suggestion made by most of my interlocutors that religious views (and the church itself) shape the way in which their families, their peers, and the larger community in Detroit view them as Black LGBT people.

Ultimately, the treatment and policing of sexuality that Black LGBT people endure from both outside and within Black communities create deep-seated internal struggles that influence how Black LGBT people treat others and themselves. Noir added, "All of my friends were secretly gay, and we were all afraid of going to Hell from getting hard [an erection] off of fantasizing about one another. I mean, it was horrible. I was a judgmental monster, and I prayed whenever I had a steamy conversation. I felt condemned." My conversations with both Tino and Noir demonstrate that explicit and implicit homophobia resulting from expectations about heteronormative gender and sexual roles directly influences the information that Black LGBT people get about HIV/AIDS.

In his study of public opinion about HIV/AIDS among African Americans, the political scientist Lester K. Spence found that Black communities' views on HIV/AIDS and its disproportionate impact on Black people are shaped mostly by how the epidemic is framed in the mass media.[18] According to Spence, mass media framing, or what he calls episodic frames, of HIV/AIDS, particularly in the Black press, draws on long-held beliefs about the sexual behavior of Black gender and sexual minorities. And for those without particular perspectives on HIV/AIDS, episodic frames help to create new ones. In both cases, this framing largely influences both the larger society and Black people's association of HIV/AIDS with the sexual behavior of sexual minorities.[19] Spence suggests further that, as a consequence, "episodic frames connect HIV/AIDS (and its spread) directly to MSM, thereby implicating the so-called deviant sexual behavior of Black men in its spread, activating or generating beliefs connecting HIV/AIDS to individuals, generating derision or 'anticare.'"[20]

It is clear that HIV/AIDS, while devastating Black LGBT communities, is having an increasingly perilous ffect on Black communities in general. Yet there is a tendency within certain sectors of Black communities, religious or otherwise, to scapegoat Black LGBT people on moral grounds as a way of demonstrating their ability to sift out and regulate the so-called deviance within our midst or, as the political scientist Cathy J. Cohen argues, to police the boundaries of blackness. These are the boundaries of Black cultural membership. As is the case in other communities throughout the African diaspora, cultural membership in various locales is lodged in heteronormativity. In effect, for Black people in Detroit, HIV/AIDS, which should be a consensus issue, is instead what Cohen calls a crosscutting issue.

According to Cohen, marginalized communities often imagine and promote a front of false consensus in constructing their public images. However, crosscutting issues such as sexuality and HIV/AIDS disrupt this false consensus, peeling back the front and revealing the hierarchies and inequities within the community, thereby exposing the fallacy of a collective community consciousness.[21] Crosscutting issues pose challenges for marginal groups disproportionately, and they directly affect particular segments *within* a marginalized population.[22] Consequently, by linking HIV/AIDS to homosexuality, Black communities are engaging in what Cohen terms secondary marginalization, a phenomenon by virtue of which select, privileged members of Black communities determine the priorities and regulate and police the margins of blackness. This shapes the community's public image while disavowing and disciplining the less privileged members or those who do not conform.[23]

Although Black heterosexuals, or at least those who do not claim gay identities, constitute a sizable number of HIV/AIDS cases, homosexuality continues to be the predominant marker of HIV/AIDS infection. And Black LGBT people make up a considerable portion of the larger African American society and serve primary roles in Black communities across the country. Nevertheless, by and large, community reactions to HIV/AIDS are seriously hampered by community prejudice against or even outright disavowal of Black LGBT people.

Capitalizing on anxieties produced by "crisis discourses" across the globe, racist, patriarchal, and homophobic technologies converge to mark Black LGBT people as the ultimate threat to the "Black nation" and society at large. Therefore, in Black communities, nonnormative sexual subjects are "offered up" in the feigned service of protecting the community from HIV/AIDS, while heteropatriarchal and homophobic renderings of blackness circulate and thrive within and outside Black domains.

Considering how dominant discourses on HIV/AIDS facilely attach the disease to Black bodies on both a global and a local scale, and how in turn Black communities suture the disease to Black homosexuality, one can see what a formidable challenge Black LGBT communities, let alone Ballroom members, face. Noir captures well how the virus is used to denigrate gay people in Black communities: "If you weren't gay you wouldn't get it, that's how Black people here think." Black homophobic discourses install HIV/AIDS as a justification for the exclusion of gender and sexual minorities from Black cultural belonging in both overt and covert ways. And this relates to my interlocutors' struggle against an internalized sense of worthlessness. Thus, as a factor that contributes to marginalization and exclusion, institutional homophobia/heterosexism and other social ramifications of HIV/AIDS can be more debilitating than the disease itself. One of the facilities of the cultural labor of community is to refract these feelings of worthlessness caused by marginalization and exclusion. Therefore, Ballroom communities are compelled to be proactive and multifaceted in their struggle against the epidemic and the stigmatized practices that accompany it.

HIV/AIDS Prevention for Whom?

Institutional homophobia/heterosexism, other forms of discrimination, and the social stigma associated with HIV/AIDS present challenges for prevention and treatment. Ballroom members who are HIV/AIDS prevention workers, some of whom are HIV positive, are very familiar with the epidemic's disproportionate impact on Black MSM. These members occupy a very important social position in the scene, as well as in the HIV prevention community in Detroit. Prevention workers are hampered by the reality that Black people infected with HIV/AIDS in large cities like Detroit do not have access to AIDS prevention and treatment resources that are equal to those available to their White counterparts.[24] This is especially the case for Black people who claim gay or nonnormative gender identities.

In 2004 I visited Mpowerment Detroit (also referred to as Young Brothers United), a Black HIV/AIDS prevention organization that works mostly with young Black MSM. Father Infiniti, a Butch Queen, was the Executive Director and also father of The House of Infiniti in the city at the time. I met with Father Infiniti at the organization's suite located on the fourth floor of a loft apartment building on Beaubien Street in the Greektown district in downtown Detroit. Just before our interview, Father Infiniti was on the phone apparently talking to one of his funders in Lansing, Michigan. Frustrated, he slammed the phone down on the receiver and said, "They want us sick!" Later in the interview, Father Infiniti described a time when many members of the Black gay community in Detroit were coming to his office asking for condoms. He called the Michigan Department of Community Health (MDCH) to request condoms so that he could distribute them since he was situated among those most in need of prevention resources in the community. Yet, for some reason, state officials would not give him the condoms. Father Infiniti's plaint (hence the title of this chapter) signifies a complex matrix of oppression characterized by aggressive targeting of the Ballroom community by public health agencies—CBOs—in their HIV/AIDS prevention efforts against a backdrop of inequitable distribution of HIV/AIDS prevention funds and resources that prioritizes White gay men's health.

At the Horizons Project, while openly HIV-positive, Noir managed 112 cases of people infected with HIV, along with his coworker and house brother, Tino, also HIV-positive. Like MOC, the Horizons Project was one of a very few HIV/AIDS prevention organizations in the city while I was conducting fieldwork.[25] Noir's and Tino's caseloads demonstrate the problem of too much need and not enough resources that is emblematic of HIV/AIDS prevention work in most cities. This is especially the case when treating Black MSM. Given that similar approaches to controlling HIV/AIDS exist throughout the United States and beyond, my experience working with HIV/AIDS prevention programs in Detroit reflects this broader problem with racism, homophobia/heterosexism, misogyny, and class biases dictating the priorities in HIV/AIDS prevention policies. I want therefore to return to my experience working at MOC, as it is an insightful example of how a CBO's organizational culture can be gripped by the same systemic phobias that necessitated its creation in the first place. In 2002 the agency received a $1.25 million grant over five years from the Centers for Disease Control (CDC) to run a program created specifically for the Ballroom community.[26] This grant constituted at least 95 percent of MOC's operating budget.

Before he was fired from MOC by upper management, Father Infiniti created HOUSSE (Helping Others Use Safer Sex Education). This was an innovative program designed to move the approach to HIV/AIDS beyond traditional prevention models and develop strategies from within the Ballroom community. Staff members worked closely with the Ballroom community to create ways to improve social conditions in the Black community by reducing the spread and impact of HIV/AIDS. Since Ballroom members have been disproportionately affected by the epidemic, the program relied heavily on Ballroom leaders' knowledge of and access to other Ballroom members and their performance practices to help disseminate a host of information related to HIV/AIDS and other sexually transmitted diseases and infections. Capitalizing on the kinship structure of Ballroom houses that is central to the overall community, MOC provided funding to selected houses to assist them in putting on their ball events—the culturally productive domain of the Ballroom community. In exchange for the funds (small grants), prominent members of the community are required to disseminate HIV/AIDS prevention messages at the balls and in the day-to-day activities of Ballroom members.

When I learned of this program, I was immediately enthusiastic. During the initial weeks at MOC, I felt as though I was able to contribute directly to the development and implementation of this valuable program. For example, as the staff consultant, I assisted in Noir Prestige's appointment at MOC as the youth program supervisor/outreach worker, and I sat on the Personnel Committee, which hired both Duchess Prestige as the HOUSSE program supervisor and a Black non-gay-identified man who was not a Ballroom member as the prevention coordinator for the entire organization. Together we set up a prevention team on which I worked closely with Noir, Duchess, and the prevention coordinator to refine the organization's HIV/AIDS prevention program. For a few months, the prevention team worked to concretize and refine the program so that it would draw from the values and practices of Ballroom culture and efficiently dispense prevention information and services throughout the community. Despite my work in HIV/AIDS prevention street-level outreach with an organization in Oakland, California, this position at MOC was new for me. While I was learning the ropes, so to speak, I saw this position as an opportunity to play a role in building a bridge between the Ballroom community and MOC to develop socially and culturally relevant HIV/AIDS prevention strategies.

However, soon after our work was under way, I was increasingly struck by the internalized racism, misogyny, and homophobia/heterosexism evident in MOC's daily operations. Let me demonstrate my point by providing a brief synopsis of an incident that occurred at MOC. It is far more complicated than I can fully elaborate here, but it is important in underscoring the limitations inherent in CBO institutional cultures and understanding how they disrupt otherwise productive prevention efforts.

On May 12, 2003, six staff members, including me, submitted a collective grievance letter to MOC management and the Board of Directors.[27] With additional written support from the HIV/AIDS prevention coordinator, this letter was essentially a "vote of no confidence" against the deputy director. The letter alleged serious misconduct on the part of the deputy director/human resources manager. About a week prior to this, the deputy director/human resources manager had distributed, via e-mail, an inappropriate photograph of Duchess to several other staff members at MOC. The picture stemmed from a series of sexually explicit photos that Duchess had taken and placed on a sex website a year or so before he joined the MOC staff. The photograph was sexually suggestive in nature and clearly a private/personal matter, or at the very least one that should not have been circulated among fellow employees without Duchess's permission. Therefore, the staff argued (appropriately, in my mind) that the distribution of the photo was a gross violation of Duchess's privacy and confidentiality and in effect amounted to sexual harassment.[28] The staff also viewed the deputy director's actions as abusive and retaliatory because Duchess is a feminine Butch Queen who had openly disagreed with the deputy director on several occasions. Furthermore, as Noir put it, the e-mail incident was just "icing on the cake." The deputy director's behavior had already resulted in numerous verbal and written complaints against him about, among other things, confrontational public outbursts toward his subordinates at conferences and public disclosures of an employee's HIV/AIDS status and other confidential information from that person's personnel file.[29] I want to emphasize that in his capacity as the deputy director, he was also the human resources manager, which gave him access to confidential information on all employees at MOC. The deputy director's inappropriate behavior apparently knew no bounds.

After the board president and the executive director launched what proved to be an entirely bogus investigation, absolutely no disciplinary actions were taken against the deputy director for his conduct. Conversely, all of the employees who signed the letter were fired, forced to resign immediately, or eventually terminated.[30] The high employee turnover rate was one of many factors that impeded MOC's ability to conduct the prevention work for which it had received funding.[31]

The Board of Directors, CDC, and MDCH were notified and sent all of the documents related to the incident. Oddly, the latter two organizations did not respond at all and the former helped to sabotage staff members' efforts to redress an insidious problem at the organization that ended up destroying it within two years.[32] What I have described is only the tip of an iceberg of core problems that result when an organization purportedly dedicated to combating an affliction that affects underrepresented populations disproportionately adopts the dominant values and practices of the larger society. Duchess, Noir, others, and I were a link between MOC and the Ballroom community, and we suffered discrimination within this HIV/AIDS prevention organization that works with Black LGBT communities. Here was an opportunity for MOC to demonstrate its commitment to the Ballroom community and Black LGBT people at large by adopting a policy of "zero tolerance" for discrimination in HIV/AIDS prevention work.

Sadly, I found in MOC, a Black LGBT organization, a profound lack of knowledge of and appreciation for not only the Ballroom community in Detroit but also the diversity of the Black LGBT community in general. The makeup of the MOC staff reflected a palpable disjuncture between the CBO and the community it was supposed to serve. One example of this is that MOC had no transgender members on its staff, yet transgender men and women constitute a substantial part of the community. Management expressed disdain for transgender men and women in general. The exclusion of transgender women, for example (this is particularly problematic given their disproportionate representation in the HIV/AIDS epidemic), is a pervasive practice in places like Detroit.[33] It is worth pointing out that the MDCH's 2003 report on HIV/AIDS infection rates in the state lists no transgender category. This demonstrates the huge gap between the public health establishment, with its attendant CBOs, and the communities on which it claims to focus its preventive energies.[34]

Of no less importance, the absence of transgender women and men in the organization coincided with an extremely hostile work environment for the feminine Butch Queens and queer and heterosexual Black women on the staff. This prevented what was a progressive and creative staff from working together to devise new ideas and strategies for HIV/AIDS prevention that would supersede the ineffective and outmoded approaches that the MOC management placed before us. Since misogyny, homophobia, and transgenderphobia permeate the organizational culture of CBOs such as MOC, not to mention the racism and elitism in the AIDS control culture in the United States, we should not expect the prevention priorities and approaches of these organizations to be free of such biases.

It is important for Ballroom members doing HIVAIDS prevention work to critique and revise HIV/AIDS discourse and the policies it undergirds. In his book *Acts of Intervention: Performance, Gay Culture, and AIDS*, performance theorist David Román argues that AIDS cannot be separated from the discourses that construct and, in fact, "sustain it."[35] Discourse regarding AIDS informs the specific priorities (defining those whose lives are worth saving) that public health institutions devise regarding prevention. Recalcitrant racism, sexism, homopohobia/hetero-sexism, poverty, and other forms of disenfranchisement are inextricably linked to scurrilous representations of AIDS as a gay disease, let alone a Black gay one. Like international NGOs, CBOs, unwittingly but in some cases deliberately, extract their prevention techniques from hegemonic discourses. As I have demonstrated, MOC became part and parcel of the perpetuation of conservative views on Black gender and sexual relations that ascribe value to heterosexual men, masculine MSM, or all those who adhere to the heteropatriarchal order. Failing to move against these dominant representations and practices occludes the emergence of more radical approaches to HIV/AIDS prevention in Detroit.[36]

Because of their pivotal role in this struggle, Ballroom members who are HIV/AIDS prevention workers in Detroit are in a good position to assert that nonprofit HIV/AIDS prevention efforts are not working and to come up with better strategies. Yet, in order to do this job while confronting other obstacles that impede progress within Black LGBT communities, prevention workers have to overcome systemic exclusion, challenge collective cultural representations and beliefs, and simultaneously try to help community members maintain a sense of value in their lives.[37]

All of my interlocutors stated that stigmatization associated with HIV/AIDS is a primary obstacle to prevention. By and large, discourses on HIV/AIDS *produce* stigma and CBOs *perpetuate* it. The late sociologist Erving Goffman suggests that stigmatization, or "stigma," refers to a deeply discrediting attribute that is ascribed to a person,[38] an identity, groups of people and their practices, and their lives in general. For those who are HIV infected or constructed as being at high risk for infection, stigma taints their lives and, joined with other categories of marginalization such as race, class, gender, and sexuality, undermines their very personhood. Stigma that interacts with other categories determines, in part, whose lives are valuable and thus worth saving. In addition, stigma is also a way in which multiply marginalized people experience themselves.[39] Thus, the stigma associated with HIV impacts the willingness of LBGT members of the Ballroom community to participate in or access prevention activities and services, respectively.

For instance, when I asked Tino whether his organization's efforts are putting a dent in the spread of the disease, he responded, "In terms of the prevention aspect, *no*. I would rather my job [peer advocate for treatment] not to have to exist, and I am very busy. Horizons has prevention aspects, but in general workers are not being effective across the city of

Detroit. To be effective you have to have mobile counseling and testing, but workers are biased." Moreover, along with other Ballroom member prevention workers, Tino states that racism, homophobia, and transgenderphobia guide CBO engagement with Black LGBT populations. And these biases exist at the organization in which they themselves work. As Tino stated:

> Organizations are not looking at the sensitivity issues; they are saying that we have certain objectives that we have to meet and okay, you need to get the numbers at all costs. The Ballroom community people are not coming to organizations like they thought they would. When the prevention tables go to the balls, the people are not flocking to them as the organizations thought they would. Organizations are not concerned about the culture, and Ballroom kids avoid and don't want the stigmatization.

Community members and workers perceive these organizations as being concerned only with meeting the quotas needed to maintain their federal and state funding. Although MOC ignored alternative views expressed by community members and even its own staff members who were a part of the Ballroom community, management made sure that its outreach workers met its quotas. In general, CBOs' efforts in Detroit are viewed as indifferent to and disconnected from the core desires and needs of Black LGBT people.

The administration of HIV/AIDS prevention efforts among youths of color illustrates again how CBOs target populations for quotas but are not interested in the views of those populations. "Everybody be grabbing info from all of these organizations and reports, but no one's talkin' to the youth. Ain't a youth on these boards," said Father Infiniti. As discussed elsewhere in this book, the Ruth Ellis Center (REC) provides outreach and residential services for underserved populations, such as young Black gays and lesbians and transgender men and women. Yet for most of the duration of my fieldwork, the agency was mired in racial scandal, and even after its organizational leadership eventually stabilized, only in recent years has it effectively reconnected with the communities of color that it primarily serves.[40] Generally, as I pointed out regarding transgender men and women, most of the CBOs do not have adequate representation from the communities with which they are working. Consequently, CBOs are always talking *about* members of the Ballroom community but

rarely talking *to* or working *with* them. This is clearly a major impedi-
ment, as Tino attests: "Prevention workers are not being effective 'cuz
prevention workers are biased even before they go into it." As a result,
members of the Ballroom community do not trust CBOs in Detroit; they
do not view their efforts as genuine. This creates and sustains the kind of
ineffective outcomes that CBOs in Detroit experience today.

The training of state and local HIV/AIDS prevention and treatment
workers contributes to, instead of mitigating, the effects of the gender
and sexual biases of workers. Discourses of HIV/AIDS and prevention
strategies are based on a gender and sexual hierarchy that marks Black
homosexuals as perpetually diseased subjects who must be separated
from "regular" people. As Duchess adamantly argued while he sat on
a couch in his small one-bedroom apartment in a "rough" northwest-
side neighborhood in Detroit, HIV/AIDS is represented in the training
discourse as a Black gay disease. Duchess's characterization of his training illustrates that the HIV/AIDS prevention information around which
outreach certification training in Michigan is configured is inherently
biased against Black LGBT people. According to Duchess:

> The people that are conducting the training don't really have a clue
> how to help gay folks. They make sweeping generalizations about
> the "activities" of Black MSM. I used to get really upset in train-
> ings when the trainer knew less about how to reach the people
> than I did. Of course they focused on the Black gay young men,
> roughly from about [age] fourteen to twenty-seven. And at first
> the emphasis was placed on not getting it. Then the focus shifted
> to not passing it. The disconnect came in the typecasting of gay
> people. I can't tell you how many conferences or trainings I have
> gone to and the so-called experts tell you what type of gay per-
> son does what. Does that make sense? Like, for instance, the City
> of Detroit certifies all HIV testers and counselors. In the training
> they discuss behavior as it relates to gender identification. "Any
> gay man that. . . . A man is gay if he . . ." they would say. The people
> in the room that represented gayness in all its different forms were
> a reflection that the truth is contrary to that. It didn't add up to
> most of the people that would be there. They would think that
> all gay people are extremely promiscuous and the only thing they
> think about is sex. As an outreach worker it was my job to sort out

the differences and apply what I did take from it to help the folks I saw day in and day out.

Duchess's statements are very important to my argument about the limitations and disconnectedness of conventional HIV/AIDS prevention efforts and the discourses from which they are drawn. According to sexuality and AIDS scholar Cindy Patton's *Fatal Advice: How Safe-Sex Education Went Wrong*, public health has based its prevention efforts on discourses of risk that mark off particular communities for a type of cultural quarantine while excluding others, as opposed to comprehensively educating the entire population.[41] Like other disease prevention regimes, especially those devoted to socially communicable diseases, AIDS education is ostensibly designed to inform members of the larger population so that they can modify their behaviors to reduce risks.[42] However, in the actual practices of many public health organizations, the aim is to identify high-risk communities and change their behaviors so that the rest of the public will be safe from "them"—or at least create the perception of safety.[43] Meanwhile, the safety of the members of the marked communities is of little concern; instead, what takes priority is the need to contain the communities, disavow them, and discipline their behaviors. As Patton further states:

> Supposedly apolitical health education strategies became the means for dividing educational subjects into those who would be formed into citizens [and therefore protected] through a national pedagogy and those who would be policed or, if they were lucky, ignored as they developed their own dissident safe-sex strategies.[44]

Therefore, as Noir emphasized firmly, "HIV kills. Why? Stigma. The people living *with it* have to make others comfortable living around it; that's a lot of work. And folks die trying to accomplish that because you end up living in secret. Support is key and very essential in living with the illness or around it." Noir demonstrates how a vicious cycle of stigmatization undermines any prevention program.

The few organizations that focus on the Black LGBT community in Detroit have enacted prevention programs buttressed by convergent racialized, classed, gendered, and sexualized discourses of risk. But it is the isolating of certain Black groups within the Black community on one level, and the characterization of Black people as a high-risk population on the other, that keeps Ballroom members from utilizing the prevention and treatment resources offered by these organizations. Simply put, Ballroom members are already stigmatized, and the prevention efforts themselves are stigmatized, so the utilization of the services stigmatizes them even more.[45] Tino Prestige underscores this when he says, "The Community Health Awareness Group has a mobile testing unit. But when the unit shows up to a ball, people won't be willing to go to it 'cuz people will think something is wrong with them, so they don't want to be seen that way."

In Michigan, at least in 2003, the scant available HIV/AIDS reduction strategies consist of distributing brochures, condoms, and other safe-sex materials, discussion groups, and safe-sex training,[46] but they ignore the crucial role that cultural values play in shaping the stigmatization associated with race, class, gender, sexuality, and AIDS. Directly related to this issue, few CBOs create programs that move beyond simply reducing individual "risk behaviors" by addressing the social conditions that contribute to them.

Duchess worked toward institutionalizing Ballroom so that it could address national issues confronting the community such as HIV/AIDS, drug abuse, and unemployment. He wanted to "develop a funding source where special populations can apply to create quality programs that provide services, and help them as they are, without prejudice and bias." Duchess endeavored to intervene in the spread of the virus within Ballroom by altering the terms on which prevention has been traditionally based.

Unfortunately, however, staff and Ballroom members like Duchess had an agenda that proved inconsistent with the prevailing aims of the MOC administration. When MOC fired Duchess, he was effectively pushed out of both the Ballroom scene (which I will discuss) and HIV/AIDS prevention altogether. And based on reactions from the Ballroom community, MOC's actions aggravated an already troubled relationship between the Ballroom community and HIV/AIDS prevention organizations at the federal, state, and local levels. Clearly, there was a relationship between the institutional culture at MOC, where its management had internalized dominant notions of HIV/AIDS that denigrate Black LGBT people, and the employees' choice to challenge both in order to develop and implement truly effective HIV/AIDS models. In the summer of 2005, MOC closed amid a scandal regarding misappropriation of funds.[47]

The central question here is: what is the connection between one's struggle to find meaning in life, a struggle exacerbated by expulsion from the social institutions from which meaning and value are often derived, and one's added vulnerability to HIV/AIDS? The rapid spread of HIV/AIDS within dispossessed communities is due in large part to the terms of dispossession. Therefore, it is important to examine what counts as health and well-being regarding Black LGBT people within the Ballroom community and larger Black society. Even when Ballroom members work for CBOs, their understanding of the needs of the community of which they are a part does not shape the interests and prevention approaches endorsed by those in charge. It is difficult to avoid concluding that this happens because CBOs' agendas do not always reflect a genuine belief that Ballroom members' lives are indeed worth saving.

Ballroom Kinship and Performance as HIV/AIDS Intravention

I have gone to great lengths to delineate the nature and terms of Black LGBT people's intersectional marginalization. For many, HIV/AIDS is a direct result of these conditions. The social conditions of HIV/AIDS weigh heavily on the self-worth of individual members and the community. As Noir believed, HIV kills because of the stigmatization associated with it. I have, then, painted a rather gloomy picture, albeit a real one, to show the gravity of the problems Ballroom members face in confronting HIV/AIDS. But what do Black LGBT members *do* about such conditions? How does Ballroom culture provide a space within which to forge alternative realities for its members as a creative response to the HIV/AIDS epidemic?

Part of what is at stake in the Ballroom community is a struggle for alternative community representation and community preservation.[48] Ballroom members pursue the aforementioned by creating an epistemology that undergirds the social support that Ballroom's kinship structure provides and by creating "prevention houses," which collaborate with CBOs to produce prevention balls. These practices are critical aspects of the overall work of forging an alternative social sphere. I draw from several Ballroom practices deployed to address HIV/AIDS, some of which reflect its members' desire for recuperative forms of self- and collective representations.[49] I contend that Ballroom's practices and potentialities unveil the difference between governmental forms of *intervention* and on-the-ground cultural forms of *intravention*.

I have written elsewhere that predominant HIV/AIDS prevention models rely on the notion of intervention. Within public health, intervention approaches are designed programmatically to facilitate individual behavioral change to reduce incidents and the prevalence of HIV infection among targeted populations that have been cast as "high risk."[50] Interventions are evidence based and have to be legitimized and authorized by public health institutions such as the CDC to receive funding.[51] These approaches tend to impose prevention strategies, knowledge, and values onto communities while assuming that populations claim little to no agency in their own daily health and well-being. But according to Francisco Roque, director of community health at Gay Men's Health Crisis (GMHC), "We are not going to be able to DEBI or test our way out of this epidemic. A great deal of the problem of HIV infection is at the community level."[52] In other words, prevention efforts are more effective if derived from within communities as opposed to being imposed by public health, such strategies are often inappropriate for the communities they are intended to benefit. Conversely, the concept of intravention captures what so-called communities of risk already do, based on their own knowledge and ingenuity, to contest, reduce, and survive the impact of HIV/AIDS on their own terms. Practices of intravention are forged by and emerge from within everyday poor and working-class communities like Ballroom.[53]

All of my interlocutors who were HIV prevention workers agree that doing HIV/AIDS prevention work within the Ballroom scene is difficult; however, some believe that it offers possibilities that otherwise are perceived not to exist. One such possibility is the notion of self-renewal. I reiterate a point Diva D made earlier that being in the Ballroom scene is akin to living a "fictitious existence." This fictitious existence is a sphere and an occasion for one to remake the self within Ballroom to contend with the negative representations of Black LGBT and the stigmatization of HIV/AIDS in the outside world.

In Ballroom communities, image is very important, even if that image is, in many ways, fleeting. It is important for one to be seen in a preferential light, and members take great pains to achieve this. In one sense, the importance placed on image and status in Ballroom make HIV/AIDS prevention work difficult because members distance themselves from anything related to HIV/AIDS for fear that it will tarnish them. Yet, in another sense, within Ballroom one's image and status are mutable and can be highly influential within the scene. As I discussed earlier in this book, many aspects of Ballroom terminology represent this point. Icons, Legends, Statements, and Stars signify the opportunity for individual members to attain community recognition and status that can alter a person's sense of self.[54] Thus, value, at least on a superficial level, is reconstituted in the Ballroom world, and this means a great deal to someone who consistently feels unimportant in the outside world.

Medical anthropologist Vinh-Kim Nguyen's study of the *milieu*, a homosocial underground scene of Ivorian men in Abidjan, Côte d'Ivoire, reveals a culture that bears striking similarities to Ballroom. According to Nguyen, members of the milieu create a social epistemology or social knowledge as a way of refashioning themselves and reshaping the cultural landscape of same-sex relations in the midst of the new reality of HIV/AIDS in an emerging African metropolis.[55] This social knowledge informs the relations and tactics used to navigate complex conditions for individual and collective benefit.[56] It is usually produced and contained within dispossessed communities and subaltern spaces and enables its members to comment on their conditions, as well as to develop strategies to alter them. Likewise, Ballroom members reconstitute themselves by creating social knowledge in the midst of the HIV/AIDS crisis in order to change its social consequences. Therefore, Ballroom social knowledge enables effective HIV/AIDS prevention that is based on the values and norms established by its community members as opposed to those established outside of it, which do not necessarily serve the best interests of the members.

In chapter 4, I described how the pleasure members get from competing is integral to Ballroom culture. Here I return to the idea of competition to emphasize its function as a form of Ballroom community social knowledge. Again, competition is a hallmark of Ballroom culture and is another means through which image and status are formed and repaired. Since individual members and houses can gain recognition and status mainly by "snatching a trophy," competition is an integral aspect of the social world of Ballroom that offers possibilities for effective HIV/AIDS prevention. Father Infiniti confirmed this when he said, "In terms of the Ballroom community in Detroit, if it ain't got nothing to do with a trophy, these girls don't care." And when I asked Pootaman, a young Butch Queen member of The House of Ninja in Detroit who was an HIV/AIDS prevention worker at MOC, why he became interested in walking balls, he said, "I enjoy the competition, the feeling of sitting someone down to prove a point, that I could take home a trophy." Father Infiniti and Pootaman speak to the centrality of the trophy, the accoutrements that come along with it, and how both represent the attainment of value and affirmation that Ballroom members are usually otherwise denied in the outside world.

Prevention Houses

The social knowledge of Ballroom culture links the balls to the community-fashioned kinship system that both sustains the community and facilitates HIV/AIDS prevention. This linkage constitutes what Ballroom refers to as *prevention houses*. A prevention house may have either a formal or an informal relationship with a CBO. Besides organizing prevention balls, a core mission of a prevention house is to develop and implement strategies for preventing HIV/AIDS and other sexually transmitted diseases and infections by fostering open and informed discussions about sex and advocating "safe-sex" practices. While I competed in prevention balls as a member of The Legendary House of Prestige, whose Detroit chapter was a prevention house, I found some of the strategies deployed to be somewhat banal and sex negative. The idea of prevention houses and balls is fascinating, but now, in retrospect, I advocate that houses and balls move away from safe sex to a notion of *risk reduction*. Risk reduction constitutes a more elaborate set of strategies that emphasize reducing risk for HIV as opposed to eliminating risk altogether.[57] Risk reduction is more realistic because members of houses are indeed having sex. Houses, particularly house parents, are in a pivotal position to encourage and provide information to help their members understand that having a satisfying sex life and a healthy one are not mutually exclusive; both should be advocated and pursued. Thus, housework, in this case, takes on a crucial HIV/AIDS prevention dimension that is not necessarily undertaken in other houses and chapters. And for those already infected with HIV, the prevention house is a safe and supportive space, providing the social, and at times material, support and care that they often do not get from their families of origin or elsewhere in the larger Black LGBT community.

Because of his unique vantage point as both a prominent member of the Ballroom scene and a supervisor of the Ballroom program at MOC, Duchess wanted to establish an autonomous Ballroom community that could utilize the features of the culture to fight HIV/AIDS on its terms. For instance, he formed the Detroit chapter of the House of Prestige as an HIV/AIDS prevention house. Many of the members in the Detroit chapter were HIV/AIDS prevention workers. "Folks in the community know that I work here [at MOC] and often call me at home or see me in the streets and ask if I have condoms on me," said Duchess. For a while, Duchess used his position as a housemother, his status in the community, and his position on the MOC staff to advance an HIV/AIDS prevention agenda. As he articulated it, Ballroom is built on social relations that redefine prevention work: "The structure of the [Ballroom] community already allows for familial prevention work, you know, just in the fact that someone can say to you, 'now you know you need to wear a condom' and it be from someone that you have built that trust factor with. People in the community do prevention work all of the time." Housemothers and housefathers in particular provide daily parental guidance for Ballroom kids regarding intimate/romantic relationships, sex, gender and sexual identities, health, hormonal therapy, and body presentation, among other issues. Yet, in prevention houses, HIV/AIDS prevention is another crucial role house parents assume as leaders of houses. I refer to this as *prevention parenting.* Noir Prestige explained how prevention parenting works in houses: "Even in the traditional sense, if I'm supposed to be the matriarch or the patriarch of the family, the head, if I see one of my kids is just out there being a whore, then it's my duty to go, 'are you protecting yourself?'" Yet, because housework in the domestic aspect of the house—nurturing and caring for the members—is typically undertaken by housemothers, HIV/AIDS prevention parenting is mostly a housemother endeavor. Prevention parenting is especially important for Femme Queens who are taking hormones. Because members of the Ballroom community have limited or no access to safe hormone injections, some Femme Queen mothers ensure that their kids use clean needles, and they draw from the experience or knowledge they have gained to guide their children through their hormone therapy. In many cases, Femme Queen housemothers can keep their kids from getting hormone shots through shady and unsafe sources on the street. Within Ballroom houses, members consult with their parents and house siblings on issues that, either by choice or by necessity, they do not discuss with their biological kin. This becomes very important for those facing HIV/AIDS issues either directly or indirectly.

For Ballroom members who are HIV positive, prevention parenting is critical, particularly for those who are not open about their status. Even more so, however, for those already infected, HIV/AIDS involves deep emotional trauma. After diagnosis, coming to terms with one's infection status is an initial hurdle that has to be faced. Overcoming the fear, the self-loathing, the despair, and the onslaught of other feelings reflects the challenge of acknowledging the multidimensionality of the epidemic's impact on people's lives. By all medical accounts, social and emotional trauma is directly and indirectly linked to physical health. For instance, recent studies show increasing rates of post-traumatic stress disorder (PTSD) among MSM who are HIV infected.[58] It is worth pointing out, however, that mental health services have proven inaccessible for poor and working-class Black LGBT people. In general mental health services have not been effectively integrated into HIV prevention and treatment services. Thus, if not treated properly, the stress brought on by the disease can seriously diminish an infected person by compromising the immune system's ability to fight off opportunistic infections that encroach upon the body. Given the already stress-ridden lives that many HIV/AIDS-infected people lead largely due to their circumstances, socially, politically, and economically vulnerable communities need to support such people in order to help them confront these challenges. Noir explained how his first housemother, a Woman, supported him when he tested positive for HIV: "My old housemother was very supportive of my situation. When I got sick she called me and said, 'What's going on, you okay?' Her and another house member would always stop by and bring me soup or whatever, just some kind of token." This is a testament to the power of Ballroom's labor of care, resonating within its social world, to prevent the trauma of HIV from taking its toll on the infected person.

I argue throughout this book that Ballroom culture forces a reexamination and expansion of the meaning of labor. Here I suggest as well that this community's practices necessitate a rethinking of what African American Studies scholar Cornel West refers to as "nonmarket values." For West, nonmarket values are love, care, and service.[59] I have drawn from West's notion to describe care, service, competition, and critique as nonmarket values in the Ballroom community. Nonmarket values do not exceed the market, but they should not be reduced to the market either. Not only do these values constitute a labor of care—housework—that becomes intensified when the community decides to deal with HIV/AIDS collectively, but they exist in the quotidian aspect of Ballroom life. To illustrate this, I want to return to the sibling relationship between Noir and Tino Prestige. Among the many aspects of their relationship, I want to highlight those that relate directly to HIV/AIDS. Both Tino and Noir were infected with HIV in their teens. They were both in long-term relationships (eight years) with partners who were not infected, partners who also struggled with the difficulties of loving someone who is HIV-positive or living with AIDS. Because Noir did not drive, Tino would drive him to his doctor appointments when Noir's partner was unable to do so. They were both treatment advocates at the Horizons Project. Most important, they provided overall treatment for each other. Clearly, Noir and Tino helped each other weather the psychic trauma that comes with HIV/AIDS infection in ways that not even their partners could offer.

Like all communities, however, the Ballroom house, even one dedicated to prevention, is a site of conflict, where members disagree on a multitude of issues—HIV/AIDS prevention is only one example. Soon after he presided over a very successful anniversary ball, things began to take a turn for the worse for Duchess. His vision and often capricious approach to things created friction within his own house, as well as within MOC. Accordingly, after the Domination Anniversary Ball, Father Alvernian removed Duchess as the mother of the Detroit chapter. When I interviewed Father Alvernian about the issue, he said that Duchess had been overstepping his bounds and not moving the house in the right direction. Conversely, Duchess said that Father Alvernian was concerned only with being "fierce" in the Ballroom scene. There were times when other concerns took precedence. According to Duchess, some members of the house were obsessed with boosting and maintaining their reputations within the Ballroom scene at the expense of developing and implementing effective HIV/AIDS prevention strategies. Unfortunately, being fierce in the scene and focusing on HIV/AIDS prevention were apparently viewed as mutually exclusive aims. Both Duchess and Alvernian said that there was no "shade" between them; they simply disagreed about the role of The Legendary House of Prestige in the fight against HIV/AIDS. In this particular case, neither the MOC leadership nor the national leadership of The Legendary House of Prestige demonstrated a genuinely sustained commitment to reducing the spread of HIV/AIDS in the Ballroom community.

Nonetheless, the features of the Ballroom community labor that I have delineated here are taken for granted by CBOs and go unaccounted for in HIV/AIDS reports. In many cases, members express love for one another and serve each other when needed, ultimately adding overall value to each other's lives, especially when facing desperate situations. These nonmarket values are an essential defense against the epidemic's perilous consequences.

Prevention Balls

Some Ballroom HIV/AIDS prevention houses have joined forces with CBOs to create *prevention balls*. For example, one of the most famous prevention houses is GMHC's The House of Latex in New York City. For almost twenty years, GMHC has organized The House of Latex Ball, one of the most popular HIV/AIDS prevention balls in the country, drawing between 2,500 and 3,000 audience members and participants. Prevention balls are designed to educate Ballroom members about healthy sexual practices and awareness, through the competitive performances at the balls.[60]

It is worth reiterating here that the Ballroom community is a place in which Black LGBT youth, especially, look for guidance, nurturing, care, and support. Given the already mentioned absence of youth voices on CBO staffs and boards, the Ballroom community's embrace of Black LGBT youth is essential to HIV/AIDS prevention work. According to Ballroom members and HIV/AIDS prevention workers, the members are getting younger and younger. These "kids," literally, are more prone to high-risk sexual behavior. As Tino suggests, "A lot of people who are involved in the community are dealing with being put out of the home 'cause of their parents, and maybe they are out at an early age and they get involved with sex and substance abuse at an early age." Consequently, for young Black LGBT people, Ballroom becomes a space that counters the social conditions that produce these risk factors. As Tino observes:

> The main reason why I got involved in Ballroom was to deal with my own biases and misinformation by observing. But also to connect with people who were infected that others in the scene didn't

Fig. 19. A Butch Queen competes in an American Runway HIV prevention category at The House of Latex Ball in New York City in 2007.
(Photograph by Frank Leon Roberts.)

know. I was able to connect with people at the balls. During a
Ninja ball, I ran into a guy who was HIV-positive who had missed
his appointment. I encouraged him to come to his appointment
to follow up on his health. He came but still has problems with
adherence with his appointments. He is eighteen years old and
probably hasn't come to grips with it and is afraid.

Since balls have major drawing power, they offer a space in which to
engage younger members in unique ways. People such as Tino's client
will not go to a place like MOC to access treatment resources, nor is he
able to discuss his status with his biological family. But the young HIV-
positive man participates in balls, and he may or may not be a member
of a house. Ballroom prevention workers such as Tino encourage their
clients to take better care of their overall health and to remember to take
their medications. Especially for Black LGBT youth in Detroit, depressed

social conditions contribute to people's engagement in high-risk sexual practices. Tino's movement between the Ballroom scene and HIV/AIDS prevention is evidence of his understanding of the magnitude of the problem of HIV/AIDS infection rates among Black LGBT youth. These issues should be considered in any prevention program.

Another example of the important role that prevention balls play is related to one in which I participated in March of 2005.

By now I've become accustomed to the whole process that is a ball, but this is a special one, a ball devoted to HIV/AIDS education and prevention. It is an annual affair, the Love Is the Message Ball, in Los Angeles, where I've been participating in the scene as a member of the Los Angeles chapter of The Legendary House of Prestige. This annual ball is cosponsored by The House of Rodeo and the Minority AIDS Project in Los Angeles. I will be walking with Pokka, the father of the chapter, in the Schoolboy Realness versus Executive Realness category for the mini-grand prize. The description of the category on the flyer reads:

> School Boy Realness—Let's see if U were paying attention in Sex Ed. Bring us School Boy realness w/a safe sex production. Props a must and you will be graded on your project and knowledge
>
> vs.
>
> Executive—U have been promoted to CEO of a condom company of your choice. U must have a prop and be prepared to sell your product to the board.

Pokka has planned our performance and is determined to win the trophy and the hundred-dollar cash prize. Since Pokka and I walk Executive Realness, I am dressed for the part, and I will be playing the role of a CEO with Pokka playing that of the president of the Board of Directors for the Lifetime Condoms Corporation. He has spent time and money preparing everything we need to mount this miniproduction.

When Kodak Kandinsky, the commentator for the evening, announces our category, members from various houses come out as Schoolboy Realness, all wearing clothes sporting several condoms, which they have attached in one way or another. Because I am in the waiting area of the hall, I cannot see them perform their miniproduction. But now it is our turn, and Pokka walks out ahead of me, dressed in an all-black suit and carrying his laptop computer case. He approaches the judges' table and reads a statement about the crisis of HIV/AIDS in the Black community, stressing that condom use is an effective strategy in the fight against the spread of the disease. "Now, I bring to you Professah Prestige, our new CEO, to make a brief statement," announces Pokka. I come strutting down the runway in a navy blue suit carrying my laptop computer in a black leather computer bag in one hand and a large black portfolio case full of billboards in the other. When I reach the judges' table, I take the microphone and declare, "My name is Professah Prestige, the new CEO of Lifetime Condoms. We have new durable condoms that do not reduce sensation. I hope you all will give them a try. Be safe and use condoms!" After my statement, the commentator asks the judges to score me. "Are they real? Do you see it? Judges, score him [all of the judges flash cards with "10" written on them]. Okay, tens across the board. Prestiges, step to the side. Next contestants please," says Kodak. "Thank God, I did not get chopped," I think to myself.

After other competitors are chopped, only five competitors remain: Pokka and me from The Legendary House of Prestige and three members from another house (who walked Schoolboy Realness). Then someone from the Minority AIDS Project poses the following question to all of us: "What is a dental dam?" Each of us is instructed to whisper the answer in Kodak's ear. When he comes to me, I explain that a dental dam is used for oral sex, providing a barrier of protection between the mouth and the anus or the vagina. After everyone has taken a turn whispering into Kodak's ear, he announces that only two of us gave the correct answer, a Schoolboy Realness kid from the other house and me. Apparently, Pokka has given him the wrong answer. I feel rather sorry because Pokka has done most of the preparation for our production.

Finally, the time has come for the judges to choose who looks more real between the Schoolboy Realness kid and me, the executive. "Who is realer?" asks Kodak. When Kodak comes to the final two of the seven judges, one of them points at me and says, "He look like a real executive." I can't believe it. I've won the category! I am shocked and thrilled at the same time. They present a trophy and the hundred-dollar prize to me. I resolve to take the trophy as a keepsake, but later I give the money to the housemother to put into our house fund. I have won the category for The Legendary House of Prestige. Most important, within the competitive spirit at the balls, members of the Ballroom community have been exposed to knowledge about safe-sex practices without singling out or stigmatizing individuals.

Fig. 20. Professah Prestige from the Los Angeles chapter of The Legendary House of Prestige poses before walking and snatching a trophy in the Executive Realness category at the Love Is the Message Ball in 2005. (Photograph by Marlon M. Bailey.)

My experience with prevention balls and Ballroom culture more generally demonstrates how Ballroom performance, kinship, and the social
knowledges that are produced through these cultural practices can constitute a radical intravention in the HIV/AIDS crisis derived from within
the community itself.

Clearly, there are deep-seated conflicts regarding the reduction of
HIV/AIDS infection within the Ballroom community; its members are
not unified in their approaches to it. But not only does Duchess's experience demonstrate the multiple contestations about HIV/AIDS prevention that exist within the Ballroom scene, but his story also reveals that
even though some CBOs have come into being "from the ground up," too
many serve as the conductors of race, class, gender, and sexual oppression "from the top down." It is the Ballroom member who is also an HIV/
AIDS prevention worker who is often situated at the intersection of these
contested domains. Over the long haul, Ballroom members perform the
labor of caring for and the valuing of lives that is integral to building and
sustaining a community in the midst of crisis.

"We Don't Die Like This Anymore"

In February 2005 I conducted a final round of interviews in Detroit at
the Mpowerment Detroit agency. During this visit, I went to see Noir
Prestige at the house in which he grew up, on the northwest side of Detroit. Noir had become seriously ill and was bedridden as he continued
to battle for his life against an emboldened HIV, which was taking over
his body. I called Noir often to check on his health. Living in California,
I felt distant and unable to care for him in the ways in which I wanted
because I lived so far away. I knew this would be a difficult moment, but I
never hesitated because of my love for a dear friend and my understanding of the commitment to one another that house membership entails.

I arrive at the duplex on Monté Vista Street, not too far from where I
grew up on Littlefield Street and directly across from the home of a very
close friend I have known since childhood. Incidentally, this friend had
introduced me to Noir twelve years previously. As I approach the entry
to the duplex I am instructed to go upstairs to the back room where Noir
is lying in bed. I am stunned when I first see him. He is so emaciated that

I hardly recognize him. He has been in the hospital for several weeks trying to overcome the opportunistic infections he caught as a result of having a compromised immune system. In addition, the medication he is taking causes him to hallucinate. As I look at Noir and try to remember him as he looked when I saw him several months prior, a part of me realizes that the virus is taking him while another part remains hopeful that he will recover. For Noir is a fighter. He has been in and out of the hospital several times before, near death on a few occasions, and he has always pulled through. As he is lying in the bed, he is surprisingly alert and humorous. Even though the disease has taken a toll on his body, he still has high spirits and he is optimistic about his prognosis. Noir says his doctor told him that once his T cell count increases, he can start a new regimen of medication. Nonetheless, during our visit I keep asking myself, "How did this happen?" When I leave Noir later that day, I refuse to accept the possibility that he is going to die.

Less than two months later, on April 17, 2005, Noir's partner of now nine years called and told me that Noir had been diagnosed with a terminal brain infection. He said Noir was deteriorating rapidly and that he did not know how long he would live. Noir's mother called me the next day and requested that I come to Detroit to see him before he passed away. I called my former partner, who was also Noir's friend, and asked if he would accompany me to see Noir because I felt that I would be unable to bear seeing him in such a state alone. I also thought it would be good for him to see as many of the people who loved him as possible.

The following week I fly to Chicago, where I meet my former partner, and we drive to Detroit in the afternoon of the following day to see Noir. When we arrive, we go upstairs to the second floor of the duplex and see Noir lying on a couch in the living room. Noir is totally incapacitated. The disease has destroyed his body to the extent that he can no longer look after himself. It is very difficult to see him in such a state; however, I am relieved and happy that I have an opportunity to be with him, to see and touch him, while he is still alive. Eventually, Noir has to be carried to his bed in the room in the back of the apartment where he falls asleep soon after. As I look at him I become increasingly frustrated and sad because I cannot understand why someone so young, someone who offers so much to the world, has to suffer so much.

Approximately two weeks later, after seeing and touching him and hearing his voice one last time, my dear friend Noir Prestige slipped into a coma and then died of complications resulting from AIDS. I was told that the hospice nurse who cared for Noir during his last days said to his partner, "We don't die like this anymore." This was a sobering but astute observation. Noir had died as several of my loved ones had died from complications of AIDS back in the late 1980s and early 1990s. Indeed, during those earlier days of the epidemic in Detroit, before the introduction of antiretroviral medication and other forms of coordinated care/treatment, the state in which I saw Noir is the way "we" used to die. But why, in 2005, did he die "like this"?

I reflect on Noir Prestige's battle with HIV/AIDS and his eventual death because it captures the challenges that members of the Ballroom community, the Black LGBT community, and the larger Black society face in the struggle against this disease and the social conditions associated with it. Given that many people lead long and healthy lives with HIV, the social conditions in which Noir lived clearly played a more critical role in his social and physical death than has been realized or acknowledged in discourses about this epidemic. As I argue throughout this book, the consequences of social exclusion from and marginalization within family and community, compounded by HIV infection or the risk thereof, contribute to the social, emotional, and spiritual destruction experienced by many Black LGBT people. It is the stigma, joined with the deleterious social conditions under which many of my interlocutors live, that prove to be far more destructive than the virus itself.

In "The Ethic of Care for the Self as a Practice of Freedom," the late French philosopher Michel Foucault elaborates on what he refers to as the "ethics of the care for self." He argues that freedom is an ethical practice, one that requires care for the self in order to know the self and improve it. This work toward knowledge and improvement of the self fosters more complex relationships with others even as it requires a more appropriate treatment of others. Most important, Foucault suggests that care of the self is inextricable from the ethical and deliberate pursuit of liberty, in terms of the individual, as well as the community.[61] Foucault's theory enables a deeper understanding of the challenges that intersectional marginalization presents for Black LGBT people and the role that cultural labor can play in enacting care for the self in the midst of the HIV/AIDS crisis.

Noir was confronted with several obstacles that perhaps prevented him from caring for himself so that he could stay alive to care for others. First, because Noir grew up in a dysfunctional family and was raised by a grandmother who was very religious and homophobic, he was policed and punished for his gay sexuality at an early age. His mother was addicted to crack cocaine, and his father abandoned him when he was very young. As Noir explained in chapter 3, his grandmother repudiated him for being gay and made him go to church in order to force him to be straight; he had to accept the Black familial ultimatum. Noir pursued intimate/romantic relationships with women but soon realized that he was not attracted to them. As is the case for many Black LGBT people in Detroit, at an early stage in his life, religious ideology made Noir regret his sexuality and in effect caused him to devalue this aspect of himself. As Foucault observes, it is a paradox of Christianity that, while the belief in salvation is fundamental to Christian theology, salvation is obtained through a renunciation of the self.[62] Hence, the homophobia/heterosexism that is deeply embedded in notions of blackness to which many people are forced to subscribe is often instantiated through religious ideology. As a result, Black LGBT people such as Noir expend substantial effort battling the residues of self-hatred. Internal self-hatred impedes one's ability to resist external forms of oppression.

Second, after Noir was diagnosed with HIV, he focused his efforts on HIV/AIDS prevention in the Black community. Having come out as a gay man a few years prior, which is no small feat in Detroit, he had to face his own HIV infection soon after. And for a person living with HIV, Noir did not have a stable support system, one that could help him focus on his emotional and physical health in order to keep his immune system strong enough to contain the HIV virus. He joined the Ballroom scene and began tireless work in HIV/AIDS prevention almost simultaneously. He worked for MOC as the coordinator of its youth HIV/AIDS prevention program, and subsequently he joined the Horizons Project as a treatment advocate, managing an inordinate number of treatment cases.

However, while Noir engaged in all of these prevention activities, his own health was deteriorating rapidly. His partner and I encouraged him to take his medications consistently, change his diet, reduce his stress, get proper rest, and take better care of himself in general. Unfortunately, as it turned out, Noir was unable to perform the same labor of care and love for himself that he performed for others. And, although Noir was very popular and always surrounded by people, as some of my interlocutors have said, living with HIV can be a very lonely experience. On the one hand, Noir was an HIV/AIDS prevention worker and activist who worked tirelessly to inform young people and others about HIV. But, on the other hand, Noir struggled with his own HIV/AIDS status and was unable to focus on his own health and well-being so as to continue to do the work of outreach.

The cultural labor that members of the Ballroom community perform makes it possible for its members to alter the discursive rendering of Black LGBT people as worthless. This counterpublic can help members of the Ballroom community develop a better relationship with themselves and others. Accordingly, such a counterpublic should be the foundation of Black belonging and, in turn, form the basis of HIV/AIDS prevention. Yet we have somehow shifted away from love, family (whatever that means for us), and community as a primary tool of social intervention. The prevention cause has been reduced to rhetoric with very little real effort behind it. Home, family, community, and HIV/AIDS prevention in Black communities must extend beyond the rhetoric. The former must be more than the racial/cultural claims of linked fate and unity that cast out those people who do not fit into or choose not to subscribe to gender and sexual normativity. The latter must extend beyond advocating condom use, promoting safe sex, and rebuking those who do not practice it. For Ballroom members, life choices and practices, including sexual ones, are negotiated and forged out of the complicated social, economic, political, spiritual, and psychic dimensions and circumstances of their lives. What Ballroom culture illustrates is that the labor through which home, family, community, and HIV/AIDS prevention are constituted has to be constantly enacted in order for these notions and entities to be truly realized.

I emphasize HIV/AIDS and its disproportionate impact on the Ballroom community in part to better understand the psychological consequences of social marginalization and exclusion. Noir Prestige's demise reflects what continues to happen to other Black LGBT members of the Ballroom community in Detroit as it relates to HIV/AIDS in particular and to their intersectional marginalization in general. I am also interested in how such factors contribute to rendering Black LGBT people vulnerable to epidemics like HIV/AIDS and therefore hampering their ability to enact cultural work to effect social change. Chiefly, this issue is not solely about forging an alternative community; it is also about saving lives.

Clearly, the Ballroom community falls short, at times, of actually sustaining the lives of many of its members. I suggest that what Ballroom culture offers is just the beginning of a cultural practice of survival that is desperately needed. Therefore, it is incumbent on those of us who study Black people, and those of us who are interested in the lives of the most marginalized people in our midst, to examine, at a much deeper level, the psychosocial impact of social exclusion on people who are already displaced.

Noir's death highlights the sobering reality that many Ballroom members of his generation have been lost to AIDS. Telling this personal story helps me to examine the social and health consequences of the mainstream exclusion that most members of the community face. These are consequences that even Ballroom culture could not overcome in Noir's case. Most of all, those of us ensconced within "at-risk" communities know that HIV/AIDS—the disease itself—does not discriminate. It has no boundaries. On the contrary, the health establishment's and sociopolitical responses to it, on a local, national, and global scale, are the true agents of discrimination. This fact marks the difference between *prevention* (from the outside) and *intravention* (from within) and the dialectic between the two that is necessary to ameliorate the disease among Ballroom communities. Part of the work of world-making is the labor of community and the structure and process of care that ultimately, over the long haul, intervene in the wake of such a multifarious crisis.

Finally, as I reflect on my own life and the lives of the Black LGBT people I know and love, it is clear that exclusion from Black belonging or marginalization within it has an indelible impact on our feelings about ourselves, as well as each other. In turn, some of us end up spending a good portion of our lives seeking this love—often in the wrong places and in many ways—to compensate for what we lost or never received. And, for me, there is a direct link between how we see ourselves, whether we value ourselves or not, and the choices we make throughout our lives. The late African American writer James Baldwin once suggested that Black Americans need witnesses in a country that thinks everything is White.[63] I would add that Black LGBT people need witnesses also in a Black society that thinks the only lives that are valuable and worth living and saving are male, straight, and HIV-negative. Ultimately, cultural labor can save lives, but we all have to be committed to performing it relentlessly.

Epilogue
The Future of Ballroom Culture

It is a beautiful spring day in late April 2012, as I enter a medium-sized ballroom on the lower level of the Renaissance Washington, DC, Downtown Hotel. Seated at tables throughout the room are prominent members of the Ballroom community representing nearly twenty houses from across the United States, and one from Toronto. Several representatives greet me, including well-known Butch Queens, some of whom were involved in the research for this book. To my pleasant surprise, seated next to me is Mother Goddess Rodeo, whom I have seen and spoken to only once or twice since my fieldwork ended. Clint Evisu, a former member of the defunct House of Ford in Detroit, is here from Atlanta, where he now lives. Among the other Butch Queens here—all now living in New York City—are Legendary Luna Luis Ortiz, Michael Garcon, and commentator Jack, formerly a Givenchy and now a Mizhrahi. Legendary Father Tommy Avant Garde is here from Chicago.[1] Here as well are some of the most respected Women Ballroom members, including Terry Revlon from Atlanta and Aisha Prodigy Iman from New York, both of whom I am meeting for the first time. Legendary Ayanna Christian, a Femme Queen from here in DC, is also in the room, and Sean Ebony, a Butch, is here from New York. I am here in part because a few months ago I accepted an invitation to join the Board of Directors of the House of Blahnik, so I am at a table with fellow members Stephaun and Kevin. We are all gathered here to do something that has been much discussed and often attempted but has yet to happen concretely: organizing on a national level.

Jay Blahnik, director of the Legacy Project and founder of The House of Blahnik, has invited me to speak at this meeting—the National House/ Ball Community Change Consultation.[2] The invitation to speak reflects my changing role within the Ballroom community since 2001, when I attended my first ball, to 2007, when I finished my fieldwork. I am no longer an active participant/ball-walker and member of The Legendary House of Prestige; instead, I am an "aged-out" Ballroom community leader and advocate for HIV/AIDS prevention and the health and wellness of its Black LGBT members. In my new role in the Ballroom scene, I am here to work with other leaders in the community to plan and organize a national entity that can design and advocate for a clinical research agenda focused on the Ballroom community. Creating such a Ballroom advocacy organization, they believe, would address the incongruity that most of the limited research on Ballroom and HIV/AIDS is conducted by neither members of the scene nor Black LGBT people. Members of the Ballroom community need to be at the table and working at all levels among those who conduct research and create and implement a public health policy agenda.

It seems fitting to end this book with an account of this meeting because of what the diversity of the participants—and the fact that they are gathered here at all—suggests about the future of Ballroom culture. In this epilogue I am talking about the Ballroom scene in general, not just Detroit's, to suggest both the limits and the possibilities of this minoritarian cultural formation. Ballroom as a community is very complex and conflicted; it is inclusive, egalitarian, and fluid in some ways while exclusionary and hierarchical in others. At a session on transgender people in the Ballroom scene at the meeting in DC, for instance, Sean Ebony made a trenchantly poignant statement in this regard: "Sex is fluid but acceptance is not, in the Ball scene." As cultural studies scholars have argued, a minoritized culture like Ballroom consistently reproduces itself and expands while simultaneously reifying within itself some of the same exclusionary and oppressive structures that brought the community into being in the first place. Ballroom culture is the means through which Black LGBT people seek to survive and challenge those limiting structures. This can be clearly seen in the proliferation of Ballroom scenes and practices throughout the globe and the various *microscenes* that have emerged from within the Ballroom community to redress, theoretically at least, the exclusions and hierarchies that are practiced and maintained in what members now call the "main scene."

First, although not all Ballroom members will agree, the scene has largely been racially/ethnically homogeneous throughout its history. Yet, as with other Black cultural formations such as hip-hop, for example, LGBT, same-sex and same-gender-loving or queer people in various geographies across the globe are taking up Ballroom culture. Made possible, in part, through networks of Black LGBT people in Detroit, Rochester, and Buffalo, there is now a growing scene in Toronto. According to Chris Cushman, who lives there currently, The House of Monroe—the inaugural house of the Toronto scene—held its first Almighty Ball in 2009. As I have argued elsewhere, Ballroom culture is an African diasporic formation; in the Toronto Ballroom scene, the majority of members are Afro-Canadian LGBT people, most likely second- or third-generation Canadians whose families emigrated from the Caribbean or Africa. The social location of Afro-Canadian LGBT people in a majority White country like Canada is similar to that of Black LGBT people in the United States, marked by multiple forms of exclusion and marginalization. Thus, Ballroom serves as a means through which Afro-Canadian LGBT people can undertake the necessary cultural labor to enhance the quality of their lives.

Beyond North America, Ballroom communities (or at least the practices associated with Ballroom) have emerged in Japan. Ms. Koppi Mizrahi, a cisgender Japanese woman who, according to my interlocutors, is straight, reportedly learned how to vogue from YouTube video clips.[3] She came to the United States to compete with members of the Ballroom scene and impressed the legendary voguers. Since then Koppi has taken vogue back to her country and is one of the pioneers of a burgeoning Ballroom scene—Japanese style. In addition, the legendary voguers Aviance Milan and Rashuan Evisu have gone to Russia and Sweden several times to teach vogue and organize balls. There are houses and smaller scenes in London and other places throughout the world. While Ballroom culture has clearly gone global, there are simultaneously virtues and problems with this expansion across cultural, national, and geographic boundaries. On the one hand, the culture becomes a space of refuge for a whole range of people and communities, no matter where they live. On the other hand, it is frustrating to contemplate how the ingenuity of the Black and Latino/a LGBT people who created Ballroom ends up being appropriated by others while the creators are denied any recognition for their creation. In this sense, Ballroom culture is recognized as a global phenomenon instead of being viewed as a phenomenon created by Black and Latino/a LGBT people in the United States that has *expanded* globally. Therefore, both the discursive and material returns to the actual creators of this cultural formation are diminished. This is no

minor issue for a community, like Ballroom, in which recognition and
representation matter, and these factors are often tied to social quality of
life for its members.

Second, as many of the Ballroom members at the meeting mentioned,
Ballroom culture was started by Femme Queens but over the years has
been taken over by Butch Queens. It is among the consequences of this
"takeover" that Women, Butches (mostly masculine lesbians), transgender men, and transgender women have been marginalized in the
scene, to the extent that there are far fewer competitive categories for
them in at any given ball. According to the founder of The House of
Iman, Aisha Prodigy Iman, a Woman who is also a lesbian, "The WBT
[Women, Butch, and Transgender] scene was started because there
weren't enough categories for cisgender women and Butches to compete in. There have always been a lot of women into Ballroom, but they
were sidelined in the scene." As a result, they started their own scene.
She further explains:

> In 2001, for example, I had an all-women's ball in New York and
> over 700 women were there. There were, and still are, all-women
> houses in Atlanta, Richmond, Philly, Baltimore, Miami/Fort Lau-
> derdale, and there are some in Texas. In 2008 the WBT scene
> started growing, and there are houses such as Divenchy, Bosses
> and Belladonna, Moulin Rouge, and Iman. The House of Iman
> has seventy members who are mostly cisgender women who are
> mostly lesbian and bi-women.

The exclusion of Women, Butches, and Femme Queens from and
marginalization within the main scene is a systemic problem because
prominence in Ballroom is typically conferred based on one's success
at winning—"slaying and snatching"—trophies and cash prizes at balls.
Lacking categories in which to compete, it becomes difficult, impossible
even, for Women, Butches, and Femme Queens to gain recognition in
the scene. The *microscene,* or the Women, Butches, and Transgender
(WBT) scene, was started, in part, to address this systemic problem. At
WBT balls, almost all of the categories are designed for Women, Butches,
and Femme Queens, with relatively few categories available for Butch
Queens. Perhaps in response to this trend, in the main scene there are
now women's chapters of established houses. The leadership of houses

such as Prada, Prodigy, Mizrahi, and Blahnik has allowed members to open an all-women chapter to compete in the WBT scene on behalf of their houses.

However, Aisha also points out that even though the creation of the WBT scene was motivated by a desire for equity and inclusion, it "replicates the forms of oppression that exists in the main scene." These are forms of oppression based on gender power relations in terms of categories and gender presentation in the community. Masculine Women and Butches marginalize and oppress feminine Women and Femme Queens. As is the case in the main scene, masculinity can be, resiliently, privileged and oppressive without regard for those to whom it is ascribed and by whom it is performed.

A third direction of Ballroom culture, which has been referred to as the Ballroom evolution, is the Kiki scene. Among Black LGBT communities, to *kiki* means to have fun, to laugh, or to "catch up." The Kiki scene consists of a racially diverse group of LGBT young people between the ages of twelve and twenty-four. While working at GMHC in 2002–3 and also serving as mother of The House of Latex in New York City, Aisha Prodigy Iman created the Kiki scene. This scene was developed chiefly as an HIV/AIDS intervention based on a social network model to address rising infection rates among young men and transgender women of color. Its HIV prevention purposes notwithstanding, the Kiki scene is an alternative to the main scene according to my interlocutors, who characterize it as "too competitive" and "too serious." The Kiki scene was created as a testing ground for the main scene, a safer way for young people to move up through the ranks and eventually make the main scene. According to Aisha, "I conceived of the Kiki scene as a youth and young adult alternative—junior varsity—to the main scene, which many young people viewed as too competitive and intense. That's why we call it the Kiki scene—a space for people to just have fun," said Aisha. "The main scene is not fun anymore."

Furthermore, in the main scene, balls are a core feature, but in the Kiki scene social networking is the most important medium of social exchange and includes balls but is not limited to them. Primarily, CBOs secure spaces for Kiki balls, which highlight the important role that this relationship plays in HIV prevention efforts among the scene's young LGBT participants. Kiki scene practices, however, unabashedly transgress the official protocol established in the main scene. In some cases,

Kiki balls are thrown at far more random times and in less traditional spaces than is characteristic of the main scene. For example, "A bunch of kids will just start a Kiki ball on the pier in the middle of the day in New York," said Aisha. This speaks to the ways in which this microscene is also engaged in courageous efforts to "take back" the pier in Greenwich Village, a space from which it has been increasingly excluded over the past three decades. Clearly, the Kiki scene has emerged as an essential means through which to target primarily young Black LGBT people for HIV prevention and as another refuge to which these young people can turn when they have been ostracized from or oppressed within their biological kin households or their communities of origin.

Yet it was a persistent theme among several of those present at the meeting in DC that the Kiki scene has become a carbon copy of the main scene by maintaining all of the harsh and "cutthroat" forms of competition for which Ballroom is notorious. Young people have begun to craft and stunt to acquire extravagant clothing and increase their chances of winning a category at a Kiki ball, and some are proclaiming legendary status without having achieved the required level of accomplishment commensurate with such status in the overall scene. This is an issue of great consternation in the scene now. Aisha believes, echoing her observations about the WBT scene, that the Kiki scene "now replicates the negative aspects of the main Ballroom scene. The Kiki scene is going to become its own mainstream scene." This was not what was intended when the Kiki scene was developed.

True to form, these, in part, unintended consequences reflect the unpredictable nature of culture but also how it is generative and dynamic. As Robin D. G. Kelley reminds us, culture is never static.[4] Yes, indeed, the social process of creating new spaces of inclusion while simultaneously reifying forms of exclusion will continue, as it is characteristic of cultural formations. However, what is generative, what is progressive, about Ballroom is the creativity that is produced at the interstices between the limits experienced in the community and the possibilities imagined by those who are stigmatized, marginalized, and oppressed in its midst. As Ballroom continues to evolve in the ongoing effort to address its limitations, innovative ways to include new kinds of gender and sexual subjectivities emerge, and as new practices are deployed to counter the increasingly perilous conditions under which Black LGBT live, we can envision more ways to create enduring communities for those located at the bottom of our society.

Considering the more than ten-year period covered in this study and the time it has taken to bring the book to print, some aspects of the Ballroom scene will have changed since I began writing. Indeed, Ballroom has and continues to be a community on the move. This may be the first book on Ballroom culture, but I sincerely hope it will not be the last. Future researchers may find it equally challenging to keep up with the constantly evolving Ballroom scene. Recently I attended a ball in Detroit during the city's Black Pride festivities. Attendance at the ball was good, and I saw people old and new, including Diva D. Bvlgari, Antawn, formerly a Ford, and Mother Goddess. There were many new people in attendance from throughout the region. As some of us "old kids" continue to age-out, we will pass the torch to the new kids. These new participants are Ballroom culture's future.

Notes

Preface

1. I use the phrase "got AIDS" because in the 1980s, neither I nor my friends understood the difference between HIV and AIDS. We thought that people "got"—were infected with—AIDS as opposed to HIV.

2. This person's name has been changed to protect his privacy. Throughout this book, I refrain from using the given names of my interlocutors unless they explicitly gave me permission to do otherwise.

3. *Seroconversion* is a term used in HIV research and prevention (blood testing) to denote the appearance of anti-HIV antibodies, which means a person has become HIV infected.

Chapter 1

1. Brian Currid, "*We Are Family:* House Music and Queer Performativity," in *Cruising the Performative: Interventions into Ethnicity, Nationality, and Sexuality,* ed. Philip Brett, Sue-Ellen C;ase, and Susan Leigh Foster (Bloomington: Indiana University Press, 1995), 192.

2. The exact URLs for these sites are www.walk4mewednesdays.com, www.the houseofballs.com, and www.getyourtens.com[0].

3. The relatively large Latino/a membership in Ballroom in cities like New York, Newark, Miami, and San Antonio is largely due to the distinct demographics and cultural geographic environments in cities where Black and Latino/a people live and socialize in close proximity to each other. For more on Latino/as in Ballroom Culture, particularly in New York City, see Arnaldo Cruz-Malavé's *Queer Latino Testimonio, Keith Haring, and Juanito Xtravaganza: Hard Tails* (New York: Palgrave Macmillan, 2007); and Edgar Rivera Colón's "Getting Life in Two Worlds: Power and Prevention in the New York City House Ball Community" (PhD diss., Rutgers University, 2009).

4. With few exceptions, Ballroom scenes in cities such as Detroit, Chicago, Atlanta, Cleveland, and Philadelphia are almost exclusively Black.

5. I use the term *interlocutors* to refer to this study's participants. I deliberately depart from using conventional terms used in qualitative methods such as subjects and informants because *interlocutors* is a more accurate way to describe the role of participants in this study. They were more akin to guides, consultants, and partners

in this study because they possessed key knowledges about the Ballroom community that they exposed me to as a coparticipant. For more on this methodological point, see D. Soyini Madison's *Critical Ethnography: Method, Ethics, and Performance* (Thousand Oaks, CA: Sage Publications, 2012).

6. Since chronological age is not emphasized among the members, I generally do not provide the ages of my interlocutors in this book. Some would not tell me their age when I asked during the interview.

7. Thomas Sugrue, *The Origins of the Urban Crisis: Race and Inequality in Postwar Detroit* (Princeton, NJ: Princeton University Press, 1996), 3.

8. Thaddeus Russell, "The Color of Discipline: Civil Rights and Black Sexuality," *American Quarterly* 60, no. 1 (2008): 106.

9. Sugrue, *Origins*, 3.

10. Ibid., 11.

11. Ibid.

12. U.S. Census Bureau, "Population Change and Distribution 1990–2000: Census 2000 Brief" http://www.census.gov/prod/2001pubs/c2kbr01-2.pdf (accessed March 3, 2013).

13. U.S. Census Bureau, American FactFinder Detroit 2010, http://factfinder2.census.gov/faces/nav/jsf/pages/community_facts.xhtml (accessed March 3, 2013).

14. For a discussion on the rankings of the top ten most segregated cities in the United States, see Daniel Denvir, "The 10 Most Segregated Urban Areas in America," *Salon*, http://www.salon.com/2011/03/29/most_segregated_cities/slide_show/7/ (accessed September 1, 2012).

15. This was the rate of unemployment as of July 2005 taken from a report created by the Department of Labor and Economic Growth for the State of Michigan, www.michigan.gov (accessed September 1, 2012). The poverty statistics are taken from the U.S. Census Bureau, Michigan: Census 2000 Profile http://www.census.gov/prod/2002pubs/c2kprof00-mi.pdf (accessed September 1, 2012).

16. See Patricia Montemurri, Kathleen Gray, and Cicil Angel, "Detroit Tops Nation in Poverty Census," *Detroit Free Press*, August 31, 2005.

17. For more on homeless LGBT youths in Detroit and the State of Michigan, see Ruth Ellis Center, http://www.ruthelliscenter.org/ (accessed July 24, 2012).

18. Kofi Natambu, "Nostalgia for the Present: Cultural Resistance in Detroit, 1977–1987," in *Black Popular Culture*, ed. Gina Dent, Michelle Wallace, and the Dia Center for the Arts (Seattle: Bay Press, 1992), 173.

19. For more on this, see James F. Wilson's *Bulldaggers, Pansies, and Chocolate Babies: Performance, Race, and Sexuality in the Harlem Renaissance* (Ann Arbor: University of Michigan Press, 2010).

20. For more on the historical practices and spaces of Black drag performance or public gender nonconformity, see Brett Beemyn, "The Geography of Same-Sex Desire: Cruising Men in Washington, DC, in the Late Nineteenth and Early Twentieth Centuries," *Left History* 9, no. 2 (2004): 141–58; Eric Garber, "A Spectacle in Color: The Lesbian and Gay Subculture of Jazz Age Harlem," in *Hidden from History: Reclaiming the Gay and Lesbian Past*, edited by Martin Duberman, Martha Vicinus, and George Chauncey Jr., 318–31 (New York: Penguin Group, 1990); and Kevin J. Mumford, *In-*

terzones: Black/White Sex Districts in Chicago and New York in the Early Twentieth Century (New York: Columbia University Press 1997).

21. George Chauncey Jr., *Gay New York: Urban Culture, and the Making of the Gay Male World,* 1890–1940 (New York: Basic Books, 1994), 248.

22. Victoria W. Wolcott describes two Great Migrations. According to her, while the first Great Migration during the 1910s and the 1920s dramatically increased Detroit's Black population, tens of thousands more Black southerners migrated to Detroit in the second Great Migration of the 1940s. Wolcott adds that, during the 1940s, Detroit was under extreme racial strife marked by Blacks' struggle against public housing discrimination in 1942. The racial turmoil escalated into one of the worse race riots in Detroit's history in 1943.

23. Ruby Walker, "Interview with Chris Albertson," audiocassette, Jersey City, 1970–71. The experience that Ruby Walker discusses took place in Detroit in the mid-1920s. I transcribed this portion of the interview.

24. Garber, "A Spectacle in Color," 325.

25. Rochella Thorpe, "'A House Where Queers Go': African-American Lesbian Nightlife in Detroit, 1940–1975," in *Inventing Lesbian Cultures in America,* ed. Ellen Lewin (Boston: Beacon Press, 1996), 43.

26. The Ruth Ellis drop-in center, where the Street Outreach Program is housed, is located in Highland Park (a small incorporated city surrounded by Detroit). The residential programs are administered at Ruth Ellis's house in Detroit, located in the North End neighborhood. The two residential programs are the Transitional Living Program and the Semi-independent Living Program. The Ruth Ellis Center is one of only four social service agencies in the country dedicated to helping LGBTQ teens and young adults who are experiencing homelessness. In an interview I conducted with Laura Hughes, the executive director of the Ruth Ellis Center, she gave me a packet of information on the agency and the services it provides. I used this document, along with my discussion with her, to describe the agency's mission. This information can also be found on the Ruth Ellis Center's website, www.ruthelliscenter.org (accessed March 1, 2013).

27. Russell, "The Color of Discipline," 109. Also see Tim Retzloff, "'Seer or Queer'? Postwar Fascination with Detroit's Prophet Jones," *GLQ: A Journal of Lesbian and Gay Studies* 8, no. 3 (2002): 271–96.

28. Russell, "The Color of Discipline," 113.

29. Both Russell and Retzloff make a similar argument about Jones in terms of his rise and fall in popularity. Also see Angela D. Dillard, *Faith in the City: Preaching Radical Social Change in Detroit* (Ann Arbor: University of Michigan Press, 2007).

30. Before his Detroit mayoral stint, Kilpatrick was in the Democratic leadership in the Michigan State House of Representatives. He won the seat that was vacated by his mother, Carolyn Cheeks Kilpatrick, who was elected to the US House of Representatives for the Thirteenth District in Michigan. Kwame Kilpatrick's father, Bernard Kilpatrick, served as chief of staff for Edward McNamara, the longtime county executive for Wayne County, in which Detroit is located.

31. For more on this, see Jan Stevenson's article "Kilpatrick Responds to LGBT Community," *Between the Lines,* June 14, 2001. See also Jason Michael, "Detroit Mayor Denounces Marriage Equality for Gays on National Television," *Between the Lines,*

March 4, 2004. It is worth noting that in 2008 Kilpatrick was removed from office in part for perjuring himself in front of a grand jury about an inappropriate sexual relationship between him and his chief of staff, Christine Beatty. Text messages on an official city phone retrieved by means of a court subpoena revealed evidence of a sexual relationship between the two. This relationship transpired while both Beatty, now divorced, and Kilpatrick had marital spouses. Kilpatrick had vociferously denied the existence of this relationship.

32. For more on theories from the flesh, see E. Patrick Johnson's "'Quare' Studies, Or (Almost) Everything I know about Queer Studies I Learned From My Grandmother" in *Black Queer Studies: A Critical Anthology*, ed. E. Patrick Johnson and Mae Henderson (Durham: Duke University Press 2005), 124–57. Johnson draws from Cherríe Moraga and Gloria Anzaldúa, eds., *This Bridge Called My Back: Writings by Radical Women of Color* (New York: Kitchen Table; Women of Color Press, 1983).

33. Robin D. G. Kelley, *Yo' Moma's Dysfunktional! Fighting the Culture Wars in Urban America* (Boston: Beacon Press, 1997), 45.

34. Ibid.

35. Siobhan B. Somerville, "Queer," in *Keywords for American Cultural Studies*, ed. Bruce Burgett and Glenn Hendler (New York: New York University Press, 2007), 190.

36. Ibid., 187.

37. For more on queer practices, particularly in relation to gender and sexuality and kinship and community, see Judith Halberstam's *In a Queer Time and Place: Transgender Bodies, Subcultural Lives* (New York: New York University Press, 2005) Richard Rodriguez's *Next of Kin: The Family in Chicano/a Cultural Politics* (Durham, NC: Duke University Press, 2009); Fiona Buckland's *Impossible Dance: Club Culture and Queer World-Making* (Middletown, CT: Wesleyan University Press, 2002); and Mary L. Gray's *Youth, Media, and Queer Visibility in Rural America* (New York: New York University Press, 2009).

38. Susan Manning, "Performance," in *Keywords for American Cultural Studies*, ed. Bruce Burgett and Glenn Hendler (New York: New York University Press, 2007), 177.

39. Here I draw from Butler's theory of gender performativity. For elaboration on this theory, see Judith Butler's *Gender Trouble: Feminism and the Subversion of Identity* (New York: Routledge, 2006).

40. José Esteban Muñoz, *Disidentification: Queers of Color and the Performance of Politics* (Minneapolis: University of Minnesota Press, 1999), 195.

41. Lisa Duggan, "The Trails of Alice Mitchell: Sensationalism, Sexology, and the Lesbian Subject in Turn-of-the-Century America," *Signs*, Vol. 18 no. 4 (1993): 792–93.

42. D. Soyini Madison and Judith Hamera, "Performance Studies at the Intersections," in *The Sage Handbook of Performance Studies*, ed. D. Soyini Madison and Judith Hamera (Thousand Oaks, CA: Sage Publications, 2006), xii.

43. Muñoz, *Disidentification*, 195–96.

44. David Román, *Performance in America: Contemporary U.S. Culture and the Performing Arts* (Durham, NC: Duke University Press, 2005), 23. Román makes a similar argument in his first book, *Acts of Intervention: Performance, Gay Culture, and AIDS* (Bloomington: Indiana University Press, 1998).

45. Margaret Thompson Drewal, "The State of Research on Performance in Africa," *African Studies Review* 34, no. 3 (1991): 2.

46. Considering that Ballroom culture is a North American phenomenon, some of the interviews are with members from other cities such as Atlanta, Philadelphia, Oakland, and Los Angeles. Even though I focus on the social geography of Detroit, my data reflect the national scope of Ballroom culture, as I have attended several balls elsewhere in the country.

47. Johannes Fabian, *Power and Performance: Ethnographic Explorations through Proverbial Wisdom and Theater in Shaba, Zaire* (Madison: University of Wisconsin Press, 1990), 5. The cultural anthropologist Johannes Fabian claims that researchers must move from informative ethnography to performative ethnography. Fabian suggests that the ethnographic process is a performance between the researcher and his or her interlocutors. It must move beyond communication and dialogue to a more interactive exchange of knowledge. According to Fabian, performative ethnography offers an opportunity to alter and negotiate the power relations that come with the territory of doing ethnographic work. Fabian suggests that doing ethnography with and not of a particular group allows for a stronger partnership to develop between the researcher and his or her informants.

48. Dwight Conquergood, "Performance Studies: Interventions and Radical Research," *TDR: The Drama Review* 46, no. 2 (2002): 146.

Chapter 2

1. Charles F. Stephens, "Performing Black and Gay: Butch Queen Radicalism," in *If We Have to Take Tomorrow: HIV, Black Men, and Same Sex Desire,* ed. Frank León Roberts and Marvin White (New York: Institute of Gay Men's Health, 2006), 31.

2. Roberto Strongman, "Syncretic Religion and Dissident Sexualities," in *Queer Globalization, Citizenship, and the Afterlife of Colonialism,* ed. Arnaldo Cruz-Malavé and Martin F. Manalansan IV (New York: New York University Press, 2002), 182.

3. Karen McCarthy Brown, "Mimesis in the Face of Fear: Femme Queens, Butch Queens, and Gender Play in the Houses of Greater Newark," in *Passing: Identity and Interpretation in Sexuality, Race, and Religion,* ed. María Carla Sánchez and Linda Schlossberg (New York: New York University Press, 2001), 209.

4. Percy C. Hintzen, *West Indian in the West: Self-Representation in an Immigrant Community* (New York: New York University Press, 2001), 34.

5. Jonathon David Jackson, "The Social World of Voguing," *Journal for the Anthropological Study of Human Movement* 12, no. 2 (2002): 27.

6. Jason Cromwell, *Transmen and FTM: Identities, Bodies, Gender, and Sexualities* (Urbana: University of Illinois Press, 1999), 32–33.

7. Ann Fausto-Sterling, *Sexing the Body: Gender Politics and the Construction of Sexuality* (New York: Basic Books, 2000), 235.

8. Enoch Page and Matt U. Richardson, "On the Fear of Small Numbers," in *Black Sexualities: Probing Powers, Passions, Practices, and Policies,* ed. Juan Battle and Sandra L. Barnes (New Brunswick, NJ: Rutgers University Press, 2010), 61.

9. In *Paris Is Burning* and the debates the film generated, there was no mention of a gender system, even though the gender subjectivities existed. In their studies, Jonathon David Jackson and Karen McCarthy Brown have come to different conclusions

about what is more commonly called the gender system. In his work on vogue performance in the Ballroom scenes of Philadelphia and New York City, Jackson suggests that there is a four-part gender system (Butch Queens, Femme Queens, Butches, and Women) and three sexes (woman, man, and intersex). Karen McCarthy Brown's study of Ballroom in Newark states that there is a five-part gender system, which includes all of the categories I identify in the text except for biologically born men. Last, New York University PhD candidate Frank Léon Roberts, who also focuses on New York, identifies a six-part gender system that adds Butch Queen with a Twist (a performance category). The gender identity system that I deploy departs, slightly, from the aforementioned. I came to my conclusions about the system after analyzing numerous category descriptions on the flyers and interviews with housefathers and housemothers who live in Detroit, Fayetteville, North Carolina, and Los Angeles. I suspect that these discrepancies are due to regional differences in Ballroom culture.

10.   For more on the inextricable linkage between gender and sexuality, see Kristen Schilt and Laural Westbrook, "Doing Gender, Doing Heteronormativity: 'Gender Normals,' Transgender People, and Social Maintenance of Heterosexuality," *Gender & Society* 23 no. 4 (2009): 440–64.

11.   I am aware that, throughout this book, I use the acronym LGBT, and thus I lump gender and sexual categories together whenever I refer to the membership of the Ballroom community. I use LGBT as a shortcut and because it best reflects the ways in which members of the community to whom I refer identify themselves.

12.   Susan Stryker, "(De)subjugated Knowledges: An Introduction to Transgender Studies," in *The Transgender Studies Reader*, ed. Susan Stryker and Stephen Whittle (New York: Routledge, 2006), 7.

13.   Stephens, "Performing Black and Gay," 31.

14.   In the Ballroom scene, as in larger LGBT communities, sexual practice is what one does sexually. Sexual practice reflects a panoply of sexual acts in which members engage, and those sexual acts tend to be categorized along lines of masculinity and femininity (at least in public discussion). For instance, as Ballroom members would say, sucking dick, eating ass or pussy, giving or receiving, are oral sexual practices. For men, getting one's dick sucked is at times associated with masculinity and sucking dick with femininity. Sexual practice is linked to sexual position, which refers to anal and vaginal penetration. Sexual position implies bottom, the one who gets fucked, and top, the one who does the fucking. Top is associated with masculinity and bottom with femininity. Again, how this is represented in the public sphere is always very different from what most people actually do. Most of the time individuals fuck, get fucked, or are sexually versatile, as mentioned earlier in this chapter.

15.   Stephens, "Performing Black and Gay," 33.

16.   Ibid.

17.   Stryker, "(De)Subjugated Knowledges," 10.

18.   Jane Ward, "Transmen, Femmes, and Collective Work of Transgression," *Sexualities* 13, no. 2 (2010): 237.

19.   I discuss this organization—which I mentioned in chapter 1—at greater length in chapter 5.

20.   Within the Ballroom community, people use the "he" and "she" pronouns inter-

changeably when referring to Butch Queens. This is different for Femme Queens and Butches, who are always referred to as "she" and "he," respectively.

21. Sherrie Inness and Michelle Lloyd, "G.I. Joes in Barbie Land: Recontextualizing Butch in Twentieth-Century Lesbian Culture," in *Queer Studies: A Lesbian, Gay, Bisexual, and Transgender Anthology*, ed. Brett Beemyn and Mickey Eliason (New York: New York University Press, 1996), 14.

22. Jackie Goldsby, "Queens of Language," in *Queer Looks: Perspectives on Lesbian and Gay Film and Video*, ed. Martha Bever, John Greyson, and Pratibha Parmar (New York: Routledge, 1994), 110.

23. Judith Butler, *Undoing Gender* (New York: Routledge, 2004), 219.

24. Peggy Phelan, *Unmarked: The Politics of Performance* (New York: Routledge, 1993), 93.

25. Robyn Wiegman, *American Anatomies: Theorizing Race and Gender* (Durham, NC: Duke University Press, 1995), 4.

26. Maurice O. Wallace, *Constructing the Black Masculine: Identity and Ideality in African American Men's Literature and Culture, 1775-1995* (Durham, NC: Duke University Press, 2002), 135.

27. E. Patrick Johnson, *Appropriating Blackness: Performance and the Politics of Authenticity* (Durham, NC: Duke University Press 2003), 9. For a discussion of race, the body, and dance performance, see Susan Manning's *Modern Dance, Negro Dance: Race in Motion* (Minneapolis: University of Minnesota Press, 2004).

28. Rashad Shabazz, "So High You Can't Get Over It, So Low You Can't Get Under It": Carceral Spatiality and Black Masculinities in the United States and South Africa," *Souls* 11 no. 3 (2009): 287.

29. Ibid.

30. Johnson, "'Quare' Studies," 137-38.

31. Ibid.

32. Karen McCarthy Brown, "Mimesis in the Face of Fear," 216.

33. For more on the notion of being "unmarked," or what members of the Ballroom community refer to as "unclockable," see Phelan, *Unmarked*.

34. Johnson, *Appropriating Blackness*, 20.

35. Similar to Butches (transgender men) who transition (although few actually do), it is not clear whether Femme Queens who transition move into the category of Woman in the Ballroom community.

36. Johnson, *Appropriating Blackness*, 90.

37. Mark McBeth, "The Queen's English: A Queery into Contrastive Rhetoric," in *Constrastive Rhetoric Revisited and Redefined*, ed. Clayann Gilliam Panetta (Mahwah, NJ: Lawrence Earlbaum Associates 2001), 105-6.

38. L. H. Stallings, *Mutha' Is Half a Word: Intersections of Folklore, Vernacular, Myth, and Queerness in Black Female Culture* (Columbus: Ohio State University Press, 2007), 261.

39. Judith Butler, *Bodies That Matter: On the Discursive Limits of "Sex"* (New York: Routledge, 1993), 125.

40. José Esteban Muñoz, *Disidentification: Queers of Color and the Performance of Politics* (Minneapolis, University of Minnesota Press, 1999), 195.

Chapter 3

1. Wayne Corbit, *Crying Holy,* in *Colored Contradictions: An Anthology of Contemporary African American Plays,* ed. Harry Elam Jr. and Robert Alexander (New York: Penguin Group, 1996), 488.

2. This quote is from an interview I conducted with Tim'm T. West in Oakland, California, in 2000.

3. Rhonda M. Williams, "Living at the Crossroads: Explorations in Race, Nationality, Sexuality, and Gender," in *The House That Race Built,* ed. Wahneema Lubiano (New York: Vintage Books, 1998), 136.

4. My use of the term *platonic* is meant to reflect the friendship and nonromantic nature of the parental relationships that lead most Ballroom houses. Conversely, my use of the term is not meant to signify any gesture toward Plato or his influence on Western philosophy.

5. In *Whose Detroit? Politics, Labor, and Race in a Modern American City* (Ithaca, NY: Cornell University Press, 2001), Heather Ann Thompson suggests that from 1910 to 1966 the number of Black Americans living outside of the South rose from 800,800 to 9.7 million and that this occurred, in large part, because labor markets in northern cities were opened to Black people between World Wars I and II.

6. Farah Jasmine Griffin, *"Who Set You Flowin'?" The African-American Migration Narrative* (Oxford: Oxford University Press, 1995), 102.

7. For more on this point, see Nicholas Lemann, *The Promised Land: The Great Migration and How It Changed America* (New York: Knopf, 1991).

8. Thomas N. Maloney and Warren C. Whatley, "Making the Effort: The Contours of Racial Discrimination in Detroit's Labor Market, 1920–1940." *Journal of Economic History* 55, no. 3 (1995): 489.

9. According to Victoria Wolcott, *Remaking Respectability: African American Women in Interwar Detroit* (Chapel Hill: University of North Carolina Press, 2001), 244, in the late 1940s Black women had broken into the industrial and white-collar labor force after years of rampant discrimination in Detroit.

10. Scott Peller, "Laboring for a Brave New World: Our Ford and the Epsilons," in *Huxley's Brave New World: Essays,* ed. David Garrett Izzo and Kim Kirkpatrick (Jefferson, NC: McFarland, 2008), 63.

11. Micaela di Leonardo, "The Female World of Cards and Holidays: Women, Families, and the Work of Kinship," in *Gender in Cross-Cultural Perspective,* ed. Caroline B. Brettell and Carolyn F. Sargent, 2nd ed. (Upper Saddle River, NJ: Prentice-Hall, 1997), 386.

12. Daniel P. Moynihan, "The Tangle of Pathology," in *The Black Family: Essays and Studies,* ed. Robert Staples, 6th ed. (Belmont, CA: Wadsworth Publishing, 1965), 7. This document can also be found at the US Department of Labor, Office of the Assistant Secretary for Administration and Management—History—www.dol.gov/oasam (accessed March 1, 2013).

13. Moynihan, "Tangle of Pathology," 7.

14. According to Wahneema Lubiano, common sense is lived ideology that is articulated in everyday understandings of the world, the community, and one's place in it. She makes this argument in "Black Nationalism and Black Common Sense: Policing

Ourselves and Others," in *The House That Race Built*, ed. Wahneema Lubiano (New York: Vintage Books, 1998), 232.

15.   Stuart Hall, "The Problem of Ideology: Marxism without Guarantees," in *Stuart Hall: Critical Dialogues in Cultural Studies*, ed. David Morley and Kuan-Hsing Chen (London and New York: Routledge, 1996), 26.

16.   Paul Gilroy, "It's a Family Affair," in *Black Popular Culture*, ed. Gina Dent (Seattle: Bay Press, 1992), 312.

17.   Ibid.

18.   There are a variety of texts written by Black scholars that advance heteropatriarchal, or at the very least heteronormative, perspectives on the Black family, especially regarding Black male sexuality. With only a few exceptions, these scholars either totally ignore same-sex sexuality or see it as a threat to the Black family structure. Some of these texts include Nathan and Julie Hare's *The Endangered Black Family: Coping with the Unisexualization and Coming Extinction of the Black Race* (San Francisco: Black Think Tank, 1984) and their edited collection, *Crisis in Black Sexual Politics* (San Francisco: Black Think Tank, 1989); Robert Staples's *Black Masculinity: The Black Man's Role in American Society* (San Francisco: Black Scholars Press, 1982); Molefi Asante's *Afrocentricity: The Theory of Social Change* (Trenton, NJ: Africa World Press 1988); Haki Madhubuti's *Black Men: Obsolete, Single, Dangerous? The Afrikan American in Transition—Essays in Discovery, Solution, and Hope* (Chicago: Third World Press, 1990); Frances Cress Welsing's *The Isis Papers* (Chicago: Third World Press, 1991); and Na'im Akbar's, *Chains and Images of Psychological Slavery* (Jersey City, NJ: New Mind Productions, 1984). While less explicitly homophobic, even the more scholarly and rigorous texts on the Black family treat the subject in heteronormative terms, as exemplified by Orlando Patterson's *Rituals of Blood: Consequences of Slavery in Two American Centuries* (New York: Basic Civitas, 1998); Robert Staples's edited collection, *The Black Family: Essays and Studies*, 6th ed. (Belmont, CA: Wadsworth Publishing); and Robert B. Hill's *Research on the African-American Family: A Holistic Perspective* (Westport, CT: Auburn House, 1993).

19.   Lester K. Spence, "Uncovering Black Attitudes about Homosexuality and HIV/AIDS," lecture presented at the National Conference of Black Political Scientists, Alexandria, Virginia, 2005, 2.

20.   Robyn Wiegman, *American Anatomies: Theorizing Race and Gender* (Durham, NC: Duke University Press, 1995), 7.

21.   Wahneema Lubiano used this term at a lecture she delivered at the University of California, Davis, in March 2002. In the article cited previously, Lubiano defines *nationalism* as the activation of a narrative of identity and interests. Whether or not it is concrete in the form of a state (or the idea of its possibility), this narrative is one according to which members of a social, political, cultural, ethnic, or "racial" group relate to themselves, and it is predicated on some understanding—however mythologized or mystified—of a shared past, an assessment of present circumstances, and a description of or prescription for a shared future. Nationalism articulates a desire—always unfulfillable—for a complete representation of the past and a fantasy for a better future. It is a social identification. Lubiano, "Black Nationalism and Common Sense," 233.

22.   Ibid., 232.

23. I attended The Million Man March. It was called for and primarily organized by the Honorable Minister Louis Farrakhan of the Nation of Islam and is one example of the propagation of the Black family ideology through intersecting discourses of religion and politics. On that day, in front of hundreds of thousands of Black people, primarily men, from a variety of socioeconomic, geographic, and regional and religious backgrounds, the minister admonished Black men to go back to their communities and reclaim their roles as providers, leaders, and protectors of the Black nation. Detroit was well represented, I might add, and there were also self-identified Black queer people there, including me and my friends. Most of the speakers viewed the Black family as ground zero in the struggle for social, political, and economic equality and thus argued for the need to resurrect the Black family as the bulwark of cultural unity and resistance against US racial oppression. Although this event has been critiqued and dismissed by a number of Black feminist and queer scholars, its ongoing sociocultural significance within Black communities, and the role it has played in reproducing heteropatriarchal discourses of the Black family, should not be underemphasized.

24. Lisa Rofel, "Qualities of Desire: Imagining Gay Identities in China," *GLQ: A Journal of Lesbian and Gay Studies* 5, no. 4 (1999): 451–74.

25. M. Jacqui Alexander, "Erotic Autonomy as a Politics of Decolonization: An Anatomy of Feminist and State Practice in the Bahamas Tourist Economy," in *Feminist Genealogies, Colonial Legacies, Democratic Futures,* ed. M. Jacqui Alexander and Chandra Talpade Mohanty (New York and London: Routledge, 1997), 84.

26. E. Patrick Johnson, *Appropriating Blackness: Performance and the Politics of Authenticity* (Durham, NC: Duke University Press, 2003), 22.

27. Angela Yvonne Davis, *Women, Culture, and Politics* (New York: Vintage Books, 1990), 74. See also Carol Stack, *All Our Kin* (New York: Basic Books, 1974).

28. Stanlie M. James, "Mothering: A Possible Black Feminist Link to Social Transformation?," in *Theorizing Black Feminisms: The Visionary Pragmatism of Black Women,* ed. Stanlie M. James and Abena P. A. Busia (New York and London: Routledge, 1993), 46.

29. Lubiano, "Black Nationalism and Black Common Sense," 245.

30. In "Unmarried America," a *Business Week* cover story (October 20, 2003), Michelle Conlin and Jessi Hempel argue that the traditional (nuclear) family model is a thing of the past. According to the US census, married couple households have slipped from 80 percent in the 1950s to only 50.7 percent today. Only 25 percent of the population consists of married couples with kids, and that is projected to drop to 20 percent by 2010.

31. Johnson, *Appropriating Blackness,* 79.

32. Historian Lisa Duggan's "Holy Matrimony," *The Nation,* February 26, 2004, is one of the most insightful commentaries on the same-sex debates. Duggan argues that powerful moral conservatives seek to deny a "flexible menu of choices for forms of households and partnership recognition open to all citizens, depending on specific and varying needs" (3). She further suggests that a flexible menu would undercut heteronormative marriage, which privileges men and family values, positioning moralism as the arbiter of social welfare policy. Unfortunately, the conservatives are winning the cultural war for now.

33. Eric Garber, "A Spectacle in Color: The Lesbian and Gay Subculture of Jazz Age

Harlem," in *Hidden from History: Reclaiming the Gay and Lesbian Past*, ed. Martha Vicinus, George Chauncey Jr., and Martin Duberman (New York: Penguin Group, 1990), 319.

34. William Hawkeswood and Alex W. Costley, *One of the Children: Gay Black Men in Harlem* (Berkeley: University of California Press, 1996), 8.

35. Douglass Martin "Pepper LaBeija, Queens of Harlem Drag Balls, Is Dead at 53," *New York Times*, May 26, 2003, http://www.nytimes.com/2003/05/26/arts/pepper-la beija-queen-of-harlem-drag-balls-is-dead-at-53.html (accessed March 3, 2013).

36. Hawkeswood and Costley, *One of the Children*, xiv.

37. Mignon R. Moore, *Invisible Families: Gay Identities, Relationships, and Motherhood among Black Women* (Berkeley: University of California Press, 2011).

38. In the article, "Pepper LaBeija Is Dead at 53" memorializes Pepper LaBeija, an icon of Ballroom culture. Struggling with diabetes for the past ten years, she died on May 14, 2003, of a heart attack in New York City. Pepper was the mother of one of the first houses, The House of LaBeija, founded in 1970. In the article, Father Junior LaBeija, at forty-six and one of the oldest original LaBeija members still alive, says, "The Harlem ball scene has existed for more than 100 years, and the balls have primarily been about cross-dressing. Junior joined The House of LaBeija in 1975. Grandfather Marcel LaBeija is the oldest active Ballroom participant at 58 years old. He got involved in Ballroom in 1963." Paul Schindler, "Pepper LaBeija Is Dead at 53," *Gay City News*, June 10, 2003, www.gaycitynews.com (accessed March 1, 2013). The *New York Times* reported that "Pepper was the last of the four great queens of the modern Harlem balls: Angie Xtravaganza, Dorian Corey, and Avis Pendavis all died in recent years." Douglas Martin, "Pepper LaBeija, Queen of Harlem Drag Balls, Is Dead at 53," *New York Times*, May 26, 2003, 1.

39. Kath Weston, *Families We Choose: Lesbians, Gays, Kinship* (New York: Columbia University Press, 1991), 106–7.

40. In recent years, some parents of houses with multiple chapters have been called overseers of a region, such as "overseer of the Midwest region."

41. Leonardo, "The Female World of Cards and Holidays," 386.

42. Other bars similar to the Woodward, such as the Continental and the Shoppers' Lounge, all located in downtown proper, closed in recent years and were replaced by Compuware's corporate headquarters and a parking structure as part of downtown renewal plans put in motion by former mayor Dennis Archer's administration (1994–2002). These bars were popular places where Black LGBT people and Ballroom members could meet, drink, and socialize.

43. Weston, *Families We Choose*, 106.

44. Early in my research, before I decided to focus on Detroit, I interviewed Lovely Mohair and Tim'm T. West at the Sexual Minority Alliance of Alameda County (SMAAC) Youth Center, then located on Telegraph Avenue in downtown Oakland, California. As of 2012, Lovely is the mother of The House of Revlon West Coast.

45. Linda M. Burton and Carol B. Stack, "Kinscripts," in *Families in the U.S.: Kinship and Domestic Politics*, ed. Karen V. Hansen and Anita Ilta Gary (Philadelphia: Temple University Press, 1998), 408. Burton and Stack also argue that "kinscripts" constitute a framework that represents the interplay of family ideology, norms, and behaviors over the life course.

46. Judith Halberstam makes this point in *Female Masculinity* (Durham: Duke University Press, 1998).

47. Ibid., 408.

48. Emily Arnold and Marlon M. Bailey, "Constructing Home and Family: How the Ballroom Community Supports African American GLBTQ Youth in the Face of HIV/AIDS," *Journal of Gay and Lesbian Social Services* 21, nos. 2–3 (2009): 180–81.

49. Unfortunately, I do not have much data on Women members of the Ballroom "gender system." Increasingly, more Women are getting involved, but, as my interlocutors told me, this increase is not a significant one in Detroit. Most of the Women in Ballroom culture are on the East Coast.

50. Evelyn Nakano Glenn, "Social Construction of Mothering: A Thematic Overview," in *Mothering: Ideology, Experience, and Agency*, ed. Evelyn Nakano Glenn, Grace Chang, and Linda Rennie Forcey (New York: Routledge, 1994), 6.

51. Arnold and Bailey, "Constructing Home and Family," 180.

52. Christopher Carrington, *No Place Like Home: Relationships and Family Life among Lesbians and Gay Men* (Chicago: University of Chicago Press, 1999), 17.

53. Arnold and Bailey, "Constructing Home and Family," 180.

54. Weston, *Families We Choose*, xviii.

55. For more information on Black queer perspectives on same-sex marriage, see Marlon M. Bailey, Priya Kandaswamy, and Mattie Udora Richardson, "Is Gay Marriage Racist?," in *That's Revolting: Queer Strategies for Resisting Assimilation*, ed. Matt Bernstein Sycamore (New York: Soft Skull Press, 2004).

56. In Ballroom, princes and princesses are the sons or daughters in houses who are most likely to become the housemothers or housefathers should the current parents not continue their roles.

57. James, "Mothering," 44–45.

58. Jonathon David Jackson, "The Social World of Voguing," *Journal for the Anthropological Study of Human Movement* 12, no. 2 (2002): 32.

59. Fiona Buckland, *Impossible Dance: Club Culture and Queer World-Making* (Middletown, CT: Wesleyan University Press, 2002), 4.

60. Carrington, *No Place Like Home*, 6.

Chapter 4

1. Selvin Kahn said this while commentating a ball in Detroit on July 26, 2010, at the St. Regis Hotel, during the city's Hotter than July Pride Festivities. Formerly a member of The House of Givenchy, Selvin is the overall mother of The House of Kahn, based in New York City. He is no doubt the most prominent and sought-after commentator in the Ballroom scene nationally and has been at least throughout the ten years that I have been conducting research on and associated with the community.

2. Neiman Marcus Escada is a very popular Ballroom commentator based in Chicago. This chant was taken from a CD of music mixes called *Bamabounce*. My interlocutors told me that Neiman Marcus performs this chant at the balls he commentates.

3. The Detroit Masonic Temple is the largest temple of its kind in the world. The temple was formally dedicated on Thanksgiving Day in 1926 by the Grand Lodge of

Michigan. For more information, see http://themasonic.com/index.html (accessed August 2011).

4. Several months after The House of Ford Ball in 2001, Eriq Christian Bazaar died from complications of AIDS. Based in New York City, Eriq was one of the leaders of the Ballroom community and a legendary member of The House of Christian Bazaar. Most of all, according to all of my interlocutors, Eriq will go down in history as one of the most outstanding commentators in the Ballroom scene ever.

5. Eric Garber, "A Spectacle in Color: The Lesbian and Gay Subculture of Jazz Age Harlem," in *Hidden from History: Reclaiming the Gay and Lesbian Past*, ed. Martha Vicinus, George Chauncey Jr., and Martin Duberman (New York: Penguin Group, 1990), 332. For more on Black LGBT life in Harlem during the mid–twentieth century, see George Chauncey's *Gay New York: Gender, Urban Culture, and the Making of the Gay Male World, 1890–1940* (New York: Basic Books, 1994).

6. Viviane K. Namaste, *Invisible Lives: The Erasure of Transsexual and Transgender People* (Chicago: University of Chicago Press, 2000), 11.

7. Eric Garber argues that drag balls and other cross-dressing events did not offer the amount of privacy that Black queer people preferred because balls attracted large numbers of people who were there to observe rather than participate. He goes on to point out that drag balls provided an arena for homosexual interaction but not for the development of a homosocial network. Garber, "A Spectacle in Color," 325. For more on this point, see Kevin J. Mumford's *Interzones: Black/White Sex Districts in Chicago and New York in the Early Twentieth Century* (New York: Columbia University Press, 1997).

8. See Paul Schindler, "Pepper LaBeija Is Dead at 53," *Gay City News*, June 10, 2003, www.gaycitynews.com (accessed March 1, 2013).

9. Eric Garber, "Tain't Nobody's Bizness: Homosexuality in 1920s Harlem," in *Black Men/White Men: Afro-American Gay Life and Culture*, ed. Michael J, Smith (New York: Harrington, 1999), 9.

10. Ibid.

11. Allen Drexel, "Before Paris Burned: Race, Class, and Male Homosexuality on the Chicago South Side, 1935–1960," in *Creating a Place for Ourselves: Lesbian, Gay, and Bisexual Community Histories*, ed. Brett Beemyn (New York: Routledge 1997), 121. In this essay, Drexel describes Halloween drag balls on the South Side of Chicago, called "Finnie Balls" named after founder Alfred Finnie. According to Drexel, these annual Finnie Balls in the 1950s originated and took place in Black working-class and poor communities in Chicago.

12. In some ways, the separation of social/sexual space between Black LBGT and straight people in Detroit and other cities throughout the country is facilitated by music. Beginning in the mid-1980s and throughout the 1990s, Black LGBT clubs played predominantly house music. Straight clubs played R&B, adult contemporary, rap and hip-hop. Ironically, now, straight people of all races and ethnicities in the United States are the primary consumers of house music, and hip-hop is the predominant music form played at Black LGBT clubs. During a brief stint in the early 2000s, the now closed Agave restaurant, which was located on Woodward Avenue and Canfield Street, held house music parties on Sunday nights. This was one of the only occasions when Black LGBT and straight people would attend a party for the music. However, this at-

tendance by both Black LGBT and straight people declined, largely due to complaints from straight-identified people that they were being sexually harassed by members of the Black LGBT community in attendance. For more on this point about the separation of social/sexual space, see Marcus Anthony Hunter, "The Nightly Round: Space, Social Capital, and Urban Black Nightlife," *City and Community* 9, no. 2 (2010): 165–86.

13. In the early 1980s, when I started going to Black gay clubs in Detroit, the drag show usually started between 11:00 p.m. and midnight. I distinctly remember this because I had a 12:30 a.m. curfew when I was a teenager. My mother certainly did not know I was going to gay bars at the age of sixteen, but I was. Regrettably, I almost always had to leave at the beginning of the drag show in order to make my curfew, so for a long time I was able to get only a glimpse of the Black drag performances in these bars and clubs.

14. An example of the perspective I am critiquing here can be found in bell hooks's "is paris burning?" in *Reel to Real: Race, Sex, and Class at the Movies* (New York and London: Routledge, 1996), 214–26.

15. Marvin K. White, "The Children," in *nothin ugly fly* (Washington, DC: Redbone Press, 2004), 70.

16. For more on this point please see Brenda Dixon Gottschild, *The Black Dancing Body: a geography from coon to cool* (New York: Palgrave Macmillan, 2003) and Thomas F. DeFrantz ed. *Dancing Many Drums: Excavations in African American Dance* (Madison: University of Wisconsin Press, 2002).

17. Moe Meyer, "Rethinking *Paris Is Burning*: Performing Social Geography in Harlem Drag Balls," *Theatre Annual: A Journal of Performance Studies* 50 (1997): 45.

18. In the late 1980s, Club Heavens, a very popular after-hours nightclub, was a unique space for primarily Black LGBT people in Detroit. There has been no other club like it since. Located on Woodward Avenue and East Seven Mile Road on the northwest side of Detroit, Heavens gained notoriety for its house music. People from all over the country, mostly gay but some straight, would come to dance. However, it was located in a rough neighborhood, on the edge of an Arab American ghetto and down the street from an area where prostitution and drug trafficking were rampant. Despite extensive violence and drug trafficking inside Heavens, the club was incredibly popular until it closed in the early 1990s.

19. Jonathon David Jackson, "The Social World of Voguing," *Journal for the Anthropological Study of Human Movement* 12, no. 2 (2002): 27.

20. As I stated at the beginning of this chapter, what I am describing is a composite ball, so everything included in the description happened at a ball, but not everything occurred at The House of Ford Ball. I have pulled these occurrences from various balls and changed the location and some of the people involved. The date, time, and location of The House of Ford Ball are all accurate.

21. In recent years, through rapid technological advancements, Ballroom has come to rely primarily on the Internet to disseminate information. Many houses have their own websites, and there are several Yahoo groups in Ballroom. The two most frequently visited websites for the Ballroom community are www.walk4mewednesdays.com and http://groups.yahoo.com/group/HouseOfBalls/ (accessed September 4, 2012).

22. Basement Jaxx, "Fly Life," *Atlantic Jaxx Recordings: A Compilation*, 1997, Atlantic Jaxx.

23. Commentators in Ballroom culture use their mouths to assimilate rhythms (music beats) in order to complement and guide the performances. In an effort to approximate the pronunciation of words and the sounds that commentators use in Ballroom, I have tried in most cases to write what they say as it sounds to me. There are some common phonic strategies that I use throughout the book to illustrate the art of the chant in Ballroom culture. For example, when I capitalize and separate each letter by a hyphen within the word, it signifies that the speaker chanted each letter one at a time in rhythm with the music, such as D-I-V-A. "Brrrrrrrrrrr" means that the commentator rolled his tongue. Hyphens between words such as *ka-kat* signify that the speaker pronounced the two words together, quickly and rhythmically. Long dashes mean that people sang parts of the chant, such as E----bo----nee. This is a chant commonly used by members of The House of Ebony. The limitations of language prevent me from capturing the true sound of what people say, but these strategies are designed to provide a sense of the chanting.

24. Ballroom members snap their fingers and gesture in the direction of a person. To throw a snap is to affirm that person or the performance.

25. Vanity 6, "Nasty Girl" *Vanity* 6, 1982, Warner Brothers.

26. I mentioned this circumstance in chapter 2.

27. In no way does this abridged version of a ball reflect their length. Full balls have about twenty to twenty-five categories, a first and a second half, and are at least five to six hours long. Balls usually end early the next morning. In recent years, more houses have hosted miniballs, which have half the categories of a full ball.

28. Ballroom members hold competitions called "battle balls" in which members compete in their categories at the local level and winners advance to a regional competition and finally a national one.

29. Masters at Work, "The Ha Dance," *Blood Vibes/Jump On It/The Ha Dance,* 1991, Cutting Records.

30. Barbara Browning, *Infectious Rhythm: Metaphors of Contagion and the Spread of African Culture* (New York: Routledge, 1998).

31. The literature on ritual is enormous, too vast to possibly cover in this chapter. However, I want to point out that, as it relates to Ballroom culture, Jonathon David Jackson refers to performances as rituals and Karen McCarthy Brown makes similar assertions about Ballroom performance as ritual.

32. L. Dale Byam "Communal Space and Performance in Africa," in *Radical Street Performance: An International Anthology,* ed. Jan Cohen Cruz (New York: Routledge, 1998), 230.

33. Karen McCarthy Brown, "Mimesis in the Face of Fear: Femme Queens, Butch Queens, and Gender Play in the Houses of Greater Newark," in *Passing: Identity and Interpretation in Sexuality, Race, and Religion,* ed. María Carla Sánchez and Linda Schlossberg (New York: New York University Press, 2001), 208.

34. Victor Witter Turner and Richard Schechner, *The Anthropology of Performance* (New York: PAJ Publications, 1986), 75.

35. Richard A. Quantz, "School Ritual as Performance: A Reconstruction of Durkheim's and Turner's Uses of Ritual," *Educational Theory* 49, no. 4 (1999): 494.

36. Manthia Diawara, "Black Studies, Cultural Studies, Performative Acts," in *Race, Identity, and Representation in Education,* ed. Cameron McCarthy and Warren Crichlow (New York and London: Routledge, 1993), 265.

37. Browning, *Infectious Rhythm*, 160.

38. Ibid.

39. According to Karen McCarthy Brown, Barbara Browning, Moe Meyer, and Roberto Strongman, these spiritual systems are not only practiced in various places throughout the African diaspora, namely, Brazil, Cuba, and Haiti, but also by a multitude of people of African descent in the United States.

40. Hunter, "The Nightly Round," 181.

41. Judith Halberstam, *In a Queer Time and Place: Transgender Bodies, Subcultural Lives* (New York: New York University Press, 2005), 6.

42. At balls members do not have to belong to a house to compete in the categories. Those competitors who do not belong to a house are called "free agents" or "007s," and they can be picked up by a house after they walk. In addition, Best-Dressed Spectator is a common category that gives people who are not involved in the Ballroom scene an opportunity to participate.

43. Jackson, "The Social World of Voguing," 34.

44. Historian Sterling Stuckey argues that since the majority of Africans brought to North America during slavery were from the western and central areas of Africa, they brought and maintain many religious and cultural traditions that are characteristic of those regions. He suggests that there is substantial evidence showing that what African Americans call the "ring shout," a counterclockwise dance ritual, comes from the cultures of West and Central Africa. He concludes that this ritual dance reveals the central function of the ritual circle to people of the African diaspora. Sterling Stuckey, *Slave Culture: Nationalist Theory and the Foundation of Black America* (Oxford and New York: Oxford University Press, 1987).

45. Henri Lefebvre, *The Production of Space* (Oxford and Cambridge, MA: Blackwell, 1991), 26.

46. Ibid., 8.

47. Dwight Conquergood, "Health Theatre in a Hmong Refugee Camp: Performance Communication and Culture," in *Radical Street Performance: An International Anthology*, ed. Jan Cohen-Cruz (London and New York: Routledge, 1998), 221.

48. Anthony Thomas, "The House the Kids Built: The Gay Imprint on American Dance Music," in *Out in Culture: Gay, Lesbian, and Queer Essays on Popular Culture*, ed. Corey K. Creekmur and Alexander Doty (Durham, NC: Duke University Press, 1995), 439.

49. MFSB, "Love Is the Message," 1973, Philadelphia International Records.

50. Brian Currid, "We Are Family: House Music and Queer Performativity," in *Cruising the Performative: Interventions into Ethnicity, Nationality, and Sexuality*, ed. Philip Brett, Sue-Ellen Case, and Susan Leigh Foster (Bloomington: Indiana University Press, 1995), 165.

51. See Denise Dalphond, "Roots of Techno: Black DJs and the Detroit Scene," *Liner Notes* 12 (2007): 6–10. This article discusses a conference that was held at Indiana University, Bloomington, in October 2006 organized by the Archives of African American Music and Culture. Although techno is a form of house music with its origins in Detroit, in the article about the conference, there is no mention of the consumption of or contributions made to the music by Black LGBT communities and DJs in Detroit. In addition, see Charlton S. Gholz's "The Search for Heaven: How Ken Collier, a Gay

Black DJ, Influenced a Generation," *Detroit Metro Times,* July 14, 2004, http://www2 .metrotimes.com/editorial/story.asp?id=6502 (accessed July 20, 2011).

52. Thomas, "The House the Kids Built," 442.

53. See John Chernoff, *African Rhythm and African Sensibility: Aesthetics and Social Action in African Musical Idioms* (Chicago: University of Chicago Press, 1979).

54. Thomas, "The House the Kids Built," 443.

55. "House-heads" are house music enthusiasts who consume house music. They are diverse in terms of race, class, gender, and sexuality.

56. In June 2007 at the It's Our Time to Shine Ball, sponsored by AIDS Project of the East Bay (APEB) in Oakland, California, Lovely, at that time the housemother of The House of Infiniti, was the commentator, along with Jay Blahnik. Lovely is the only Femme Queen I have seen commentate at a ball.

57. Marlon M. Bailey, "Performance as Intravention: Ballroom Culture and the Politics of HIV/AIDS in Detroit," *Souls* 11, no. 3 (2009): 253.

58. The minstrel tradition has three phases. The first phase was a survival mechanism for enslaved African Americans. Deploying techniques of signification, the slaves would imitate the slave master and critique the institution of slavery without the master's knowledge. During the second phase, White people co-opted the practices of minstrelsy and turned them against African Americans. White entertainers would perform in blackface, supposedly portraying Black people in what was called "Negro minstrels." In this practice, White performers corked their faces and embellished their features to create a grotesque portrayal of Black people as buffoons and subhumans. The final phase of minstrelsy is when the entertainment industry, controlled by Whites, recruited Black people to cork their own faces and embellish their own features and perform as themselves in a degrading fashion. The practice during this phase was thought to create more authenticity regarding these stereotypical images of Black people and to ostensibly demonstrate the so-called subhumanity of Black people and therefore justify Jim Crow laws and other forms of racial oppression. For more elaboration on this final point, see Marlon Riggs's documentary *Ethnic Notions* (San Francisco, California Newsreel, 1987).

59. Carlton W. Molette and Barbara J. Molette, *Black Theatre: Premise and Presentation* (Bristol, IN: Wyndham Hall Press, 1986), 65.

60. Geneva Smitherman, *Talkin and Testifyin: The Language of Black America* (Boston: Houghton Mifflin, 1977), 102.

61. Ibid., 104.

62. Margaret Thompson Drewal, *Yoruba Ritual: Performers, Play, Agency.* (Bloomington: Indiana University Press, 1992), 7.

63. Kimberly W. Benston, "The Aesthetics of Modern Black Drama: From Mimesis to Methexis," in *The Theatre of Black Americans: A Collection of Critical Essays.* ed. Errol Hill (New York; Applause, 1987), 63.

64. Typically, the identity of Men within the gender system is not a main heading for categories at balls. However, Men usually walk "realness" categories such as Thug or Men's Body categories such as Sex Siren.

65. Jessica Carreras, "Just Dance: Ruth Ellis Center Documentary Shows Why, for Some Youth, Voguing Is Life," *Between the Lines (BLT),* September 16, 2010, 21.

66. Jackson, "The Social World of Voguing," 32.

67. For an example of Old Way Vogue, see http://www.youtube.com/watch?v=T7 r27xQpdco&feature=results_main&playnext=1&list=PL7D1C827DB34D1C05 (accessed March 1, 2013).

68. "What Is Vogue," The Underground Culture of Balls by Aaron Enigma. http://balls.houseofenigma.com/what_vogue.html (accessed March 1, 2013).

69. For an example of "New Way Vogue," see http://www.youtube.com/watch?v=ctzJ92E-mtU&feature=related (accessed March 1, 2013).

70. Jackson, "The Social World of Voguing," 36.

71. Ibid., 37.

72. Ibid., 36.

73. Wolfgang Busch, dir., *How Do I Look*, DVD, Art from the Heart, 2006.

Chapter 5

1. I interviewed Wolfgang Busch on November 30, 2003, in New York City. He is the director of *How Do I Look*, a documentary on Ballroom culture, which was released in January 2006. Wolfgang said that he wants the proceeds from the film to be dedicated to HIV/AIDS prevention. For more information and updates, see http://www.howdoilooknyc.org (accessed March 2, 2013).

2. Most cities with large Black LGBT populations hold Black Pride celebrations separately from White Pride celebrations. These events are designed to celebrate LGBT lives in the African American and African diasporic contexts. Most city Black Pride organizations are part of the International Federation of Black Prides, an umbrella organization for Black Pride organizations throughout the world. For more information on this organization, see http://www.ifbprides.org/ (accessed March 2, 2013).

3. Although I am very critical of CBOs in Detroit throughout this chapter, I want to point out that it is very difficult for these organizations to provide high-level prevention and treatment services under increasingly harsh and deep structural and systemic inequalities, particularly in Detroit. As discussed in chapter 1, Detroit residents are among the most impoverished in the country, and many do not have access to quality health care. This means that CBOs are often overwhelmed with clients and woefully understaffed and underresourced. I am concerned, however, with the policy decisions and priorities that are made by public health institutions on national, state, and local levels that further stigmatize, marginalize, and exclude Black LGBT people.

4. Nancy E. Stoller, *Lessons from the Damned: Queers, Whores, and Junkies Respond to AIDS* (New York: Routledge, 1998), 103.

5. For an elaboration of her argument, see Kimberly Crenshaw, "Mapping the Margins: Intersectionality, Identity Politics, and Violence against Women," in *The Public Nature of Violence*, ed. Martin A. Fineman and Roxanne Mykitiuk (New York: Routledge 1994), 93–118. In coining the term *intersectional marginalization* I draw from theories developed by feminists of color that examine multiple forms of oppression that women of color experience simultaneously. Central to this feminist theory of color intervention is Crenshaw's theorization of Black women's experiences with a legal system that compartmentalizes their experiences by focusing on race or sex instead of taking

into account how Black women's oppression functions through race, sex, and gender simultaneously (98).

6. Michele Tracy Berger, *Workable Sisterhood: The Political Journey of Stigmatized Women with HIV/AIDS* (Princeton, NJ: Princeton University Press, 2004), 18.

7. In a chapter of her book, *Infectious Rhythm: Metaphors of Contagion and the Spread of African Culture* (New York: Routledge, 1998), Barbara Browning theorizes HIV/AIDS and the Ballroom community primarily in her critique of Jennie Livingston's film *Paris Is Burning*. Karen McCarthy Brown examines HIV/AIDS and the Ballroom scene in Newark, New Jersey, in her essay "Mimesis in the Face of Fear: Femme Queens, Butch Queens, and Gender Play in the Houses of Greater Newark," in *Passing: Identity and Interpretation in Sexuality, Race, and Religion,* ed. María Carla Sánchez and Linda Schlossberg (New York: New York University Press, 2001), 208–27. Besides the essays of mine on Ballroom and HIV/AIDS prevention that I cite here, I also theorize the epidemic's impact on the Ballroom community and Black queer people in the diaspora in "Rethinking the African Diaspora and HIV/AIDS Prevention from the Perspective of Ballroom Culture," in *Global Circuits of Blackness: Interrogating the African Diaspora,* ed. Jean Muteba Rahier, Percy C. Hintzen, and Felipe Smith (Urbana: University of Illinois Press, 2010), 96–126.

8. Brett C. Stockdill, *Activism against AIDS: At the Intersections of Sexuality, Race, Gender, and Class* (Boulder, CO: Lynne Rienner Publishers, 2003), 4.

9. "HIV among African Americans," National Center for HIV/AIDS, Hepatitis, STD, and TB Prevention, Division of HIV/AIDS Prevention, Centers for Disease Control, September 2010. These stats can also be found in Henry Kaiser Family Foundation, "Fact Sheet: Black Americans and HIV/AIDS," HIV/AIDS Policy, http://www.kff .org/hivaids/upload/6089-8.pdf. (accessed May 29, 2012).

10. Public health officials created MSM as a "risk category" to describe men who have sex with men but do not identify as gay. It is not an identity; rather, it is believed to capture sexual behavior. I use it in this chapter because it is the predominant way in which CBOs refer to gay men, as well as men who do not identify as gay.

11. "Fact Sheet: Black Americans and HIV/AIDS."

12. These statistics are taken from the Michigan Department of Community Health MCDH) website, May 2003, http://www.michigan.gov/mdcdh (accessed Aug. 4, 2012). These statistics comprise two categories: those living with AIDS and those living with HIV but not AIDS. The total number of reported cases constitutes the combined totals from both categories. In 2003 MCDH estimated that there were up to 15,500 people living in Michigan who were infected with HIV (including those living with AIDS).

13. Cathy J. Cohen, "Contested Membership: Black Gay Identities and the Politics of AIDS," in *Queer Theory/Sociology,* ed. Steven Seidman (Malden: Blackwell Publishers, 1996), 372.

14. "Quarterly HIV/AIDS Analysis," Bureau of Epidemiology, HIV/AIDS Surveillance Section, Communicable Disease and Immunization Division, Michigan Department of Community Health, October 2003, 1–4. MCDH, http://www.michigan .gov/mdch/0,4612,7-132-2940_2955_2982_46000_46003---,00.html (accessed May 17, 2012).

15. Annual Review of HIV Trends in SE Michigan (2003–2007) Bureau of Epidemi-

ology, HIV/STD/VH/TB Epidemiology Section, MCDH (July 2009). MCDH, http://www.michigan.gov/mdch/0,4612,7-132-2940_2955_2982_46000_46003---,00.html (accessed May 17, 2012).

16. Marlon M. Bailey, "Performance as Intravention: Ballroom Culture and the Politics of HIV/AIDS in Detroit," *Souls* 11, no. 3 (2009): 262.

17. Annual Review HIV Trends in Michigan (2004–2007) Bureau of Epidemiology HIV/STD/VH/TB Epidemiology Section, MCDH (May 2010). See also Focus on Detroit: A Supplemental Fact Sheet to the Annual Review of HIV Trends in SE Michigan (2004–2008). http://www.michigan.gov/mdch/0,4612,7-132-2940_2955_2982_46000_46003---,00.html (accessed May 17, 2012).

18. Lester K. Spence, "Episodic Frames, HIV/AIDS, and African American Public Opinion," *Political Research Quarterly* 63, no. 2 (2009): 258.

19. Ibid., 260.

20. Ibid.

21. Cathy J. Cohen, *The Boundaries of Blackness: AIDS and the Breakdown of Black Politics* (Chicago: University of Chicago Press, 1990), 70.

22. Ibid., 13.

23. Ibid., 70.

24. Roy Cain, "Gay Identity Politics in Community-Based AIDS Organizations," in *Inside the Academy and Out: Lesbian, Gay, Queer Studies, and Social Action,* ed. Janice L. Ristock and Catherine G. Taylor (Toronto: University of Toronto Press, 1998), 200. More elaboration on this can be found in Cathy Cohen's *The Boundaries of Blackness;* Steven Seidman's edited collection *Queer Theory/Sociology* (Cambridge, MA: Blackwell Publishers, 1996); and Brett C. Stockdill's *Activism against AIDS.*

25. Mpowerment Detroit opened shortly after my tenure at MOC, so it was not around while I was in the field during my eight-month stint in 2003.

26. It received additional funds from the MDCH Title I Ryan White Fund.

27. According to MOC policy and protocol, because the prevention coordinator is the immediate supervisor of all the staff members who filed the grievances, he decided not to sign the collective letter but instead submitted a report of misconduct as a result of a series of grievances filed, including two of his own, against the deputy director. As the staff consultant, I had advised the prevention coordinator to follow MOC policies and procedures, strictly. The prevention coordinator's previous written complaints, as well as numerous other complaints registered by other employees against the deputy director, were never addressed by the executive director. I had also attached a letter explaining my support of the collective grievance and offering some suggestions about how to address the employees' concerns. I might add that this was not the first time I had discussed these issues with the executive director.

28. For more information on the incident, see Brent Dorian Carpenter, "Sexual Harassment Allegations Rock Men of Color: Funding Could Be at Risk," *Between the Lines,* June 12–18, 2003, www.pridesource.com (accessed May 17, 2012).

29. In an interview, Father Infiniti described a conflict between him and the deputy director at an HIV/AIDS conference that he claims resulted in his firing. Noir Prestige and staff members present at the conference corroborated that the deputy director instigated a confrontation that compelled Father Infiniti to respond. Afterward, the deputy director went to the executive director and demanded that Father Infiniti be fired. I later witnessed and experienced firsthand the deputy director's belligerence and

confrontational manner (both verbal and physical) toward women, feminine gay men, and anyone who disagreed with him.

30. On June 3, 2003, I was terminated and escorted out of the building by the deputy director. I had no prior warning or indication that this would happen, and I was not given a reason for my termination.

31. On a site visit at MOC conducted by the CDC (April 25, 2003), the project officer, Lisa W. Kimbrough, said that MOC's outreach prevention work was unsatisfactory, and one of the key problems cited was the organization's inability to recruit and retain employees (this was in her written report, dated May 9, 2003).

32. On October 22, 2003, the National Labor Relations Board found MOC in violation of the National Labor Relations Act, which protects employees' right to engage in concerted activity for their benefit without reprisal. Soon afterward, the executive director, deputy director, and chief financial officer were asked to resign, apparently by the board, in the midst of allegations regarding the mismanagement of funds.

33. Viviane K. Namaste, *Invisible Lives: The Erasure of Transsexual and Transgender People* (Chicago: University of Chicago Press, 2000), 194.

34. Even today, in most states, self-identified transgender women are officially categorized as MSM. This state practice is profoundly problematic in many ways. First, transgender is a gender identity, and it is neither a sexual identity nor a sexual practice. Yet MSM is used to identify both sexual "risk" (i.e., mode of infection) and a non-gay-identified category for HIV/AIDS reporting. Nonetheless, MSM is not a gender identity (it includes gender identity, but it is not in and of itself one).

35. David Román, *Acts of Intervention: Performance, Gay Culture, and AIDS* (Bloomington: Indiana University Press, 1998), xxiii.

36. Cain, "Gay Identity Politics in Community-Based AIDS Organizations," 208–9.

37. Stockdill, *Activism against AIDS*, 2.

38. Ervin Goffman, *Stigma: Notes on the Management of Spoiled Identity* (New York: Simon and Schuster, 1963), 3.

39. Berger, *Workable Sisterhood*, 23.

40. During the time I conducted fieldwork at MOC in 2003, REC was reeling from a controversial administrative shakeup. Imani Williams, director of street outreach at REC, who is an African American "same gender loving" woman, was abruptly fired by the board. As a result of her dismissal, the entire outreach staff walked out, forcing the drop-in center at the organization to close temporarily. These staff members organized a protest in support of Williams, claiming that she was fired because of racial conflicts with the executive director, Grace McClellend, who is White. This controversy and protest created division among REC clients (largely LGBT youths of color) and the organizational leadership. For more information on this controversy, see Brent Dorian Carpenter and Jason Michael, "Firing, Resignations Cause Ruth Ellis Center to Suspend Services for a Week," *Between the Lines (BTL)*, October 23, 2003; and Brent Dorian Carpenter, "Ruth Ellis Center Scrambles to Reorganize," *Between the Lines (BTL)*, October 30, 2003. It is important to note that since 2003 REC has recovered successfully from the scandal and continues to render necessary services to homeless LGBT youths in Detroit. In 2008 REC received almost two million dollars in federal funds to enhance its programs. In October 2008 Grace McClellend was asked to step down from her post under mysterious circumstances. After an interim director ran

the organization for several months, in September 2009 the center appointed Laura Hughes as its new executive director.

41. Cindy Patton, *Fatal Advice: How Safe-Sex Education Went Wrong* (Durham, NC: Duke University Press, 1996), 23.

42. This logic of containment functioned much like it did during the tuberculosis epidemic among Black communities in the early twentieth century. Samuel Kelton Roberts Jr., in *Infectious Fear: Politics, Disease, and the Effects of Segregation* (Chapel Hill: University of North Carolina Press, 2009), makes a compelling argument about the ways in which discourses of disease joined with race and class oppression go into the making of an epidemic. Wende Elizabeth Marshall also makes this point in her essay "AIDS, Race, and the Limits of Science," *Social Science and Medicine* 60, no. 11 (2005): 2515–25.

43. Jan Zita Grover argues that the "general population" is marked as heterosexual. For more on her point see her essay, "AIDS: Keywords," in *AIDS: Cultural Analysis, Cultural Activism*, ed. Douglas Crimp, 17–30 (Cambridge, Mass: MIT Press, 1998), 27.

44. Patton, *Fatal Advice*, 23.

45. Cain, "Gay Identity Politics in Community-Based AIDS Organizations," 200.

46. Stoller, *Lessons from the Damned*, 2.

47. Jason Michael, "The Mystery of MOC: Agency Apparently Closed but Officials Aren't Talking," June 30, 2005, http://www.pridesource.com/article.html?article=14869, (accessed May 29, 2012).

48. Stuart Hall, "What Is This 'Black' in Black Popular Culture?" in *Black Popular Culture*, ed. Gina Dent (Seattle: Bay Press, 1992), 24.

49. Kim D. Butler, "Defining Diaspora, Refining a Discourse," *Diaspora* 10, no. 2 (2001): 192.

50. Bailey, "Performance as Intravention," 259.

51. Diffusion of effective behavioral interventions (DEBIs) are authorized science-based, community- and individual-level interventions authorized by the CDC to be implemented by CBOs and state and local health departments. At the time of my research, there was no authorized intervention for Black MSM. However, in recent years, Many Men; Many Voices (3MV) and D'Up are two DEBIs authorized by the CDC that specifically target Black MSM. For more information, see http://www.effectiveinterventions.org/en/home.aspx (accessed March 1, 2013).

52. Francisco Roque said this at a presentation in January 2009 at the National African American MSM Conference on HIV/AIDS and other Health Disparities in Atlanta.

53. Bailey, "Performance as Intravention," 259.

54. For more discussion of these, see www.balls.houseofenigma.net (accessed March 1, 2013).

55. Vinh-Kim Nguyen, "Uses and Pleasures: Sexual Modernity, HIV/AIDS, and Confessional Technologies in a West African Metropolis," in *Sex in Development: Science, Sexuality, and Morality in Global Perspective*, ed. Vincanne Adams and Stacy Leigh Pigg (Durham, NC: Duke University Press, 2005), 246.

56. Ibid., 247.

57. For further elaboration on risk reduction models of HIV/AIDS prevention, see Marlon M. Bailey et al., "HIV (STDs, STIs, and Viral Hepatitis) Prevention and

Men who have Sex with Men (MSM) Needs Assessment," Indiana State Department of Health, http://www.policyresourcegroup.com/documents/MSMBaileyNA_2010 .pdf (accessed February 2010). See also UCSF AIDS Health Project, "Sex without Condoms," *HIV Counselor Perspectives* 10, no. 2 (2001): 1–8.

58. For more on this point, see Brian Kelly et al., "Posttraumatic Stress Disorder in Response to HIV Infection," *General Hospital Psychiatry* 20, no. 6 (1998): 245–52; and Eve M. Sledjeski et al., "Incidence and Impact of Posttraumatic Stress Disorder and Co-morbid Depression and Adherence to HAART and CD4 Counts in People Living with HIV," *AIDS Patient Care and STDs* 19, no. 11 (2005): 728–36.

59. Cornel West, "Nihilism in Black America," in *Black Popular Culture,* ed. Gina Dent (Seattle: Bay Press, 1992), 42.

60. Ironically, when I spoke with Francisco Roque after his presentation at a National AIDS and Education Services for Minorities (NAESM) meeting in 2009, he informed me that the organization's long-standing House of Latex Ball is not recognized by the CDC as an intervention, and thus it is not federally funded.

61. Michel Foucault, "The Ethic of Care for the Self as a Practice of Freedom," trans. J. D. Gauthier, in *The Final Foucault,* ed. James Bermauer and David Rasmussen (Cambridge, MA: MIT Press, 1988), 5.

62. Ibid.

63. Karen Thorsen, dir., *James Baldwin: The Price of the Ticket,* California Newsreel, San Francisco, 1990.

Epilogue

1. Father Tommy Avant Garde is the founder of the School of Opulence, a leadership, advocacy, and HIV prevention agency that focuses on the Ballroom community in Chicago.

2. In October 2011 another national meeting was held in Los Angeles, convened by ReachLA, a youth services agency. I was unable to attend that meeting.

3. See Ms. Koppi Mizrahi vogue during a House Dance International vogue competition in New York City at http://www.youtube.com/watch?v=TrJRnsdCHlk&featur e=relmfu (accessed July 23, 2012).

4. Robin D. G. Kelley, *Yo' Mama's Disfunktional! Fighting the Culture Wars in Urban America* (Boston: Beacon Press, 1997), 9.

Glossary

Ballroom Community Terms and Phrases

Age-Out: Although chronological age is not emphasized to the extent that it is in society generally, there is a point at which one is too old to actively participate in the community or at least at which one's participation changes or wanes dramatically.

Banji: Looking like rough "trade" (see "Trade").

Being shady or **throwing shade:** Underhanded or indirect actions or someone's attempt to undermine a person without being overt; to call judges shady is to accuse them of judging unfairly or in a biased manner. It can also be an indirect critique of someone.

Bring it: To put forth the best presentation or performance.

C-A-N-I-C: A commentator chant meaning "Can I see?"

Chop: To be disqualified as a contestant from the category.

Cisgender: One whose gender identity is the same as his or her sex assignment at birth.

Craft or **crafted:** Signifies fraudulent activities or the acquisition of items or services (clothing, plane tickets, hotel rooms, cars, etc.) through illegal means—mainly identity theft (also known as "stunts" or "stunkus"). This activity is rampant in Ballroom culture and constitutes a secret economy within the scene, persisting even though some members are caught and serve jail time.

Cunt or **cunty:** Ultimate femininity.

Drama: Messy or unnecessarily complicated practices and situations.

Fierce: When used positively, it is said of a characteristic that is exceptionally good or of behavior that is well done; when used ironically, it expresses a negative judgment.

Fish or **fishy:** A girl or feminine.

Get your tens: Achieving a perfect score during the first competitive round of a category.

Kids: Relatively inexperienced members of the Ballroom scene or the larger gay world. Sometimes refers to the members of the scene in general.

Kiki: To have fun, play, catch up, or "shoot the shit."

Ovah: A person or a performance that is very impressive, extraordinary, or remarkable.

Pussy: Femininity.

Serve the kids: To perform or put forth the best performance and presentation for the audience.

Sickening: Someone or something that is so exceptional, so over the top, that it is difficult to accept or look at.

Slay and snatch: To beat your competitors and snatch (win) a trophy.

Tees: Gossip.

To decree: To set the performance standard for a category; also said of a person whose performances consistently decide a category.

Trade: A masculine, male-bodied man who identifies as straight; in the Ballroom gender system, *trade* is another term for the "men who do not identify as gay" category.

Turn it: Like *werk,* to give a grand or exceptional performance or to "bring" the crowd to its feet.

Bibliography

Akbar, Na'im. *Chains and Images of Psychological Slavery*. Jersey City, NJ: New Mind Productions, 1984.

Alexander, M. Jacqui. "Erotic Autonomy as a Politics of Decolonization: An Anatomy of Feminist and State Practice in the Bahamas Tourist Economy." In *Feminist Genealogies, Colonial Legacies, Democratic Futures*, edited by M. Jacqui Alexander and Chandra Talpade Mohanty, 63–100. New York and London: Routledge, 1997.

Anzaldúa, Gloria and Cherríe Moraga, eds., *This Bridge Called My Back: Writings by Radical Women of Color*, New York: Kitchen Table; Women of Color Press, 1983.

Arnold, Emily, and Marlon M. Bailey. "Constructing Home and Family: How the Ballroom Community Supports African American GLBTQ Youth in the Face of HIV/AIDS." *Journal of Gay and Lesbian Social Services* 21, nos. 2–3 (2009): 171–88.

Asante, Molefi. *Afrocentricity: The Theory of Social Change*. Trenton, NJ: Africa World Press 1988.

Bailey, Marlon M. "Performance as Intravention: Ballroom Culture and the Politics of HIV/AIDS in Detroit." *Souls* 11, no. 3 (2009): 253–74.

Bailey, Marlon M. "Rethinking the African Diaspora and HIV/AIDS Prevention from the Perspective of Ballroom Culture." In *Global Circuits of Blackness: Interrogating the African Diaspora*, edited by Jean Muteba Rahier, Percy C. Hintzen, and Felipe Smith, 96–126. Urbana: University of Illinois Press, 2010.

Bailey, Marlon M., Xavier Livermon, Joshua Thompson, George Kraus, Katie Dieter, and Patrick Battani. "HIV (STDs, STIs, and Viral Hepatitis) Prevention and Men Who Have Sex with Men (MSM) Needs Assessment." Indiana State Department of Health, http://www.policyresourcegroup.com/documents/MSMBaileyNA_2010 .pdf (accessed February 2010).

Bailey, Marlon M., Priya Kandaswamy, and Mattie Udora Richardson. "Is Gay Marriage Racist?" In *That's Revolting: Queer Strategies for Resisting Assimilation*, edited by Matt Bernstein Sycamore, 87–93. New York: Soft Skull Press, 2004.

Basement Jaxx. *Fly Life, Atlantic Jaxx Recordings: A Compilation*. Atlantic Jaxx, 1997.

Beemyn, Brett. *Creating a Place for Ourselves: Lesbian, Gay, and Bisexual Community Histories*. New York: Routledge, 1997.

Beemyn, Brett. "The Geography of Same-Sex Desire: Cruising Men in Washington, DC, in the Late Nineteenth and Early Twentieth Centuries." *Left History* 9, no. 2 (2004): 141–59.

Benston, Kimberly W. "The Aesthetics of Modern Black Drama: From Mimesis to Methexis." In *The Theatre of Black Americans: A Collection of Critical Essays*, edited by Errol Hill, 61–78. New York: Applause, 1987.

Berger, Michele Tracy. *Workable Sisterhood: The Political Journey of Stigmatized Women with HIV/AIDS.* Princeton, NJ: Princeton University Press, 2004.

Black Pride. http://www.ifbprides.org/ (accessed April 27, 2011).

Brown, Karen McCarthy. "Mimesis in the Face of Fear: Femme Queens, Butch Queens, and Gender Play in the Houses of Greater Newark." In *Passing: Identity and Interpretation in Sexuality, Race, and Religion,* edited by María Carla Sánchez and Linda Schlossberg, 208–27. New York: New York University Press, 2001.

Browning, Barbara. *Infectious Rhythm: Metaphors of Contagion and the Spread of African Culture.* New York: Routledge, 1998.

Buckland, Fiona. *Impossible Dance: Club Culture and Queer World-Making.* Middletown, CT: Wesleyan University Press, 2002.

Burton, Linda M., and Carol B. Stack. "Kinscripts." In *Families in the U.S.: Kinship and Domestic Politics,* edited by Karen V. Hansen and Anita Ilta Gary. Philadelphia: Temple University Press, 1998, 405–18.

Busch, Wolfgang, dir. *How Do I Look.* DVD. Art from the Heart, 2006.

Butler, Judith. *Bodies That Matter: On the Discursive Limits of "Sex."* New York: Routledge, 1993.

Butler, Judith. *Gender Trouble: Feminism and the Subversion of Identity.* New York: Routledge, 2006.

Butler, Judith. *Undoing Gender.* New York: Routledge, 2004.

Butler, Kim D. "Defining Diaspora, Refining a Discourse." *Diaspora* 10, no. 2 (2001): 189–219.

Byam, L. Dale. "Communal Space and Performance in Africa." In *Radical Street Performance: An International Anthology,* edited by Jan Cohen Cruz, 230–37. New York: Routledge, 1998.

Cain, Roy. "Gay Identity Politics in Community-Based AIDS Organizations." In *Inside the Academy and Out: Lesbian, Gay, Queer Studies, and Social Action,* edited by Janice L. Ristock and Catherine G. Taylor, 199–219. Toronto: University of Toronto Press, 1998.

Carpenter, Brent Dorian. "Ruth Ellis Center Scrambles to Reorganize." *Between the Lines (BTL),* October 30, 2003.

Carpenter, Brent Dorian. "Sexual Harassment Allegations Rock Men of Color: Funding Could Be at Risk." *Between the Lines (BTL),* June 12–18, 2003, www.pridesource.com (accessed July 24, 2012).

Carpenter, Brent Dorian, and Jason Michael. "Firing, Resignations Cause Ruth Ellis Center to Suspend Services for a Week." *Between the Lines (BTL),* October 23, 2003.

Carreras, Jessica. "Just Dance: Ruth Ellis Center Documentary Shows Why, for Some Youth, Voguing Is Life." *Between the Lines (BLT),* September 16, 2010, 21.

Carrington, Christopher. *No Place Like Home: Relationships and Family Life among Lesbians and Gay Men.* Chicago: University of Chicago Press, 1999.

Chauncey, George, Jr. *Gay New York: Urban Culture, and the Making of the Gay Male World, 1890–1940.* New York: Basic Books, 1994.

Chernoff, John. *African Rhythm and African Sensibility: Aesthetics and Social Action in African Musical Idioms.* Chicago: University of Chicago Press, 1979.

Cohen, Cathy J. *The Boundaries of Blackness: AIDS and the Breakdown of Black Politics.* Chicago: University of Chicago Press, 1999.

Cohen, Cathy J. "Contested Membership: Black Gay Identities and the Politics of AIDS." In *Queer Theory/Sociology*, edited by Steven Seidman, 362–94. Malden, MA, and Oxford: Blackwell Publishers, 1996.

Colón, Edgar Rivera. "Getting Life in Two Worlds: Power and Prevention in the New York City House Ball Community." PhD diss., Rutgers University, 2009.

Conlin, Michelle, and Jessi Hempel. "Unmarried American." *Business Week*, October 20, 2003.

Conquergood, Dwight. "Health Theatre in a Hmong Refugee Camp: Performance Communication and Culture." In *Radical Street Performance: An International Anthology*, edited by Jan Cohen-Cruz, 220–29. London and New York: Routledge, 1998.

Conquergood, Dwight. "Performance Studies: Interventions and Radical Research." *TDR: The Drama Review* 46, no. 2 (2002): 145–53.

Corbit, Wayne. *Crying Holy*. In *Colored Contradictions: An Anthology of Contemporary African American Plays*, edited by Harry Elam Jr. and Robert Alexander, 453–522. New York: Penguin Group, 1996.

Crenshaw, Kimberly. "Mapping the Margins: Intersectionality, Identity Politics, and Violence against Women." In *The Public Nature of Violence*, edited by Martin A. Fineman and Roxanne Mykitiuk, 93–118. New York: Routledge 1994.

Cromwell, Jason. *Transmen and FTM: Identities, Bodies, Gender, and Sexualities*. Urbana: University of Illinois Press, 1999.

Cruz-Malavé, Arnaldo. *Queer Latino Testimonio, Keith Haring, and Juanito Xtravaganza: Hard Tails*. New York: Palgrave Macmillan, 2007.

Currid, Brian. "We Are Family: House Music and Queer Performativity." In *Cruising the Performative: Interventions into Ethnicity, Nationality, and Sexuality*, edited by Philip Brett, Sue-Ellen Case, and Susan Leigh Foster, 165–96. Bloomington: Indiana University Press, 1995.

Dalphond, Denise. "Roots of Techno: Black DJs and the Detroit Scene." *Liner Notes* 12 (2007): 6–10.

Davis, Angela Yvonne. *Women, Culture, and Politics*. New York: Vintage Books, 1990.

DeFrantz, Thomas F., ed. *Dancing Many Drums: Excavations in African American Dance*, Madison: University of Wisconsin Press, 2002.

Denvir, Daniel. "The 10 Most Segregated Urban Areas in America." *Salon*, http://www.salon.com/2011/03/29/most_segregated_cities/slide_show/7/ (accessed September 1, 2012).

Department of Labor and Economic Growth for the State of Michigan. "Unemployment Rate for the State of Michigan (2005)." http://www.michigan.gov/midashboard/0,4624,7-256-58012_58014_58420-,00.html (accessed October 7, 2011).

Detroit Masonic Temple., http://themasonic.com/index.html (accessed August 2011).

Diawara, Manthia. "Black Studies, Cultural Studies, Performative Acts." In *Race, Identity, and Representation in Education*, edited by Cameron McCarthy and Warren Crichlow, 262–67. New York and London: Routledge, 1993.

"Diffusion of Effective Behavioral Interventions (DEBI)." http://www.effectiveinterventions.org/en/home.aspx (accessed on April 27, 2011).

Dillard, Angela D. *Faith in the City: Preaching Radical Social Change in Detroit*. Ann Arbor: University of Michigan Press, 2007.

Drexel, Allen. "Before Paris Burned: Race, Class, and Male Homosexuality on the Chicago South Side, 1935–1960." In *Creating a Place for Ourselves: Lesbian, Gay, and Bisexual Community Histories*, edited by Brett Beemyn, 119–44. New York: Routledge, 1997.

Drewal, Margaret Thompson. "The State of Research on Performance in Africa." *African Studies Review* 34, no. 3 (1991): 1–64.

Drewal, Margaret Thompson. *Yoruba Ritual: Performers, Play, Agency.* Bloomington: Indiana University Press, 1992.

Duggan, Lisa. "Holy Matrimony." *The Nation*, February 26, 2004.

Duggan, Lisa. "The Trails of Alice Mitchell: Sensationalism, Sexology, and the Lesbian Subject in Turn-of-the-Century America," *Signs* 18, no. 4 (1993): 791–814.

Fabian, Johannes. *Power and Performance: Ethnographic Explorations through Proverbial Wisdom and Theater in Shaba, Zaire.* Madison: University of Wisconsin Press, 1990.

Fausto-Sterling, Ann. *Sexing the Body: Gender Politics and the Construction of Sexuality.* New York: Basic Books, 2000.

Foucault, Michel. "The Ethic of Care for the Self as a Practice of Freedom." Translated by J. D. Gauthier. In *The Final Foucault*, edited by James Bermauer and David Rasmussen, 1–20. Cambridge, MA: MIT Press, 1988.

Garber, Eric. "A Spectacle in Color: The Lesbian and Gay Subculture of Jazz Age Harlem." In *Hidden from History: Reclaiming the Gay and Lesbian Past*, edited by Martha Vicinus, George Chauncey Jr., and Martin Duberman, 318–31. New York: Penguin Group, 1990.

Garber, Eric. "Tain't Nobody's Bizness: Homosexuality in 1920s Harlem." In *Black Men/White Men: Afro-American Gay Life and Culture*, edited by Michael J. Smith, 7–16. San Francisco: Gay Sunshine Press, 1999.

Gholz, Charlton S. "The Search for Heaven: How Ken Collier, a Gay Black DJ, Influenced a Generation." *Detroit Metro Times*, http://www2.metrotimes.com/editorial/story.asp?id=6502 (accessed July 20, 2011).

Gilroy, Paul. "It's a Family Affair." In *Black Popular Culture*, edited by Gina Dent, 303–16. Seattle: Bay Press 1992.

Glenn, Evelyn Nakano. "Social Construction of Mothering: A Thematic Overview." In *Mothering: Ideology, Experience, and Agency*, edited by Grace Chang, Linda Rennie Forcey, and Evelyn Nakano Glenn, 1–32. New York: Routledge, 1994.

Goffman, Ervin. *Stigma: Notes on the Management of Spoiled Identity.* New York: Simon and Schuster, 1963.

Goldsby, Jackie. "Queens of Language." In *Queer Looks: Perspectives on Lesbian and Gay Film and Video*, edited by Martha Gever, John Greyson, and Pratibha Parmar, 108–15. New York: Routledge, 1994.

Gottschild, Brenda Dixon. *The Black Dancing Body: a geography from coon to cool.* New York: Palgrave Macmillan, 2003.

Gray, Mary L. *Youth, Media, and Queer Visibility in Rural America.* New York: New York University Press, 2009.

Griffin, Farah Jasmine. *"Who Set You Flowin'?" The African-American Migration Narrative.* Oxford: Oxford University Press, 1995.

Grover, Jan Zita. "AIDS: Keywords." In *AIDS: Cultural Analysis, Cultural Activism*, ed. Douglas Crimp, 17–30. Cambridge, MA: MIT Press, 1988.

Halberstam, Judith. *Female Masculinity*. Durham: Duke University Press, 1998.

Halberstam, Judith. *In a Queer Time and Place: Transgender Bodies, Subcultural Lives*. New York: New York University Press, 2005.

Hall, Stuart. "The Problem of Ideology: Marxism without Guarantees." In *Stuart Hall: Critical Dialogues in Cultural Studies*, edited by David Morley and Kuan-Hsing Chen, 25–46. London and New York: Routledge, 1996.

Hall, Stuart. "What Is This 'Black' in Black Popular Culture?" In *Black Popular Culture*, edited by Gina Dent, 21–36. Seattle: Bay Press, 1992.

Hare, Nathan, and Julia Hare, eds. *Crisis in Black Sexual Politics*. San Francisco: Black Think Tank, 1989.

Hare, Nathan, and Julia Hare. *The Endangered Black Family: Coping with the Unisexualization and Coming Extinction of the Black Race*. San Francisco: Black Think Tank, 1984.

Hawkeswood, William, and Alex W. Costley. *One of the Children: Gay Black Men in Harlem*. Berkeley: University of California Press, 1996.

Henry Kaiser Family Foundation. "Fact Sheet: Black Americans and HIV/AIDS." HIV/AIDS Policy, www.kff.org (accessed November 2010).

Hill, Robert B. *Research on the African-American Family: A Holistic Perspective*. Westport, CT: Auborn House, 1993.

Hintzen, Percy C. *West Indian in the West: Self-Representation in an Immigrant Community*. New York: New York University Press, 2001.

"HIV among African Americans." National Center for HIV/AIDS, Hepatitis, STD, and TB Prevention, Division of HIV/AIDS Prevention, Centers for Disease Control, September 2010.

hooks, bell. "is paris burning?" In *Reel to Real: Race, Sex, and Class at the Movies*. New York and London: Routledge, 1996.

Hunter, Marcus Anthony. "The Nightly Round: Space, Social Capital, and Urban Black Nightlife." *City and Community* 9, no. 2 (2010): 165–86.

Inness, Sherrie, and Michelle Lloyd. "G.I. Joes in Barbi Land: Recontextualizing Butch in Twentieth-Century Lesbian Culture." In *Queer Studies: A Lesbian, Gay, Bisexual, and Transgender Anthology*, edited by Brett Beemyn and Mickey Eliason, 9–34. New York: New York University Press, 1996.

Jackson, Jonathon David. "The Social World of Voguing." *Journal for the Anthropological Study of Human Movement* 12, no. 2 (2002): 26–42.

James, Stanlie M. "Mothering: A Possible Black Feminist Link to Social Transformation?" In *Theorizing Black Feminisms: The Visionary Pragmatism of Black Women*, edited by Stanlie M. James and Abena P. A. Busia, 45–56. New York and London: Routledge, 1993.

Johnson, E. Patrick. *Appropriating Blackness: Performance and the Politics of Authenticity*. Durham, NC: Duke University Press, 2003.

Johnson, E. Patrick. "'Quare' Studies, or (Almost) Everything I Know about Queer Studies I Learned from My Grandmother." In *Black Queer Studies: A Critical Anthology*, edited by E. Patrick Johnson and Mae G. Henderson. Durham, NC: Duke University Press, 2005, 124–57

Kelly, Brian, Beverley Raphael, Fiona Judd, Michael Perdices, Graeme J. Kernutt, Paul C. Burnett, and Graham Burrows. "Posttraumatic Stress Disorder in Response to HIV Infection." *General Hospital Psychiatry* 20, no. 6 (1998): 245–53.

Kelley, Robin D. G. *Yo' Moma's Dysfunktional! Fighting the Culture Wars in Urban America*. Boston: Beacon Press, 1997.

Lefebvre, Henri. *The Production of Space*. Oxford and Cambridge, MA: Blackwell, 1991.

Lemann, Nicholas. *The Promised Land: The Great Migration and How It Changed America*. New York: Knopf, 1991.

Leonardo, Micaela di. "The Female World of Cards and Holidays: Women, Families, and the Work of Kinship." In *Gender in Cross-Cultural Perspective*, edited by Caroline B. Brettell and Carolyn F. Sargent, 2nd ed., 385–94. Upper Saddle River, NJ: Prentice-Hall, 1997.

Livingston, Jennie, dir. *Paris Is Burning*. Film/DVD. Miramax, 1990.

Lubiano, Wahneema. "Black Nationalism and Black Common Sense: Policing Ourselves and Others." In *The House That Race Built*, edited by Wahneema Lubiano, 232–45. New York: Vintage Books, 1998.

Madhubuti, Haki. *Black Men: Obsolete, Single, Dangerous? The Afrikan American in Transition—Essays in Discovery, Solution, and Hope*. Chicago: Third World Press, 1990.

Madison, Soyini D. *Critical Ethnography: Method, Ethics, and Performance*. Thousand Oaks, CA: Sage Publications, 2012.

Madison, Soyini D., and Judith Hamera. "Performance Studies at the Intersections." In *The Sage Handbook of Performance Studies*, edited by D. Soyini Madison and Judith Hamera, xii–xxv. Thousand Oaks, CA: Sage Publications, 2006.

Maloney, Thomas N., and Warren C. Whatley. "Making the Effort: The Contours of Racial Discrimination in Detroit's Labor Market, 1920–1940." *Journal of Economic History* 55, no. 3 (1995): 465–93.

Manalansan IV, Martin F. *Global Divas: Filipino Gay Men in the Diaspora*. Durham, NC: Duke University Press, 2003.

Manning, Susan. *Modern Dance, Negro Dance: Race in Motion*. Minneapolis: University of Minnesota Press, 2004.

Manning, Susan. "Performance." In *Keywords for American Cultural Studies*, edited by Bruce Burgett and Glenn Hendler. New York: New York University Press, 2007, 177–80.

Marshall, Wende Elizabeth. "AIDS, Race, and the Limits of Science." *Social Science and Medicine* 60, no. 11 (2005): 2515–25.

Martin, Douglas. "Pepper LaBeija, Queen of Harlem Drag Balls, Is Dead at 53." *New York Times*, May 26, 2003.

Masters at Work. *The Ha Dance, Blood Vibes/Jump On It/The Ha Dance*. Cutting Records, 1991.

McBeth, Mark. "The Queen's English: A Queery into Contrastive Rhetoric." In *Contrastive Rhetoric Revisited and Redefined*, edited by Clayann Gilliam Panetta, 95–112. Mahwah, NJ: Lawrence Earlbaum Associates, 2001.

Meyer, Moe. "Rethinking *Paris Is Burning*: Performing Social Geography in Harlem Drag Balls." *Theatre Annual: A Journal of Performance Studies* 50 (Fall 1997): 40–71.

MFSB. *Love Is the Message*. Philadelphia International Records, 1973.

Michael, Jason. "Detroit Mayor Denounces Marriage Equality for Gays on National Television." *Between the Lines (BTL)*, March 4, 2004.

Michael, Jason. "The Mystery of MOC: Agency Apparently Closed but Officials Aren't

Talking," June 30, 2005. http://www.pridesource.com/article.html?article=14869 (accessed May 29, 2012).

Michigan Department of Community Health, http://www.michigan.gov/mdch/ 0,4612,7-132-2940_2955_2982_46000_46003-,00.html (accessed May 17, 2012).

MDCH Bureau of Epidemiology, Focus on Detroit: A Supplemental Fact Sheet to the Annual Review of HIV Trends in SE Michigan (2004–2008) http://www.michigan .gov/mdch/0,4612,7-132-2940_2955_2982_46000_46003-,00.html (accessed May 17, 2012).

MDCH Bureau of Epidemiology, Annual Review HIV Trends in SC Michigan (2004–2007) HIV/STD/VH/TB Epidemiology Section, http://www.michigan.gov/ mdch/0,4612,7-132-2940_2955_2982_46000_46003-,00.html (accessed May 20, 2010).

MDCH, Bureau of Epidemiology. *Annual Review of HIV Trends in SE Michigan (2003–2007), HIV/STD/VH/TB Epidemiology Section, MCDH,* July 2009.

MDCH, Bureau of Epidemiology, HIV/AIDS Surveillance Section, Communicable Disease and Immunization Division. "Quarterly HIV/AIDS Analysis," October 2003, 1–4.

Molette, Carlton W., and Barbara J. Molette. *Black Theatre: Premise and Presentation.* Bristol, IN: Wyndham Hall Press, 1986.

Montemurri, Patricia, Kathleen Gray, and Cicil Angel. "Detroit Tops Nation in Poverty Census." *Detroit Free Press,* August 31, 2005.

Moore, Mignon R. *Invisible Families: Gay Identities, Relationships, and Motherhood among Black Women.* Berkeley: University of California Press, 2011.

Moynihan, Daniel P. "The Tangle of Pathology." In *The Black Family: Essays and Studies,* edited by Robert Staples, 6th ed., 7–17. Belmont, CA: Wadsworth Publishing, 1965.

Moynihan, Daniel P. "U.S. Department of Labor—History—Chapter IV.: The Tangle of Pathology." www.dol.gov/oasam/programs/history/moynchapter4.htm[1/11/2009 11:10:14 AM] (accessed May 9, 2011).

Mumford, Kevin J. *Interzones: Black/White Sex Districts in Chicago and New York in the Early Twentieth Century.* New York: Columbia University Press, 1997.

Muñoz, José Esteban. *Disidentification: Queers of Color and the Performance of Politics.* Minneapolis: University of Minnesota Press, 1999.

Namaste, Viviane K. *Invisible Lives: The Erasure of Transsexual and Transgender People.* Chicago: University of Chicago Press, 2000.

Natambu, Kofi. "Nostalgia for the Present: Cultural Resistance in Detroit, 1977–1987." In *Black Popular Culture,* edited by Gina Dent, Michelle Wallace, and the Dia Center for the Arts, 173–86. Seattle: Bay Press, 1992.

Nguyen, Vinh-Kim. "Uses and Pleasures: Sexual Modernity, HIV/AIDS, and Confessional Technologies in a West African Metropolis." In *Sex in Development: Science, Sexuality, and Morality in Global Perspective,* edited by Vincanne Adams and Stay Leigh Pigg, 245–68. Durham, NC: Duke University Press, 2005.

Page, Enoch, and Matt U. Richardson. "On the Fear of Small Numbers." In *Black Sexualities: Probing Powers, Passions, Practices, and Policies,* edited by Juan Battle and Sandra L. Barnes, 57–81. New Brunswick, NJ: Rutgers University Press, 2010.

Patterson, Orlando. *Rituals of Blood: Consequences of Slavery in Two American Centuries.* New York: Basic Civitas, 1998.

Patton, Cindy, *Fatal Advice: How Safe-Sex Education Went Wrong*. Durham, NC: Duke University Press, 1996.

Peller, Scott. "Laboring for a Brave New World: Our Ford and the Epsilons." In *Huxley's Brave New World: Essays*, edited by David Garrett Izzo and Kim Kirkpatrick, 62–72. Jefferson, NC: McFarland, 2008.

Phelan, Peggy. *Unmarked: The Politics of Performance*. New York: Routledge, 1993.

Quantz, Richard A. "School Ritual as Performance: A Reconstruction of Durkheim's and Turner's Uses of Ritual." *Educational Theory* 49, no. 4 (1999): 493–513.

Retzloff, Tim. "'Seer or Queer'? Postwar Fascination with Detroit's Prophet Jones." *GLQ: A Journal of Lesbian and Gay Studies* 8, no. 3 (2002): 271–96.

Riggs, Marlon. *Ethnic Notions*. San Francisco, California Newsreel, 1987.

Roberts, Samuel Kelton, Jr. *Infectious Fear: Politics, Disease, and the Effects of Segregation*. Chapel Hill: University of North Carolina Press, 2009.

Rodriguez, Richard. *Next of Kin: The Family in Chicano/a Cultural Politics*. Durham, NC: Duke University Press, 2009.

Rofel, Lisa. "Qualities of Desire: Imagining Gay Identities in China." *GLQ: A Journal of Lesbian and Gay Studies* 5, no. 4 (1999): 451–74.

Román, David. *Acts of Intervention: Performance, Gay Culture, and AIDS*. Bloomington: Indiana University Press, 1998.

Román, David. *Performance in America: Contemporary U.S. Culture and the Performing Arts*. Durham, NC: Duke University Press, 2005.

Roque, Francisco. Presentation ("4Real/Community Promise: Working with the House and Ball Community") given at the National African American MSM Conference on HIV/AIDS and Other Health Disparities, Atlanta, 2009.

Russell, Thaddeus. "The Color of Discipline: Civil Rights and Black Sexuality." *American Quarterly* 60, no. 1 (2008): 101–28.

Shabazz, Rashad. "So High You Can't Get Over It, So Low You Can't Get Under It": Carceral Spatiality and Black Masculinities in the United States and South Africa." *Souls* 11, no. 3 (2009): 276–94.

Schilt, Kristen, and Laurel Westbrook. "Doing Gender, Doing Heteronormativity: 'Gender Normals,' Transgender People, and the Social Maintenance of Heterosexuality," *Gender & Society* 23, no. 4 (2009): 440–64.

Schindler, Paul. "Pepper LaBeija Is Dead at 53." *Gay City News*, June 10, 2003.

Seidman, Steven, ed. *Queer Theory/Sociology*. Cambridge, MA: Blackwell Publishers, 1996.

Shaw, Todd C. *Now Is the Time! Detroit Black Politics and Grassroots Activism*. Durham, NC: Duke University Press, 2009.

Sledjeski, Eve M., D. L. Delahanty, and L. M. Bogart. "Incidence and Impact of Posttraumatic Stress Disorder and Co-morbid Depression and Adherence to HAART and CD4 Counts in People Living with HIV." *AIDS Patient Care and STDs* 19, no. 11 (2005): 728–36.

Smitherman, Geneva. *Talkin and Testifyin: The Language of Black America*. Boston: Houghton Mifflin, 1977.

Somerville, Siobhan B. "Queer." In *Keywords for American Cultural Studies*, edited by Bruce Burgett and Glenn Hendler, 187–91. New York: New York University Press, 2007.

Spence, Lester K. "Episodic Frames, HIV/AIDS, and African American Public Opinion." *Political Research Quarterly* 63, no. 2 (2009): 257–68.

Spence, Lester K. "Uncovering Black Attitudes about Homosexuality and HIV/AIDS." Lecture delivered at the National Conference of Black Political Scientists, Alexandria, Virginia, 2005.

Stack, Carol. *All Our Kin*. New York: Basic Books, 1974.

Stallings, L. H. *Mutha' Is Half a Word: Intersections of Folklore, Vernacular, Myth, and Queerness in Black Female Culture*. Columbus: Ohio State University Press, 2007.

Staples, Robert, ed. *The Black Family: Essays and Studies*. 6th ed. Belmont, CA: Wadsworth Publishing.

Staples, Robert. *Black Masculinity: The Black Man's Role in American Society*. San Francisco: Black Scholars Press, 1982.

Stephens, Charles F. "Performing Black and Gay: Butch Queen Radicalism." In *If We Have to Take Tomorrow: HIV, Black Men, and Same Sex Desire*, edited by Frank León Roberts and Marvin White, 31–34. New York: Institute of Gay Men's Health, 2006.

Stevenson, Jan. "Kilpatrick Responds to LGBT Community." *Between the Lines (BTL)*, June 14, 2001.

Stockdill, Brett C. *Activism against AIDS: At the Intersections of Sexuality, Race, Gender, and Class*. Boulder, CO: Lynne Rienner Publishers, 2003.

Stoller, Nancy E. *Lessons from the Damned: Queers, Whores, and Junkies Respond to AIDS*. New York: Routledge, 1998.

Strongman, Roberto. "Syncretic Religion and Dissident Sexualities." In *Queer Globalization, Citizenship, and the Afterlife of Colonialism*, edited by Arnaldo Cruz-Malavé and Martin F. Manalansan IV, 171–94. New York: New York University Press, 2002.

Stryker, Susan. "(De)Subjugated Knowledges: An Introduction to Transgender Studies." In *The Transgender Studies Reader*, edited by Susan Stryker and Stephen Whittle, 1–18. New York: Routledge, 2006.

Stuckey, Sterling. *Slave Culture: Nationalist Theory and the Foundation of Black America*. Oxford and New York: Oxford University Press, 1987.

Sugrue, Thomas. *The Origins of the Urban Crisis: Race and Inequality in Postwar Detroit*. Princeton, NJ: Princeton University Press, 1996.

Thomas, Anthony. "The House the Kids Built: The Gay Imprint on American Dance Music." In *Out in Culture: Gay, Lesbian, and Queer Essays on Popular Culture*, edited by Corey K. Creekmur and Alexander Doty, 437–46. Durham, NC: Duke University Press, 1995.

Thompson, Heather Ann. *Whose Detroit? Politics, Labor, and Race in a Modern American City*. Ithaca, NY: Cornell University Press, 2001.

Thorpe, Rochella. "'A House Where Queers Go': African-American Lesbian Nightlife in Detroit, 1940–1975." In *Inventing Lesbian Cultures in America*, edited by Ellen Lewin, 40–61. Boston: Beacon Press, 1996.

Thorsen, Karen, dir. *James Baldwin: The Price of the Ticket*. California Newsreel, San Francisco, 1990.

Turner, Victor Witter, and Richard Schechner. *The Anthropology of Performance*. New York: PAJ Publications, 1986.

UCSF AIDS Health Project. "Sex without Condoms." *HIV Counselor Perspectives* 10, no. 2 (2001): 1–8.

"Underground Culture of Balls." www.balls.houseofenigma.com (accessed April 27, 2011).

Vanity 6. *Nasty Girl*. Warner Brothers, 1982.

Voguing's Expansion to Japan. http://www.youtube.com/watch?v=QGuPzT5lks8and feature=related and http://www.youtube.com/watch?v=ZVuRysgYMSwandNR=1 (accessed October 7, 2011).

Walker, Ruby. "Interview with Chris Albertson." Audiocassette. Jersey City, NJ, 1970–71.

Wallace, Maurice O. *Constructing the Black Masculine: Identity and Ideality in African American Men's Literature and Culture, 1775–1995*. Durham, NC: Duke University Press, 2002.

Ward, Jane. "Transmen, Femmes, and Collective Work of Transgression." *Sexualities* 13, no. 2 (2010): 236–54.

Welbon, Yvonne, dir. *Living with Pride: Ruth Ellis @ 100*. VHS. 1999. Our Film Works.

Welsing, Frances Cress. *The Isis Papers*. Chicago: Third World Press, 1991.

West, Cornel. "Nihilism in Black America." In *Black Popular Culture*, edited by Gina Dent, 37–47. Seattle: Bay Press, 1992.

Weston, Kath. *Families We Choose: Lesbians, Gays, Kinship*. New York: Columbia University Press, 1991.

"What Is Vogue." The Underground Culture of Balls by Aaron Enigma, http://balls.houseofenigma.com/what_vogue.html (accessed August 23, 2011).

White, Marvin K. "The Children." In *nothin ugly fly*, 68–71. Washington, DC: Redbone Press, 2004.

Wiegman, Robyn. *American Anatomies: Theorizing Race and Gender*. Durham, NC: Duke University Press, 1995.

Williams, Rhonda M. "Living at the Crossroads: Explorations in Race, Nationality, Sexuality, and Gender." In *The House That Race Built*, edited by Wahneema Lubiano, 136–56. New York: Vintage Books, 1998.

Wilson, James F. *Bulldaggers, Pansies, and Chocolate Babies: Performance, Race, and Sexuality in the Harlem Renaissance*. Ann Arbor: University of Michigan Press, 2010.

Wolcott, Victoria. *Remaking Respectability: African American Women in Interwar Detroit*. Chapel Hill: University of North Carolina Press, 2001.

Index

265